CORRA

A

DETROIT'S ARCHITECTURAL SCULPTOR

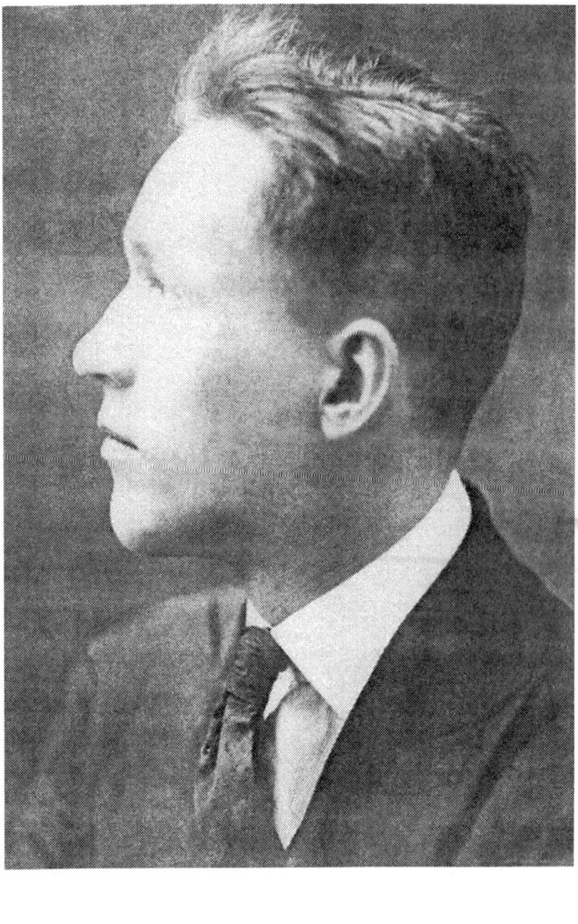

Dale A. Carlson with Einar Kvaran

Manufactured in the United States of America.

ISBN 978-0-578-61982-8

Library of Congress Control Number:2019919733

All photographs by Dale A. Carlson except where otherwise indicated.

This book is dedicated to the memory of Carolin Venegas Jones.

ACKNOWLEDGEMENTS

I would like to thank the following people for their invaluable contributions to my half-decade long Parducci project: First and foremost, the master, Corrado Giuseppe Parducci, whose ghost I often felt was riding in my passenger seat as I motored across the country in search of his works; my mother, Sherry McGinnis-Schmalenberg, my father, Anton Wayne Carlson, my step-parents, Daniel Schmalenberg and Patricia Carlson, and my brothers, Gregory, Jeff and Chris Carlson; Allen Parducci, Einar Kvaran (my personal guru of American art and architectural history), Charlotte Haynes-Dively, Michael G. Smith, Dan Austin and Jeff Morrison; Rob Kangas (my personal guru of photography), Nick Valenti, Carrie Acosta, Mark Einhaus, Jessica Dietz and Heather Gardner, all of the Oakland Community College Photography Department; Raelene Bugaj of Grosse Pointe Shores, Mat Grau, Jr. of Jesuit High School New Orleans, Mario Einaudi of The Huntington Library in San Marino, California, Matt Wendell of Bedrock Detroit, Angela and Tom Bass of New Baltimore, Michigan, Heather Jackson and John Henry of the Flint Institute of Arts, Father Jim Lowe and the late Father Livius Paoli, both of St. Scholastica Parish Detroit, Steve Genther of The Masonic Temple Detroit, Father Victor Clore of Christ the King Parish Detroit, Jeremy Kemp of the Belle Isle Conservatory Detroit, Sharon E. Venier of the Immaculate Heart of Mary Sisters in Monroe, Michigan, Rev. Darryl Lee Andrzejewski of Historic Trinity Lutheran Detroit, Father Athanasius Fornwalt of St. Mary of Redford Parish Detroit, Chaplain Jacob T. Belton of Via Christi Health in Wichita, Kansas, Madelyn Rzadkowolski of Meadow Brook Hall in Rochester Hills, Michigan, Erica Ginter of Kirk in the Hills Presbyterian Church in Bloomfield Township, Michigan, Beth Ann Dalrymple, Ted Groustra of The Players Detroit, N. Charles Anderson of the Urban League of Detroit and Southeastern Michigan, Lisa Worley and Sarah Kornacki of The Edsel and Eleanor Ford Estate in Grosse Pointe Shores, Michigan, Jeremy Dimick of the Detroit Historical Museum, Father John Libens of Colombiere College and Conference Center in Clarkston, Michigan, Nicole Lakatos of the Colony Club Detroit, Linda Robinson of First Presbyterian Church in Ann Arbor, Michigan, the late Dr. Thomas Brunk, Jeffery Tong and my other fellow members of the Berkley Historical Committee, the Midland County Historical Society, Jennifer Baross, Jack Johnson, Benjamin Gravel, and the late Balthazar Korab for inspiring me to shoot architecture like a pro.

Einar Kvaran would like to thank: My parents, first and foremost, without whom nothing, certainly not this book, would have been possible; my kids Eila and Kara, one of whom uttered the immortal words, "Going sculpting with Dad is no picnic"; my brothers, Ragnar, Hannes and Geir, and my wife, Violet Hill, for many things, but mostly for the many miles they put in with me on the road; a long list of friends who thought it would be fun to take a road trip with me and then found that, actually, one was enough; Dale Carlson, Rosemary Elias, Deborah Parducci; and special recognition to Allen Parducci, who gave me unlimited access to his father's library, work records, scrapbooks, dozens of maquettes and other small works, as well as hundreds of his own photographs and his own insights into his father.

FOREWORD

In this book we reveal the results of over five years of exhaustive and painstaking research into the life and work of Detroit's preeminent architectural sculptor, Corrado Giuseppe Parducci. We set out to create the most expansive, all-inclusive, and beyond thorough compendium of Parducci's lifetime output possible. We believe we can now confidently assert our success, and brazenly claim that nowhere else on Earth, online or off, will you find such a detailed enumeration of Parducci's life-long creative efforts. This sublimely engrossing endeavor grew into an obsession, and took us as far east as Brooklyn, as far west as Los Angeles, as far north as Minneapolis, as far south as New Orleans, and so many unexpected places in between. Our local and cross-country investigations bore beautiful fruit in the form of over 300 unique commission sites visited in fifteen states and over 70 municipalities. Our examinations of individual sculptural works modeled by Parducci ran quite easily into the 1000s, all photographed and archived for the sake of both posterity and preservation; but more importantly, for the sake of just plain knowing all we can know about this mammoth presence within Detroit's lavish cultural legacy. Over the next 125 pages, we will present photographs, and in some cases brief written analyses, of the 300+ Parducci commissions we have examined personally since 2014, each cataloged in a loosely chronological order, starting with Parducci's earliest known apprenticeship era works and ending with his very last confirmed job, executed in the year preceding his death. But the story won't end here. Not by a long shot. We promise you there are most definitely more undiscovered Parduccis waiting to be brought to light by other capable researchers, to whom we will offer complete and unfettered access to our research archive upon publication of this volume. We look forward to learning of the additions our readers and our peers in the field of Detroit architectural history will surely compel us to include in our second edition.

RESEARCH

The primary sources that have facilitated our journey of Parducci discovery are varied. First, and most important, there is Parducci's personal ledger, enumerating over 600 commissions from 1924 to 1972, with just a handful of gaps, 1932 to 1936 being the most confounding (*See Figures D, E, and F, pages 132-134*). Endless hours of protracted examination convince us the information contained within, while absolutely priceless, is also replete with errors, inconsistencies, discrepancies and downright inaccuracies. We theorize, in fact, that Parducci didn't actually keep accurate ledgers from year to year, but instead put together this lengthy registry of his career output from memory and incomplete records sometime over the course of a couple weeks or months in the early 1970s. Still, they remain the most valuable element in our palette of Parducci research resources. Photocopies of these ledgers were acquired by the co-author of this book, Mr. Einar Kvaran of Sun City, Arizona, when, around 1998, he made a trek to Southern California to meet Allen Parducci, son of Corrado, who was living in a Los Angeles neighborhood, retired from a professorship at UCLA. Along with his father's ledgers, Allen was also willing to share and allow Kvaran to photocopy over 700 images of works photographed in Parducci's studios over the course of his career. The scrapbooks from which these images came span nearly the same dates as his ledgers, though the later era of Parducci's career, 1948 and beyond, is much more thoroughly archived therein. Our thanks go out to Allen for his invaluable contributions to our understanding of his father's life and work. Kvaran also invested untold months and miles, between 1984 and 2006, hunting down and personally photographing hundreds of Parducci commissions, during the very unforgiving era of film photography no less, thereby developing his own unequaled grasp of Parducci's stylistic tendencies. He also sought out and interviewed numerous individuals with whom Parducci had personal contact over the course of his career, most notably architect Harold H. Fisher, in his 90s and, remarkably, still working. Additionally, Kvaran was the half of our research duo that did, by far, the most work in compiling the exhaustive bibliography found at the end of this book.

Included in this bibliography are two in-depth interviews with Parducci, one conducted by Dennis Barrie of the Smithsonian Institute in Washington, D.C., and one conducted by Fay Hendry, an independent researcher who in 1980 published three excellent volumes focused on outdoor sculpture found in the Michigan cities of Grand Rapids, Kalamazoo, and Lansing. Both interviews took place in Parducci's Sibley Street studio, late in his life, 1975 and 1979 respectively. Barrie's was taped and is fully transcribed. Though rife with name mis-spellings, it is readily available to all online. Hendry's is preserved only through the handwritten notes found within her archives held at Conrad Hall on the campus of Michigan State University. We consider the information contained in both to be absolutely indispensable to our understanding of Parducci's career in its entirety, but most specifically to the timeline of Parducci's activities spanning the years of 1904 to 1924. A tedious list of useful but less essential Parducci related books, pamphlets, news clippings and online web posts fills out our bibliography, should any of our readers care to delve into the murkiest depths of our research. And finally, when it comes to filling in the many blanks presented when studying a far less than flawlessly documented artist of the past, it is our own very highly trained eyes, developed over countless hours of poring over endless Parducci creations, in person and in photocopies, that most thoroughly inform our many theorizings regarding the lesser known aspects of Parducci's life and career. The time invested lent us a deserved liberty, in our opinion, to engage in deductive and inductive reasoning, as well as highly educated speculation, where we felt necessary.

BIOGRAPHY

"I think most of my skill became from starting very young. When you're very young, you're like a blotter; you absorb things. And when I was still in my early twenties, instead of being a student, I was a dean in my profession...Due to the fact that I started as a child." ~Corrado Parducci

Parducci's story begins in the small mountain town of Buti, Italy, in the province of Tuscany, approximately 10 miles to the east of Pisa. Here he was born on the 18th of March, in the year 1900, to parents Giulio and Zelinda (*See Figure A, page 129*). At the very young age of four, Parducci made the trans-Atlantic voyage with father Giulio to New York City. The family settled in the Lower Manhattan neighborhood of Greenwich Village, on Minetta Lane, just a few blocks away from MacDougal Alley, which, at the time, was a hub, if not the very center, of the United States' sculpture community. Though far too young to grasp the distinctions of his neighborhood and its residents, Parducci observes, in his 1975 interview with Smithsonian historian Dennis Barrie: *"[T]hat was my playground, that and Washington Square, and also MacDougal Alley, where all the sculptors and all the great, you know, [Augustus] Saint-Gaudens and [Daniel Chester] French, you know, that generation are all in that area."*

Impressions made at a local elementary school resulted in Gertrude Vanderbilt Whitney (Mrs. Harry Payne Whitney), an accomplished sculptor in her own right, personally approaching the parents of young Parducci to request permission for him to attend sculpture classes at the nearby Richmond Settlement House. One of Parducci's primary instructors during these most impressionable early years, Albín Polášek, would go on to attain lasting fame as the head of the sculpture department at the Art Institute of Chicago. In Parducci's words: *"Well, at the time, of course, I didn't recognize their stature; you know, I was a child. But there was a Mrs. Harry Payne Whitney at that time that was very much interested in the slum children, and she inquired at the school and got the names of a dozen or so boys that had showed aptitude in the arts. And she came over to the house and asked my parents if they would...permit me to attend a class at the settlement house on MacDougal Street. A class was formed and there was a sculptor, very able sculptor, by the name of Albín Polášek...He had just come back from the Academy in Rome, and he took charge of the class there...I must have been about eight or nine."*

Parducci continued sculptural studies at the Richmond Settlement House and other neighborhood locales throughout a large portion of his adolescence and graduated from New York City's Public School 95 at the age of 15.

Shortly thereafter, while employed as a modeler at an artificial flower factory, he turned down undesirable apprenticeship offers from famed sculptors Karl Bitter and Adolph Weinman. He instead attended classes at the Beaux-Arts Institute of Design in Manhattan, while awaiting an apprenticeship offer he viewed more favorably. Additionally, Parducci studied at Manhattan's Art Students League from 1922 to 1923 or 1924. At both schools Parducci enjoyed the mentoring of legendary figures within New York's rich art education culture of the day. He took drawing classes led by George Bridgman at the Art Students League, and studied plant anatomy under Frank Tolles Chamberlin at Beaux-Arts. The Beaux-Arts Institute was founded by a group of American architects who had attended the Ecolé des Beaux-Arts in France and its focus, sculpturally speaking, was on applied and decorative architectural arts, as opposed to pure fine art. It was run by another respected educator, Lloyd Warren, an architect himself, who was also the brother of the Warren & Wetmore architectural firm's namesake, Whitney Warren. Given the school's founding year of 1916, it is likely that Parducci was counted among its very first class. Regarding his years at these schools, Parducci states in the Smithsonian interview: *"I started to go to Beaux-Arts in about 1916, and I continued there until I came here [Detroit]. I was there about seven years. But during that time, I divided my courses with the Art Students League. There was George Bridgman there. I was in his class for three semesters, you know, drawing. I thought at the time that drawing was very important, and you didn't get that at the Beaux-Arts. They had sketch classes, but they didn't have any anatomist teaching anatomy, you know, like George Bridgman. So I divided; I attended both places, see. I went a couple of times a week at the Art Students League and the rest of the time at the Beaux-Arts. At the Beaux-Arts, they had classes both in sculpture and in ornament...Beaux-Arts was entirely free of any academic instruction, and there wasn't any fee to it. Lloyd Warren was the benefactor of the school. You know, he created the school, and he was there almost every evening, giving advice to students. I had a lot of conferences with him. And he'd have a...for instance, on Mondays he'd bring some flowers—roses or fresh flowers—and he had an artist by the name of Chamberlin, Tolles Chamberlin, and a very fine artist, and he instructed us on the anatomy of a flower."*

Parducci's lengthy interviews with Barrie and Hendry help us establish a solid timeline of his engagements in apprenticeship and employment during the seven years preceding his move to Detroit in October of 1924. As much or more than his impressive post-secondary educators, numerous non-academic influences color this crucial but somewhat shadowy developmental period. On March 9th, 1917 Parducci, his father, and architectural sculptor Ulysses Ricci signed a notarized apprenticeship agreement. Over the next four years, in addition to the guidance of Ricci, Parducci would enjoy mentorship provided by a revolving door of firm partners that included John Donnelly, Ricci's uncle Elisio, Edward Ardolino,

Angelo Zari, and culminated with the addition of Anthony DiLorenzo, the catalyst for Parducci's eventual permanent relocation to the city of Detroit.

Around 1918 or 1919 Ricci was commissioned to design architectural sculpture for several important structures at the University of Michigan in Ann Arbor. There Ricci produced works for York and Sawyer's Law Quadrangle (1923-1933) as well as Albert Kahn's Harlan Hatcher Graduate Library (1920), Angell Hall (1924), and the East Medical Building also known as the C.C. Little Science Building (1925). It is likely that around this time Parducci came to the attention of Kahn, and perhaps also to Wirt Rowland. Rowland was, at the time, a designer at Kahn's firm and one of the Hatcher Library's primary designers. He would later enlist Parducci's touch for several buildings he designed while employed by Smith, Hinchman & Grylls from 1922 to 1930 as their 'Head of Modern Design'.

Parducci speaks upon his time with Ricci's firms in the 1975 interview: *"At the time I started to work there as an office boy, they were carving the large group over at Grand Central Station...And they carved...Oh, that granite work! They had an enormous studio and an enormous business. And they had different departments; they had the sculptors and...And that's where I really got my first training, because I was in charge of the blueprints, and all these sculptors and all these ornamentalists would call on me to furnish them the drawings they needed to proceed to do work. And I was able to listen in on these architects that came in to inspect the work—the most renowned architects in the country. You know, Carrère & Hastings and Warren & Wetmore, McKim, Mead & White, and Cass Gilbert. Every day there was so much going on, and there I was, you know, a youngster listening."*

Sometime around 1921 DiLorenzo and Ricci split. Parducci chose to throw in his lot with DiLorenzo. Regarding these years of his sculpture career's genesis, Parducci states in the Smithsonian interview: "*Well, Ricci—that's Ulysses Ricci—he got a lot of ornamental work besides sculpture, so he got his old pal [Anthony] DiLorenzo to go in with him to do that part of the work. So I became an employee of Ricci and DiLorenzo...And then later on they got [Edward] Ardolino. Ardolino was a stone carver...he did the reredos of the St. Thomas Cathedral there...Well, that firm became Ricci and DiLorenzo and Ardolino. And later on, they got the uncle, so there were two Riccis there, see...And then later on, they broke up again...Ricci, Senior, also left. And they had a man by the name of Zari; he left. Ulysses Ricci opened up a separate studio. I didn't go with him. I remained with DiLorenzo because DiLorenzo was an ornamentalist and I was more interested in the sculpture. So I had the opportunity of doing all the figure work in DiLorenzo's contract...I got to know Kahn...You know, Kahn used to come at least once a month to New York...And he got interested in me and he started to give DiLorenzo contracts providing that I should do it. So work that was indirectly for Albert Kahn through DiLorenzo...DiLorenzo paid me a flat salary a week and I did work on contract...at the end of the year, I had a surplus coming to me, because the contracts were over and above my weekly wage. So even as a youngster, I was the most highly paid sculptor in New York City."*

In October of 1924 DiLorenzo sent Parducci to Detroit to complete a commission for which the architects insisted he be present, and likely, to also put in some time on George D. Mason's elaborately embellished Masonic Temple, constructed in the years 1920 to 1926. This set into motion a chain of events that would land Parducci in Detroit permanently, for as the calendar turned to August of 1925, and Parducci found himself inundated with endless local work, he made an agreement to buy out DiLorenzo's remaining Detroit interests and opened his own studio here in the young, booming Motor City.

Parducci remarks upon this transition to Detroit in the 1975 Smithsonian interview: *"And while I was here, George D. Mason and Donaldson and Meier and Smith, Hinchman & Grylls and Albert Kahn just showered me with work and I couldn't get away. I couldn't get away, and it kept up and kept up and I finally called my wife. I said, 'You'll have to come here; I haven't even got time to come to pick you up.' And I stayed here. I had a studio on Congress Street, not too far away from the Marquette Building...And I used to have Albert Kahn visit me once or twice a week."* Parducci further states in the interview that he spent his first several months in Detroit as an employee of DiLorenzo, and then goes on to say: *"So my file here shows the work I did under his name, and that was 1924. And in the middle of 1925, I was on my own. I gave him $5,000 for anything, for any interest he might have had in the work I was doing, and we called it quits."* Thus began Parducci's permanent residency in the Paris of the Midwest and an epic career that would span over a half century, his last known commission completed in 1980.

TIMELINE of the LIFE of CORRADO PARDUCCI

1900 ~ Birth: Buti, Tuscany, Italy
1904 ~ Immigration to United States
1906-1909* ~ Attends Sullivan School
1908-1911* ~ Richmond Settlement House Sculpture classes
1909*-1915 ~ Attends New York City Public Schools
1912*-1915 ~ Sculpture classes at New York City Public School No. 8
1915 ~ Graduation from New York City Public School No. 95
1916-1924 ~ Attends Beaux-Arts Institute of Design in Manhattan, NY
1917-1921* ~ Apprentice to Ulysses Ricci
1921* ~ Marriage to Rebecca
1921*-1925 ~ Employee of Anthony DiLorenzo
1922-1924* ~ Attends Art Students League in Manhattan, NY
1924 ~ Moves to Detroit
1925 ~ Buys out Anthony DiLorenzo; opens independent studio in Detroit
1925 ~ Son Allen Born
1927 ~ Twin Sons David and Harry Born
1927 ~ Tenth Street studio opens
1927-1936 ~ Employs Brother Rudolph Parducci
1928 ~ Grosse Pointe Shores home constructed
1928 ~ Father Giulio Dies
1937 ~ Mother Zelinda Dies
1947 ~ Sibley Street studio opens
1957* ~ Son Harry Dies
1958 ~ AIA Honorary Member Induction Ceremony
1962 ~ Son David Dies
1969 ~ Wife Rebecca Dies
1973 ~ Brother Rudolph Dies
1981 ~ Death: Detroit, Michigan, USA

(* = estimate)

PROCESS

A modicum of analysis befits Parducci's artistic process before one goes diving into the ocean that is his career-long output. Perhaps the most important detail of Parducci's day-to-day, so easily mis-envisioned by those who take a casual interest in him, is that he rarely worked on site. Parducci was primarily a clay and plaster modeler who spent his long work days in the studio creating original pieces out of a combination of the creative loam of his mind, the established symbolisms and expressed desires of the interests for whom he created, and the historical precedents of so many architectural sculptors that preceded him. When completed, studio assistants packed and shipped models to clients, usually construction companies closely associated with the commissioning architectural firms, who would then have Parducci's models rendered on site by other skilled artisans, usually employees or sub-contractors, often using a variety of tools specific to the task of precise reproduction. Materials in which Parducci models have been rendered include concrete, stone, marble, terra cotta, brass, iron, bronze, wood, plaster and even fiberglass. Many degrees of relief are expressed, from the shallowest to three-quarter figures, and rarely, fully disengaged elements, as seen in his 'Stations of the Cross' at Royal Oak's Shrine of the Little Flower. Free-standing statues make up a small percentage of his repertoire, while pure applied ornamentation is replete. Highly ornate plasterworks present an intriguing occasional exception to the general rule of Parducci works being rendered on site by others, the Christopher Wren ceiling at Meadow Brook Hall and the relocated Midland Theatre History Mural being the most notable.

Also worth considering here is Parducci's specialization in the applied art of structures, a discipline fraught with nuance all but lost upon fine art sculptors creating primarily for gallery and museum display. Parducci expounds briefly regarding these distinctions in the 1975 interview: *"[A]rchitectural work is so different from easel work, or the work that was done in MacDougal Alley—they were all statues for public squares...it's applied work. You have to have an understanding of scale, and you have to have understanding of the style, and of the period...You can't make a Greek figure on a Gothic building, or vice versa...And it's a specialized sort of work. The average sculptor that tried—even Daniel Chester French. I got in my scrapbook somewhere something that Daniel Chester French had to do on an architectural building. It was simply amateurish. But when he made a complete piece of sculpture in the [soap] without application that was his field."* Yet, Parducci himself possessed hardly the most refined skill of his peers, often engaging in rush jobs to accommodate the break-neck pace of the rapidly growing industrial powerhouse that was Detroit in the 1920s (perhaps Parducci's most prolific decade, despite operating his own studio for just over half of it). Anatomical imperfections within his work abound; but what he sometimes lacked in technique, he made up for with quantity. A total of well over 600 commissions fill the original ledgers of his Detroit studios. Few, if any, of his contemporaries can boast of such a voluminous and geographically far-reaching portfolio of extant works.

LEGACY

Parducci's career, sadly, represents the very end of the line of a patrimonial tradition of architectural sculptural arts that began centuries earlier in the Old World, its zenith most aptly exemplified by stonemasonry guilds of the Middle Ages. The very need for architectural sculpture was, in fact, a primarily European precedent brought to the United States by many of the very same European-educated architects that formed the core of New York City's early 20th-century architectural arts education community in which Parducci participated. Certainly Parducci's flirtations with Art Deco trends of his day exhibit an element of his style more modern than classic, but it is the architectural aspect of his craft, in our opinion, that places his career more firmly within the line of a tradition that precedes Deco by, arguably, millennia. With the advent of architectural modernism, and sculptural embellishment having fallen out of style, the fine art sculptor is what remains of the sculptural world, and Parducci himself would tell you that the culture of modern fine art sculpture is only slightly invested in the traditions of past masters, and looks more favorably upon that which is without precedent. Parducci expresses these points best, but hardly succinctly, when asked to speak upon his generation's style in the 1975 Smithsonian interview: *"[T]here was actually no style. It was a revival or resurrection of a number of styles. We worked in the Greek, in the Roman, in the Romanesque, in the early Renaissance, late Renaissance...in the English Revival of the seventeenth century, and also in the Adams, the later Georgian. And all these styles were at our fingertips, which is very unique. I mean, it was a unique experience...That revival, that resurrection, occurred near the turn of the century, several generations before I came along, and it took continuous development. The people I was working for were the pupils of the previous generation...it progressed from that, and it took several generations. Now, I happened to be the last of that group, because I was about ten years younger than my peers—that's in the early twenties. There weren't any apprentices any longer...I actually was the last one, and after myself, there wasn't very much. There was, you know, in 1929, there was a depression, and then there was very little built...some of the old designers were still alive, were still doing some work, but it was always diminishing. And then the war came along, when there was absolutely nothing. And, you know, when twenty or thirty years go by without any apprenticeships, it becomes a lost art...I can't imagine anybody today being as vitally interested as we were at that time...there was a criteria then which isn't in existence today. Today, everyone wants to create something new. So, at that time we had something. There was something that already had been developed. We were just carrying on...We had a base. I don't see any base today...there isn't a base. And I believe each generation tries to account for itself by refuting its elders. That's what causes the cycle really. The present generation is on its own; it has nothing to do with the past. And the next generation will want that prerogative."* On a less pessimistic note, an unknown author at Smith, Hinchman & Grylls, in a very short Parducci bio written around 1975, observes, "[Parducci] is not embittered by the trend away from architectural ornament, but is confident that the design pendulum will one day swing back, propelled by man's need for beauty in his environment." Though isolated pockets of activity do exist in the miniscule present-day world of architectural sculpture, for the time being Parducci's 1975 statements on the matter impart more truth, however distressing; architectural sculpture is, for the most part, a lost and dead art, Parducci most definitely being one of the very last practitioners to make an entire career of it. Furthermore, the limited architectural sculpture that is produced in the present day is far less likely to draw upon, and therefore preserve, the same age-old historical precedents that informed Parducci and his peers.

UNDERSTANDING THIS GUIDE

Each entry in this field guide to the known, extant work of Corrado Parducci is ordered in a loosely chronological fashion and contains nine to eleven parts: (1) a black and white photograph of either the structure for which sculpture was created, sculpture applied to or integrated into that structure, or, for works independent of a structure, sculpture only; (2) the name of the structure at the time of the commission (or its most commonly known name where appropriate); (3) where necessary, present-day or other former names of the structure; (4) the year or years of the structure's construction; (5) the structure's architect where known; (6) the structure's address; (7) a notation indicating the source or sources that confirm the entry as a Parducci commission; (8) the job number or numbers assigned to the commission in Parducci's ledgers; (9) the year or years in which the commission is recorded in Parducci's ledgers; (10) in quotes, the title or titles given to the commission by Parducci, verbatim, as they appear in their earliest entries within the ledgers; and (11), where necessary, concise notes regarding the commission.

For commissions created independent of a structure, a place name or other relevant identifying detail is entered in part (2).

A question mark (?) is added to the end of reported years of construction where they are less than certain.

"Architect undetermined" is entered for part (5) when the architect is unknown to us and "N/A" (meaning "not applicable") in the rare cases where no architect was involved with the commission. A question mark (?) follows the architect's name when the attribution is likely accurate but less than certain.

Key to notations used in part (7):

[L] = Parducci's ledgers
[SB] = Parducci's scrapbook
[DB] = Parducci's 1975 interview with Smithsonian historian Dennis Barrie
[FH] = Parducci's 1979 interview with independent researcher Fay Hendry or Hendry's Outdoor Sculpture Project Records
[DFP] = Detroit Free Press article
[AP] = Authors' interviews with Parducci's eldest son, Allen
[WK] = William Kapp's presentation notes for Parducci's American Institute of Architects honorary membership award ceremony in 1958

[HF] = Co-author Einar Kvaran's interviews with architect Harold H. Fisher
[C] = Written correspondence between Parducci Studios and the commissioning client
[SHG] = Condensed Parducci biography penned by unnamed author in the employ of Smith, Hinchman & Grylls in 1975
[MSA] = Michigan Society of Architects Monthly Bulletin, October 1975
[JB] = Joan Boddie's 1978 Master's Essay, 'Géza Maróti and the Decoration of the Fisher Building Lobby'
[DHM] = Detroit Historical Museum Collection

Commissions lacking a primary source that proves Parducci's involvement beyond a reasonable doubt will be indicated as such by the word [Speculative] in place of a notation.

For commissions not recorded in Parducci's ledgers the notation "N/A" will be entered for parts (8), (9) and (10).

Where appropriate, Parducci's 1975 interview with Smithsonian historian Dennis Barrie will be referred to generically in the text as "the Smithsonian interview", "the Barrie interview, or "the 1975 interview", and Parducci's 1979 interview with independent researcher Fay Hendry will be referred to as "the Hendry interview" or "the 1979 interview".

Our guide's entry numbers do not correspond to Parducci's job numbers reported in the ledgers. We respectfully request that our readers be mindful of the difference.

Where necessary, pertinent commentary will be inserted between entries to elucidate common circumstances applicable to particular groups of commissions. Space, time, money, and will preclude us, however, from engaging in extended analyses of each individual commission site. We invite our readers to engage in their own explorations of the many commissions enumerated herein, and, in tandem with thorough analysis of Parducci's scrapbook images, to familiarize themselves, as we have, with his stylistic tendencies, and then draw their own conclusions as to the extent of Parducci's contributions to each.

THE COMMISSIONS

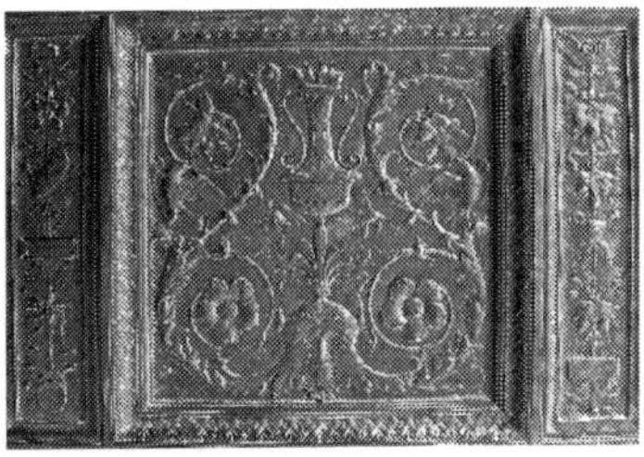

1. Huntington Library
(c.1920; Myron Hubbard Hunt)
1151 Oxford Rd
San Marino, CA
[FH, AP]
Ledger details: N/A

In his 1979 interview with Fay Hendry, Parducci attests to sculpting, during his apprenticeship years, colophons for this structure's bronze doors.

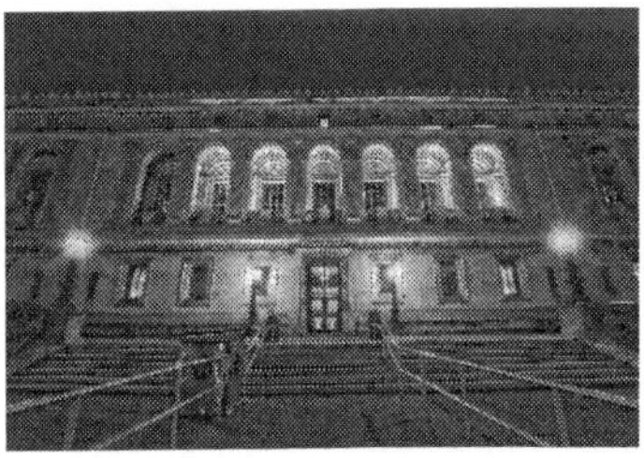

2. Detroit Public Library ~ Main Branch
(1921; Cass Gilbert)
5201 Woodward Ave
Detroit, MI
[DFP]
Ledger details: N/A

A 1973 article in the *Detroit News* reports that Parducci created a portion of the Detroit Public Library's architectural sculpture as an apprentice. We assume this claim was made by Parducci directly to the article's author. The article identifies no specific sculptural works as Parducci's, however. A wealth of embellishments is therefore open to speculation, except for the zodiacs along the roofline on the main façade and the bronze doors. Parducci names Oswald Hoepfner and Geremia Grandelis as the artists who created them in his 1975 Smithsonian interview. Some have speculated that the lintel above the main entrance is Parducci's contribution but we have uncovered no evidence to substantiate that attribution.

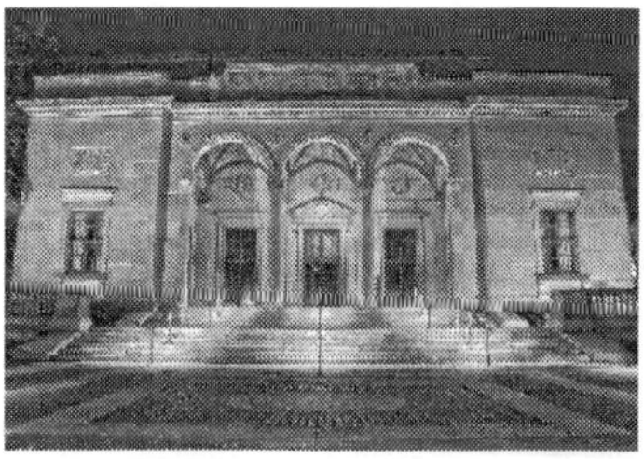

3. William L. Clements Library at University of Michigan
(1923; Albert Kahn)
909 S University Ave
Ann Arbor, MI
[WK]
Ledger details: N/A

Apprenticeship era work confirmed by William E. Kapp's presentation notes for Parducci's American Institute of Architects honorary membership award ceremony in 1958.

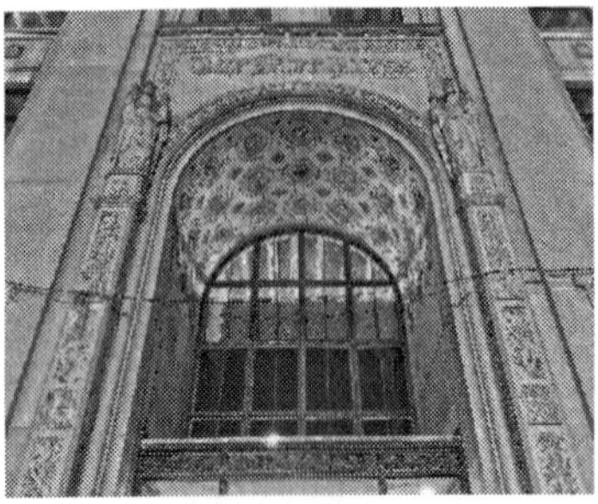

4. Detroit Free Press Building
(1923; Albert Kahn)
301 W Lafayette Blvd
Detroit, MI
[DFP]
Ledger details: N/A

A caption in a 1953 issue of the *Detroit Free Press* specifically attributes this structure's arched, rosette medallion embellished entrance loggia ceiling to Parducci. We assume this attribution was given based on statements made to the writer by Parducci himself, and that the work was executed by Parducci while in the employ of either Ulysses Ricci or Anthony DiLorenzo.

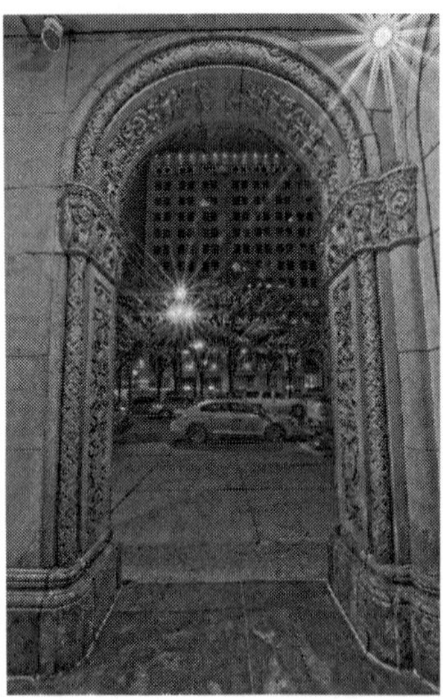

5. Chancery Building
(1924; Donaldson & Meier)
1234 Washington Blvd
Detroit, MI
[WK]
Ledger details: N/A

Work executed while most likely an employee of Anthony DiLorenzo, confirmed by William E. Kapp's presentation notes for Parducci's American Institute of Architects honorary membership award ceremony in 1958.

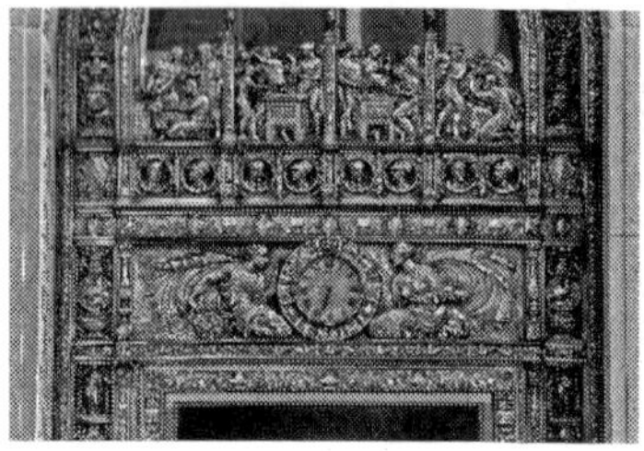

6. First National Bank Building
(1924; Childs & Smith)
201 W Second St
Davenport, IA
[SB, DB]
Ledger details: N/A

Parducci's personal scrapbook notes his specific contributions to this building's ornate exterior: the "History of Money" in bronze and the carved stone reveals directly to the left and right of the front door. Multiple works by Adolph Weinman also grace this structure's façade.

An excerpt from Parducci's 1975 Smithsonian interview regarding this commission:

"CORRADO PARDUCCI: *[T]his is a job where Weinman... Weinman made these figures, see, and I did this—that was in 1922—and these...*
DENNIS BARRIE: *Figures over the door and you did the door...*

CORRADO PARDUCCI: *Yeah, I did the bronze and these figures on the reveal.*"

Though Parducci cites the year of 1922 in the interview, his scrapbooks report 1923 as the year he executed this work.

7. Buhl Building
(1925; Wirt Rowland of Smith, Hinchman & Grylls)
535 Griswold St
Detroit, MI
[SB, FH, WK]
Ledger details: N/A

Conspicuously absent from the ledgers, the models for this commission were most likely executed by Parducci during his last months in New York City working under DiLorenzo.

Parducci's first ledger page, dated October 1, 1924 to August 16, 1925, records around 40 commissions secured during the time in which he worked as Anthony DiLorenzo's Detroit-based employee. Entries #8 through #29 in our guide are taken from this 1924-1925 page and each job number cited is marked with an asterisk, as Parducci re-started the numbering of his commissions at #1 on August 17, 1925, at the outset of his independent studio ownership. At this point in history DiLorenzo was most likely engaged with his own roster of jobs back in New York City and other Eastern locales, making the probability these works were created solely by Parducci very high. We concede the possibility, however unlikely, that DiLorenzo may have contributed to any of them.

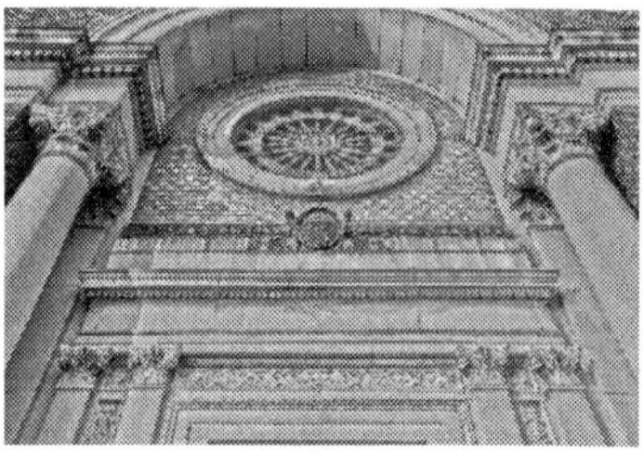

8. Church of the Nativity of Our Lord
(1924-1925; Edward A. Schilling of Van Leyen, Schilling & Keough)
5900 McClellan Ave
Detroit, MI
[L, DB]
Ledger details: Job #1*; 1924-1925 "Nativity of Our Lord"

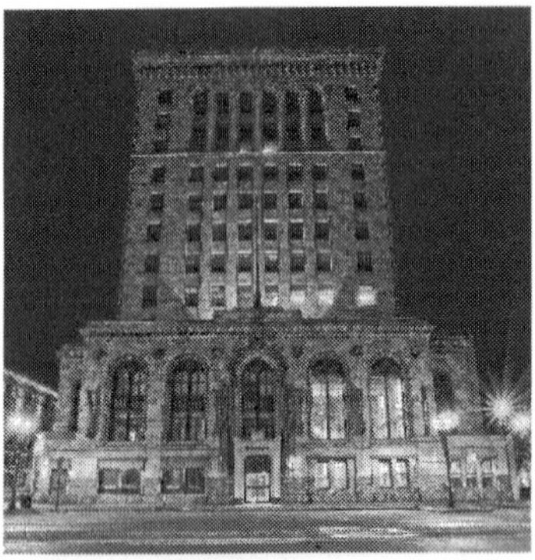

9. Second National Bank Building
(1925; Wirt Rowland of Smith, Hinchman & Grylls)
101 N Washington Ave
Saginaw, MI
[L, DB, WK]
Ledger details: Jobs #2*/#22
1924-1925/1925
"Second Nat. Bk Saginaw Mich"

An excerpt from the 1975 Smithsonian interview regarding the two preceding commissions:

"DENNIS BARRIE: *What was your first job here (Detroit)? First job as an independent organization.*
CORRADO PARDUCCI:...*I have to go way back. Let's see. Yeah, that Schilling, Nativity of Our Lord, that was the first. And the Second National Bank of Saginaw was the second. That was Smith, Hinchman & Grylls.*"

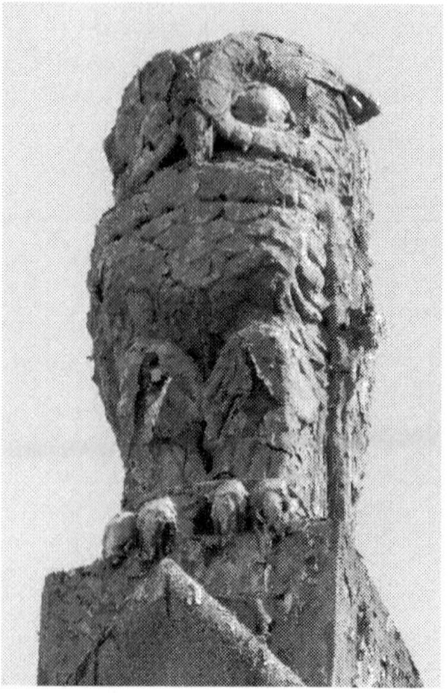

10. Psi Upsilon Fraternity House ~ Exterior Elements
(1924-1925; Albert Kahn)
1000 Hill St
Ann Arbor, MI
[L]
Ledger details: Job #7*; 1924-1925
"Psi Upslon (sic) House"

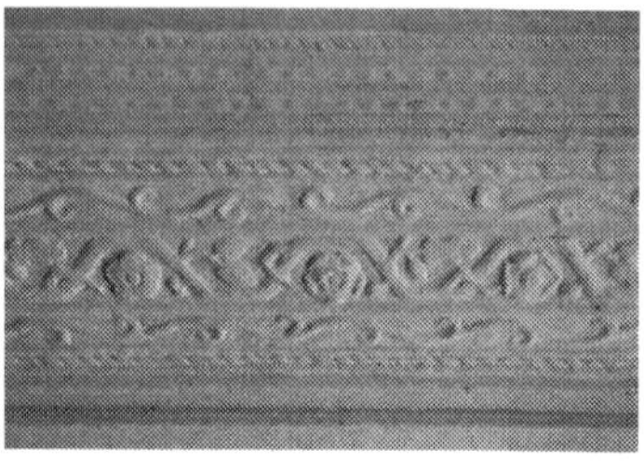

11. Psi Upsilon Fraternity House ~ Interior Elements
(1924-1925; Albert Kahn)
1000 Hill St
Ann Arbor, MI
[L]
Ledger details: Job #7*; 1924-1925
"Psi Upslon (sic) House"

In our opinion, it is highly likely that Parducci created the original patterns for all or some of this house's interior plaster works.

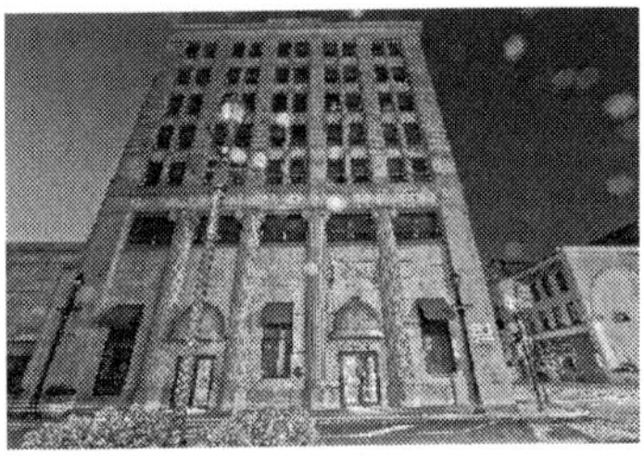

12. Citizens Title and Trust Building
(c.1924; Albert Kahn)
2 W Main St
Uniontown, PA
[L]
Ledger details: Job #9*; 1924-1925 "Citizens Title & Trust Uniontown PA"

The column capitals appear to us the last vestige of any exterior sculpture created for this structure by Parducci or DiLorenzo.

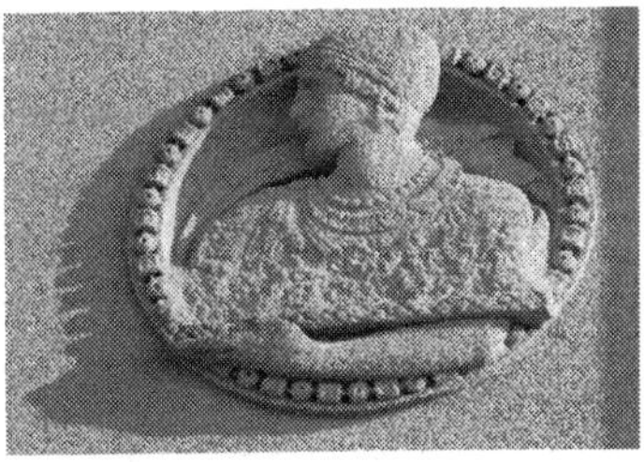

13. Paige-Detroit Motor Company Offices and Plant
(1925; Albert Kahn)
8505 W Warren Ave
Dearborn, MI
[L]
Ledger details: Job #10*; 1924-1925 "Paige Motor Co"

What object the sculpted lady above the main entrance held in hand at one time is open to speculation. We're guessing a Paige-Detroit brand automobile.

Regarding entries #14 through #18:

Parducci's myriad interior works at Detroit's Masonic Temple are widely celebrated. They are rendered in wood, metal and stone, but most importantly, plaster. In the majority of cases, where the creation of his plaster works are concerned, at the Masonic Temple and elsewhere, a pattern was first created by Parducci, in person and on site, and then duplicated to completion by other skilled artisans employed or sub-contracted by the construction company. Exceptions exist, generally his most elaborate plasters, which were created in full solely by his hand, and we would suspect that tendency to have been no different here at the Masonic Temple. Which of the Temple's many ornate works possess that distinction, however, is unknown to us. In our opinion nearly all of them qualify as potential candidates.

Regarding his work at the Masonic Temple, Parducci states in the Smithsonian interview: *"Now all the interior of the Masonic Temple...I better talk about that to you because that's kind of interesting. There are about a dozen large rooms, very large, you know, lodges, and every one is a different style. There's a Greek and there's a...The ballroom is Renaissance, and there's a cathedral in there which is Gothic, and then there's some Tudor rooms, there's an Egyptian room, and there's the Doric room...Now all these rooms are in the character and style of a particular period! And I had them all on my fingertips."*

Later in the interview: *"[T]he Masonic Temple, which came in*

1924, you know…It was actually DiLorenzo's job, which I took over when I bought him out. That was challenging in the sense that every room was different, you see…I had to skip from one generation to another. I just had to hop like an acrobat. And at the same time I was doing that, I was doing other work."

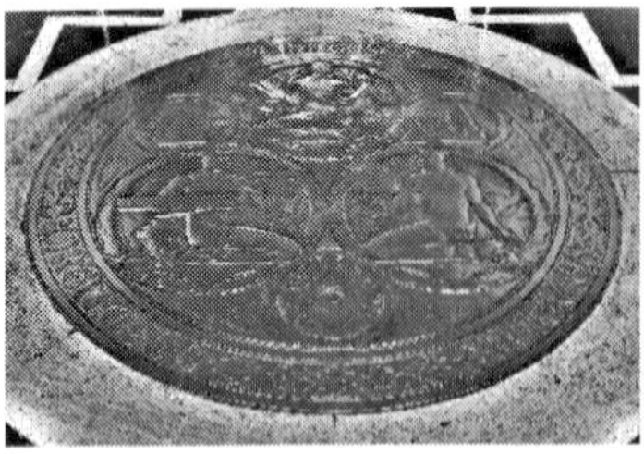

14. Detroit Masonic Temple ~ Lobby Medallion
(1920-1926; George D. Mason)
500 Temple St
Detroit, MI
[L, SB, DB, WK]
Ledger details: Jobs #11*/#2, #39/#52, #56/#156/#290
1924-1925/1925/1926/1928/1930
"Masonic Temple"

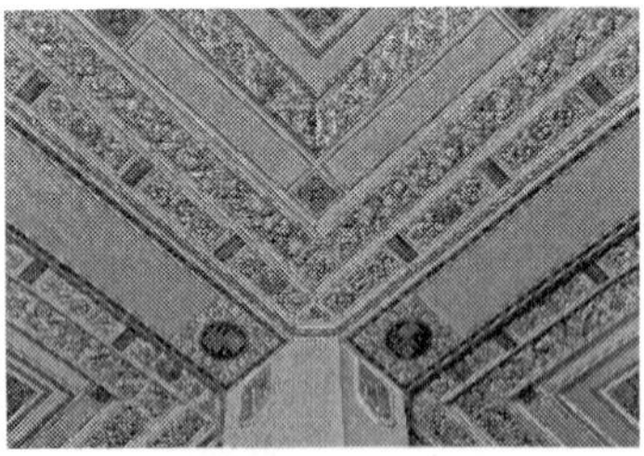

15. Detroit Masonic Temple ~ Plaster
(1920-1926; George D. Mason)
500 Temple St
Detroit, MI
[L, SB, DB, WK]
Ledger details: Jobs #11*/#2, #39/#52, #56/#156/#290
1924-1925/1925/1926/1928/1930
"Masonic Temple"

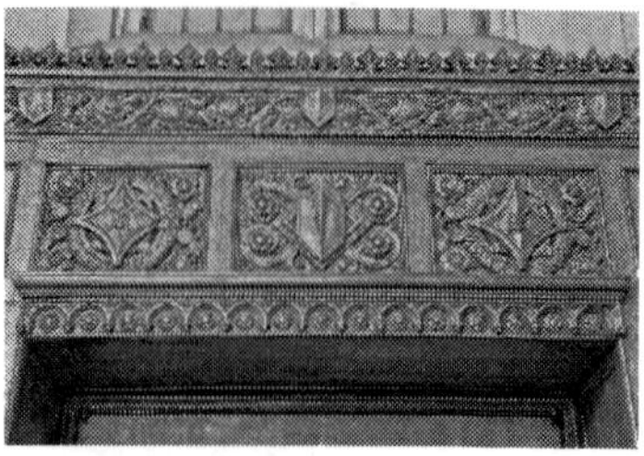

16. Detroit Masonic Temple ~ Wood
(1920-1926; George D. Mason)
500 Temple St
Detroit, MI
[L, SB, DB, WK]
Ledger details: Jobs #11*/#2, #39/#52, #56/#156/#290
1924-1925/1925/1926/1928/1930
"Masonic Temple"

17. Detroit Masonic Temple ~ Bronze
(1920-1926; George D. Mason)
500 Temple St
Detroit, MI
[L, SB, DB, WK]
Ledger details: Jobs #11*/#2, #39/#52, #56/#156/#290
1924-1925/1925/1926/1928/1930
"Masonic Temple"

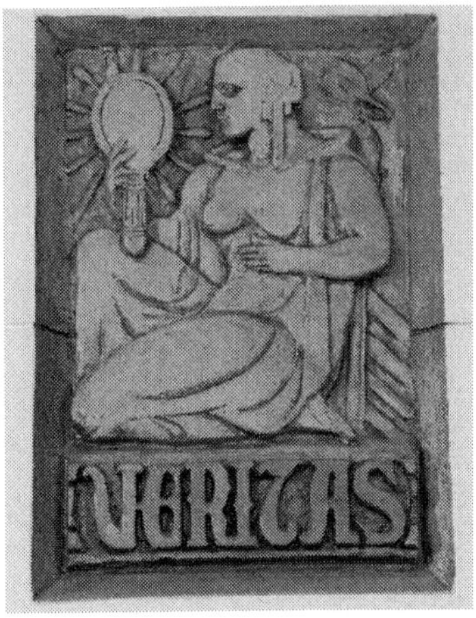

18. Detroit Masonic Temple ~ Stone
(1920-1926; George D. Mason)
500 Temple St
Detroit, MI
[L, SB, DB, WK]
Ledger details: Jobs #11*/#2, #39/#52, #56/#156/#290
1924-1925/1925/1926/1928/1930
"Masonic Temple"

A portion of Parducci's 1975 Smithsonian interview in which he references the sculptural work pictured above:

"CORRADO PARDUCCI: *Now, Detroit Decorating and Supply...You've heard of Bill [William] Kapp?*
DENNIS BARRIE: *Yeah.*
CORRADO PARDUCCI: *Well, this is a catalogue mailed to the architects, and Bill Kapp brought it to me and says, "You get this. I'll give it to you." He had his name written in gold on the cover. Let's see whether you see Bill Kapp's name. Yeah, you see it here. There's William Kapp, barely make it out.*
DENNIS BARRIE: *Um hmm.*
CORRADO PARDUCCI: *Now, Bill Kapp went page by page...He went page by page and he told me all the work I've done that they use in their catalogue. Now these two panels were in the Masonic Temple. They were stone. I don't know how they got the models, but they...I think it was artificial stone; they reproduced it.*
DENNIS BARRIE: *Oh my God.*
CORRADO PARDUCCI: *And Bill Kapp was able to point out everything that I've done that was in this catalogue.*
DENNIS BARRIE: *Oh my!*
CORRADO PARDUCCI: *Work that was special work, that was...You probably could identify some of it, because...Most of the work is very crude there, you see.*
DENNIS BARRIE: *They had a right to do this?*
CORRADO PARDUCCI: *They had no right, but there's no way of defending yourself.*"

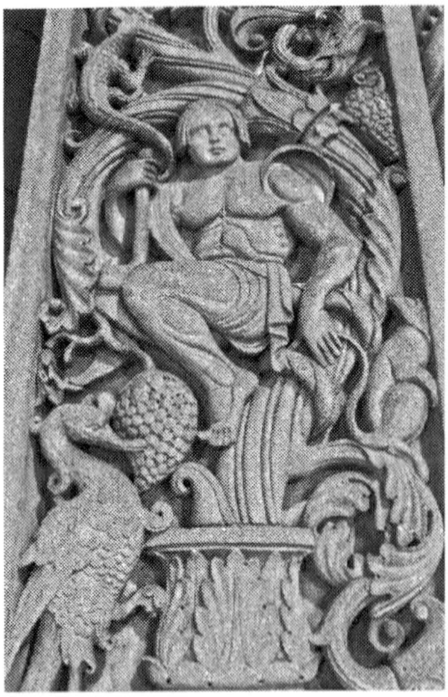

19. Security Trust Company Building
(1925; Albert Kahn)
735 Griswold St
Detroit, MI
[L, SB, DB, FH, WK]
Ledger details: Job #12*; 1924-1925 "Security Bk Bldg"

Some have speculated that the front door reveal sculpture found here was created by Ulysses Ricci. It bears an uncanny similarity to a door surround found upon the City National Bank Building in Lansing, a known Ricci commission. In our opinion, Anthony DiLorenzo is a possible contributor, as well, though less likely. Parducci specifically states in the 1975 Smithsonian interview that the Security Trust Company and First State Bank Buildings on Griswold are among the very last structures for which he created sculpture while still working in New York, solidly establishing DiLorenzo's firm as one of the architectural sculptors of record, and Parducci, of course, as one of the architectural sculptors. We must also take into account, however, statements from both the 1975 and 1979 interviews which clearly establish the fact that throughout the 1920s it was very common for Albert Kahn to contract all three sculptors (and sometimes a fourth) for a single building and split the sculptural work evenly among them. In our opinion, this division of labor likely applies to a host of other Kahn-designed structures built in the 1920s. In fact, Parducci specifically ascribes this distinction to the Fisher, Maccabees, and Kalamazoo Gazette Buildings in the Hendry interview. Other entries in our guide that we believe likely to also fit the description: #3, #4, #23, #24, #58, #59, #67, #72, and #78. So while it is indeed provable that Parducci contributed to much of the Security Trust Company Building's sculptural embellishment, it is far more difficult to say with complete accuracy which exact works are his. In short, the nature of the master-apprentice relationship deeply complicates the task of accurate attribution where the aforementioned entries are concerned, as works created in the 1920s by Ricci, DiLorenzo and Parducci are often nearly indistinguishable. We can say with absolute certainty, however, that Parducci created the model for the griffins applied to this building's façade, as he specifically states this as a fact in the 1979 interview.

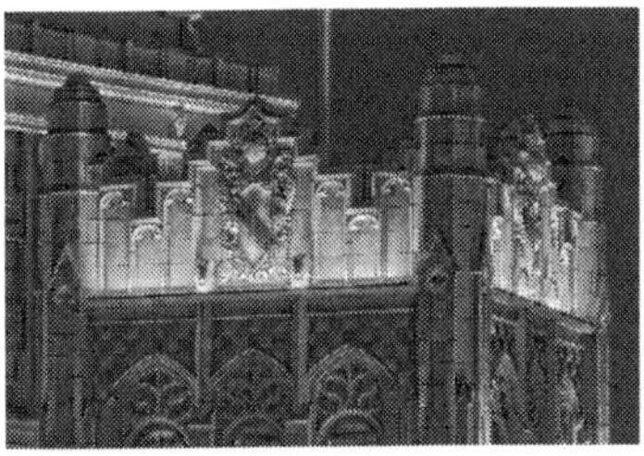

20. Metropolitan Building
(1925; Weston & Ellington)
33 John R St
Detroit, MI
[L]
Ledger details: Job #18*; 1924-1925
"Metropolitan Bldg"

21. Detroit Public Library ~ Monteith Branch
(1926; Smith, Hinchman & Grylls)
14100 Kercheval Ave
Detroit, MI
[L]
Ledger details: Jobs #21*/#6
1924-1925/1925
"Regional Bank (sic) Library"
"Regional Branch Library"

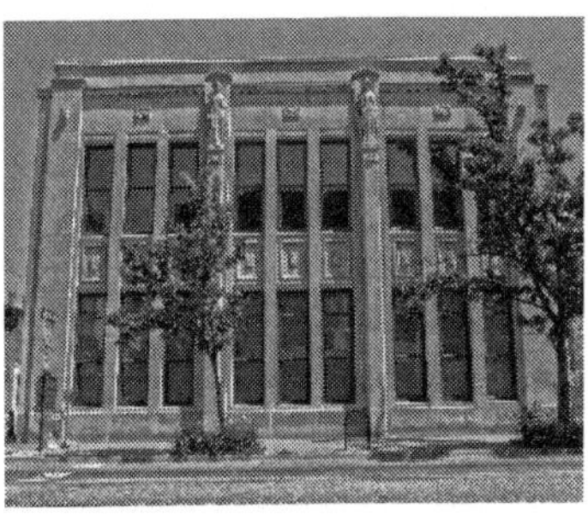

22. Kalamazoo Gazette Building
(1925; Albert Kahn)
401 S Burdick St
Kalamazoo, MI
[L, FH]
Ledger details: Job #22*; 1924-1925
"Kalamazoo Gazette"

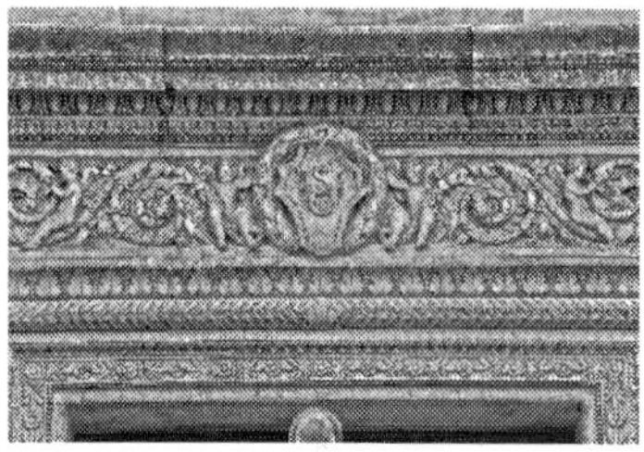

23. Standard Club
(1926; Albert Kahn)
320 S Plymouth Ct
Chicago, IL
[L, DB]
Ledger details: Jobs #23*/#5/#54
1924-1925/1925/1926
"Standard Club Chicago"

Regarding this commission, Parducci states in the 1975 Smithsonian interview: *"[T]here was a Standard Club of Chicago. That was Albert Kahn. You remember the case of Leopold and Loeb?...They were the organizers of that Standard Club...And when the work was in progress, they got involved in that murder. So the work was stopped for a number of months, until finally someone else took it over...if these buildings would talk, there's an awful lot there."*

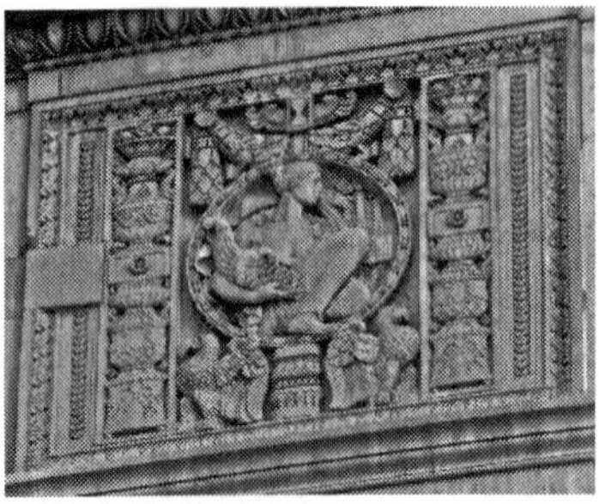

24. First State Bank Building formerly known as Olde Building now known as MarxModa Building
(1925; Albert Kahn)
751 Griswold St
Detroit, MI
[L, SB, DB]
Ledger details: Job #29*; 1924-1925
"First State Bk"

Regarding this commission and the Security Trust Company Building (entry #19), Parducci states in the 1975 interview: *"The last work I did for [DiLorenzo] before I came here were the two banks on Griswold, across the street where the old city hall was, the...Romanesque bank that they ruined with that addition up above. And there's a corner bank, which is the sort of classic, you know; it's sort of Roman...the two buildings were built at the same time. They were designed at the same time, and they went up at the same time. But that was just about the time, just before I came to Detroit...the carving on the corner building—up above you see those figure patterns and all that—it was carved during the wintertime, and they had it enclosed with canvas. And Albert Kahn didn't want to climb the scaffold to inspect the work, so he had me do that for him. And I couldn't do it very well because I couldn't get away for more than three feet. The scaffold was right up against...and you can't judge anything when you're up against it."*

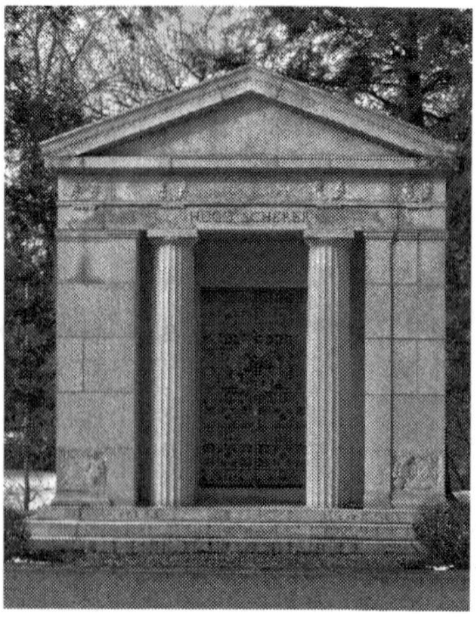

25. Hugo Scherer Mausoleum at Woodlawn Cemetery
(1925; George D. Mason)
19975 Woodward Ave
Detroit, MI
[L]
Ledger details: Job #33*; 1924-1925
"Schere (sic) Maus"

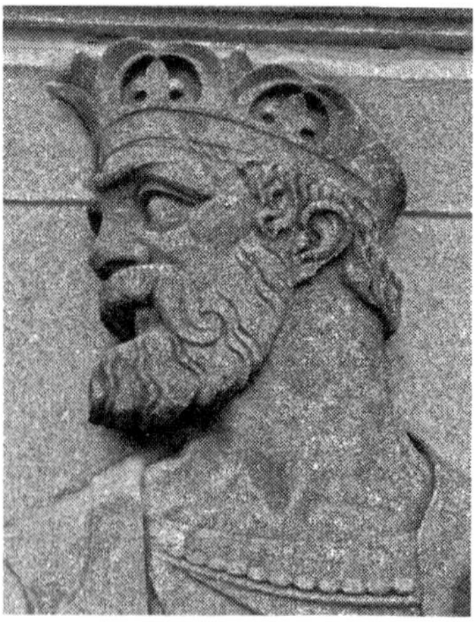

26. Acacia Park Cemetery Gates
(c.1926; George D. Mason)
31300 Southfield Rd
Beverly Hills, MI
[L]
Ledger details: Jobs #36*/#12
1924-1925/1925
"Acacia Park Cemetery"

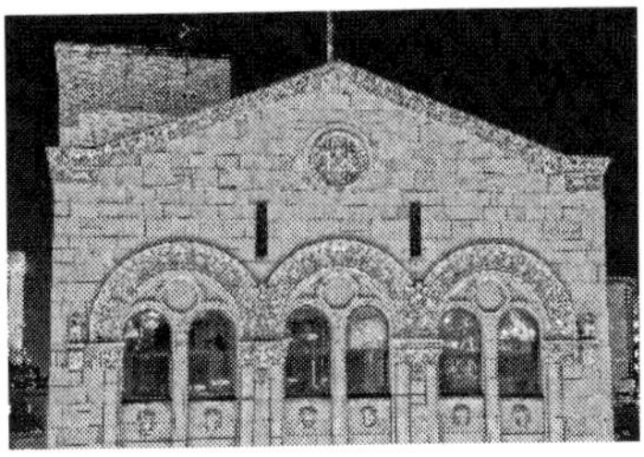

27. Broadway Exchange Building also known as American Radiator Building now known as Harvard Square Center
(1925-1926; George D. Mason)
1342-1346 Broadway St
Detroit, MI
[L]
Ledger details: Jobs #39*/#31
1924-1925/1925
"Scherer Building"

Hugo Scherer's widow, Clara, financed the construction of this building.

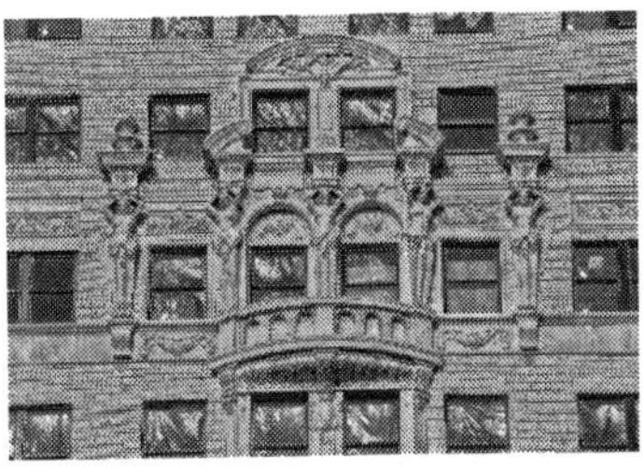

28. Book Tower
(1926; Louis Kamper)
1265 Washington Blvd
Detroit, MI
[L]
Ledger details: Jobs #40*/#15/#51
1924-1925/1925/1926
"Book Tower Add."

Margin notations in the ledgers lead us to believe Parducci also created interior plaster patterns at this site. In our opinion it is likely that sculptors other than Parducci contributed to this building's exterior embellishments, and furthermore, it is difficult to say with certainty which specific sculptural works are his.

29. Alfred J. Fisher Residence
(1926; Richard Marr)
1771 Balmoral Dr
Detroit, MI
[L, DB]
Ledger details: Jobs #41*/#16, #20/ #44, #46, #48
1924-1925/1925/1926
"A.J. Fisher Res"

In August of 1925 Parducci bought out all of DiLorenzo's Detroit interests and opened his own studio, located on Congress Street, a short distance from the Marquette Building. As previously stated, at the outset of his solo enterprise, Parducci restarted the numbering of jobs in his ledgers at #1.

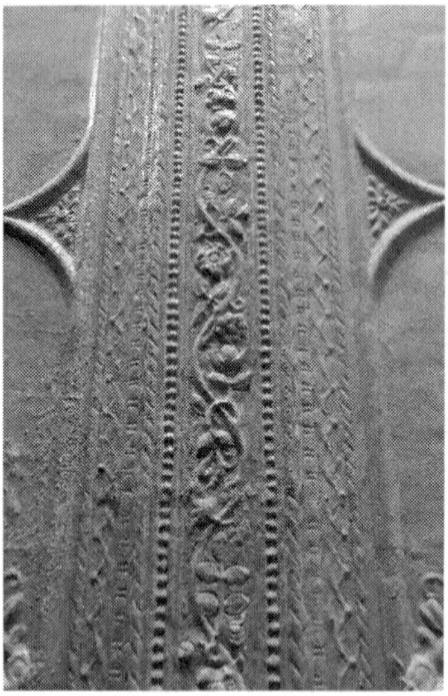

30. Albert Kahn Residence now known as Detroit Urban League ~ Gallery and Garage Additions
(1928; Albert Kahn)
208 Mack Ave
Detroit, MI
[L]
Ledger details: Jobs #3/#84
1925/1927
"Albert Kahn Res"

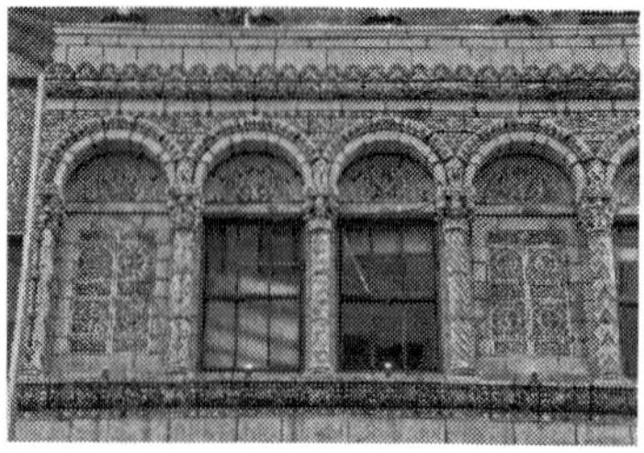

31. Bankers Trust Company Building
(1925; Wirt Rowland of Smith. Hinchman & Grylls)
211 W Congress St
Detroit, MI
[L]
Ledger details: Job #17; 1925
"Bankers Trust Co"

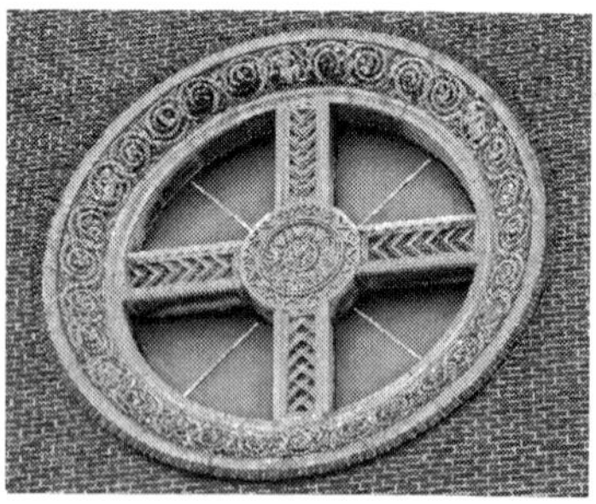

32. St. Theresa of Avila Catholic Church
(1924; Van Leyen, Schilling & Keough)
8666 Quincy St
Detroit, MI
[L]
Ledger details: Jobs #23/#880
1925/1952
"St Theresa Ch"

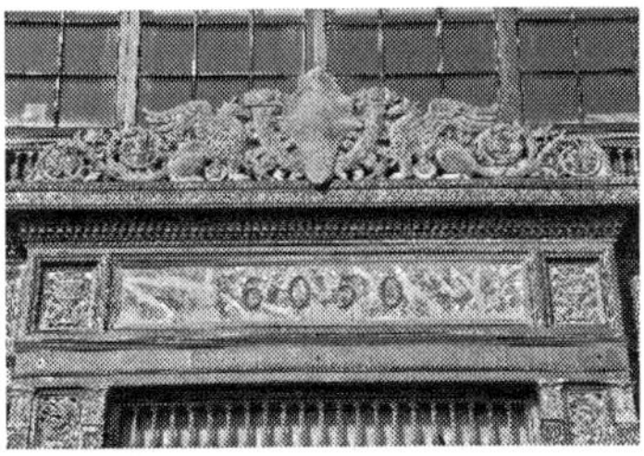

33. Stewart-Warner Speedometer Company Building now known as Wayne State University Police Headquarters
(1925; Charles Noble)
6050 Cass Ave
Detroit. MI
[L, DB]
Ledger details: Jobs #30/#49
1925/1926
"Stewart Warner"

In the 1975 Smithsonian interview Parducci speaks of a plaster ceiling he created for this structure's interior. Its current status is unknown to us.

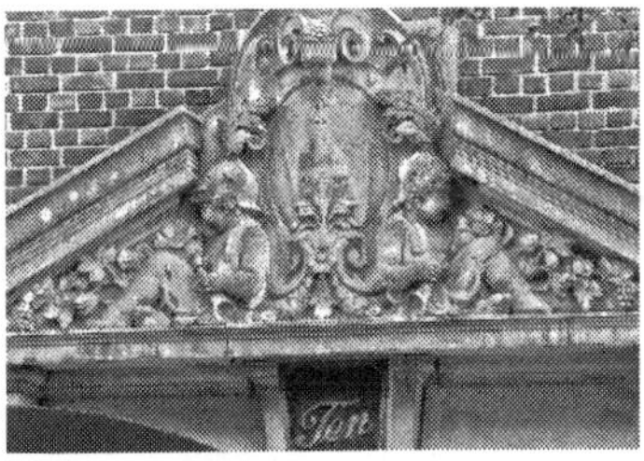

34. Walbri Court Apartments
(1926; Albert Kahn)
1001 Covington Dr
Detroit, MI
[L]
Ledger details: Job #34; 1925
"Briggs Apts"

This building's construction was financed by former Detroit Tigers owner Walter Briggs.

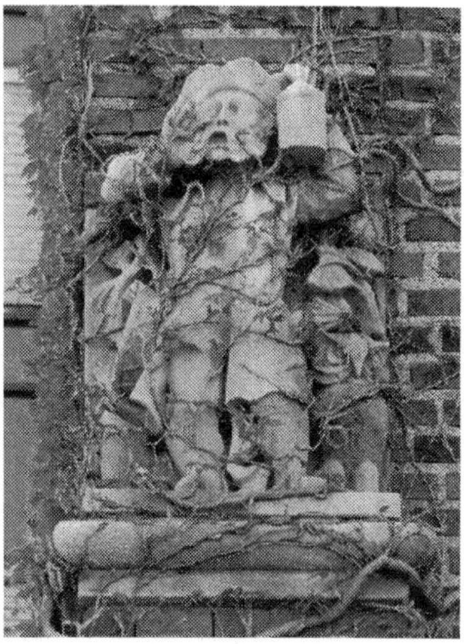

35. George Harrison Phelps, Inc. Studio and Office Building
(1926; Wirt Rowland of Smith, Hinchman & Grylls)
2761 E Jefferson Ave
Detroit, MI
[L]
Ledger details: Job #41; 1925
"George H. Phelps Radio Studio"

The first substantial gap in Parducci's ledgers is recorded on the 1926 page, between jobs #44 and #45. We believe the following fourteen commissions (entries #36 through #49) fall within this gap. Eleven of the fourteen are recorded in the ledgers on dates significantly later than 1926. As a general rule we have found that if a commission site appears in the ledgers, regardless of the year it is first recorded, it is also very likely that Parducci produced the architectural sculpture for its original construction. In most of these cases, in addition to their late entries in the ledgers, we cite nearly undeniable stylistic similarities to other Parducci works as the most compelling evidence supporting our attribution. Well established and well documented professional relationships with nearly all of the commissioning architectural firms also support our cases.

36. Calvin Coolidge Elementary School
(1925; Charles M. Valentine?)
16501 Elmira St
Detroit. MI
[L]
Ledger details: Job #250; 1929
"Coolidge High Sch"

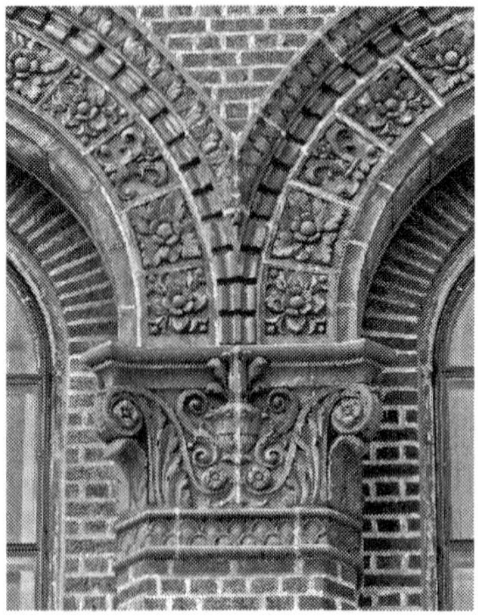

37. Michigan Bell Central Office
(1925; Wirt Rowland of Smith, Hinchman & Grylls)
325 E Washington St
Ann Arbor, MI
[L]
Ledger details:
Jobs #750/#763/#787
1946/1947/1948
"Telephone Bldg Ann Arbor"

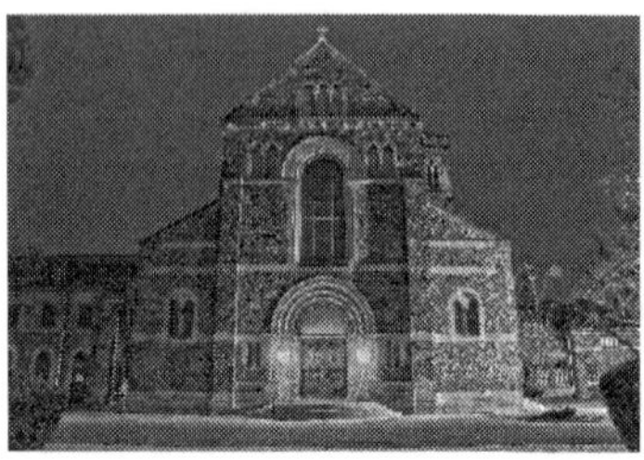

38. St. Mary of Redford Catholic Church ~ Exterior Elements
(1925; Cram & Ferguson with McGrath, Dohmen & Page)
14750 St Marys St
Detroit, MI
[L]
Ledger details: Job #775; 1947
"St Mary's Redford"

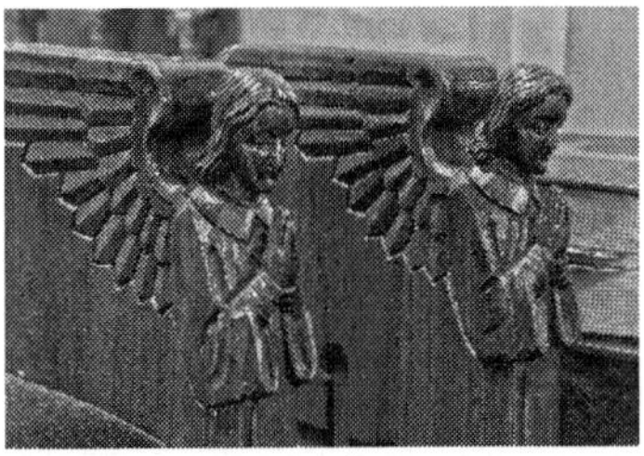

39. St. Mary of Redford Catholic Church ~ Interior Elements
(1925; Cram & Ferguson with McGrath, Dohmen & Page)
14750 St Marys St
Detroit, MI
[L]
Ledger details: Job #775; 1947
"St Mary's Redford"

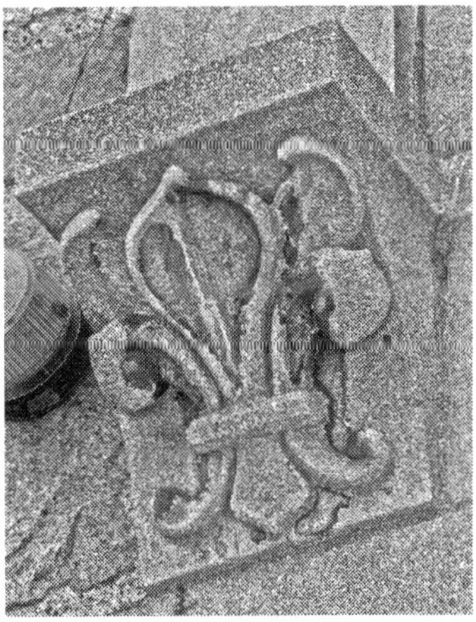

40. St. Mary of Redford Catholic Church ~ Rectory
(1925; Cram & Ferguson with McGrath, Dohmen & Page)
Mansfield St at Eaton Ave
Detroit, MI
[L]
Ledger details: Job #775; 1947
"St Mary's Redford"

41. Benjamin A. Nolan School
(1926; Wirt Rowland of Smith, Hinchman & Grylls)
1150 E Lantz St
Detroit, MI
[L]
Ledger details: Job #310; 1931
"Noland (sic) Sch"

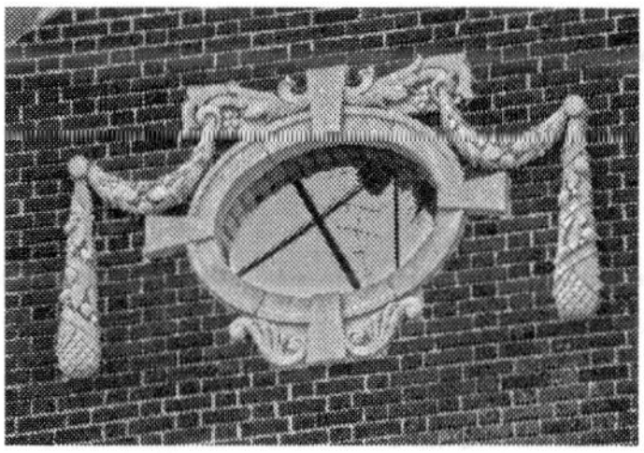

42. Hannan Memorial Y.M.C.A.
(1927; Robert O. Derrick)
10401 E Jefferson Ave
Detroit. MI
[L]
Ledger details: Job #312; 1931
"YMCA"

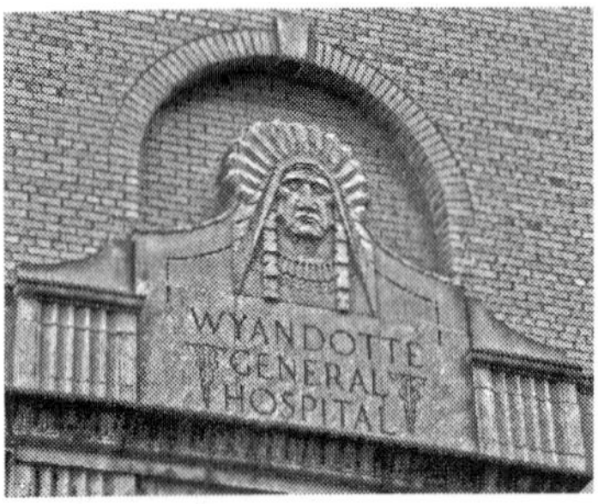

43. Wyandotte General Hospital
(1926; Stratton & Snyder)
2333 Biddle Ave
Wyandotte, MI
[L]
Ledger details: Job #313; 1931
"Wyandott (sic) Hospt"

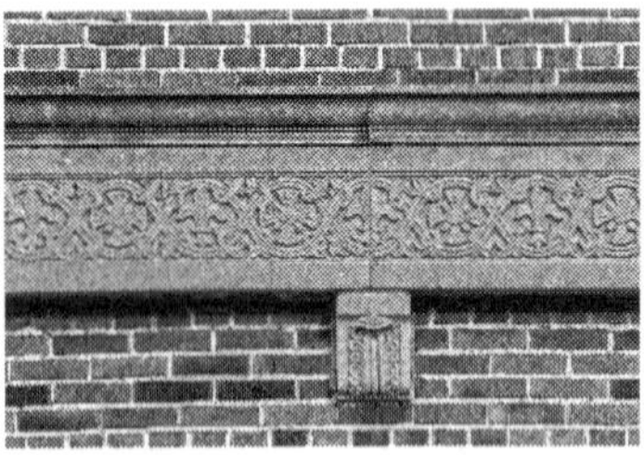

44. St. Rita School
(1926; Charles M. Valentine?)
19660 Cameron St
Detroit, MI
[L]
Ledger details: Job #315; 1931
"St Rita Sch"

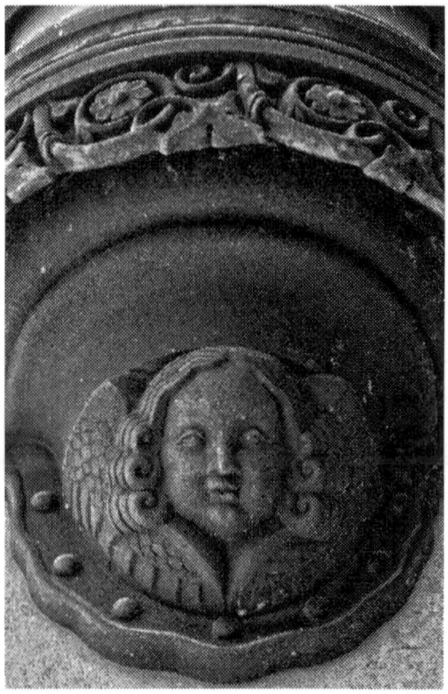

45. St. Ambrose Catholic Church
(1926; Donaldson & Meier)
15050 Hampton St
Grosse Pointe Park, MI
[L]
Ledger details: Job #671; 1942
"St Ambrose Ch"

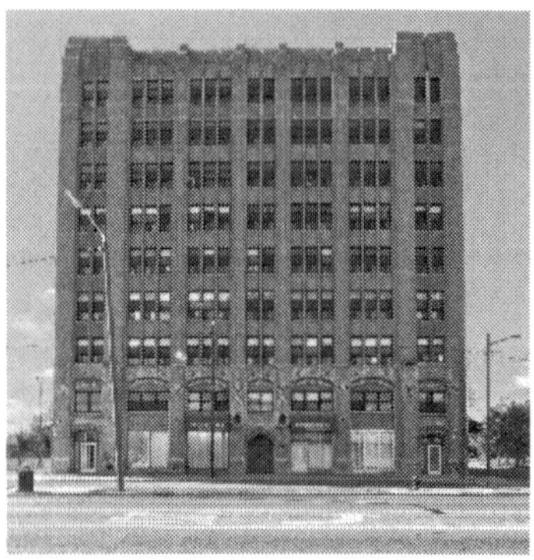

46. Boulevard Temple Methodist Episcopal Church
(1926; J. Ivan Dise)
2567 W Grand Blvd
Detroit, MI
[L]
Ledger details: Job #886; 1952
"Methodist Ch"

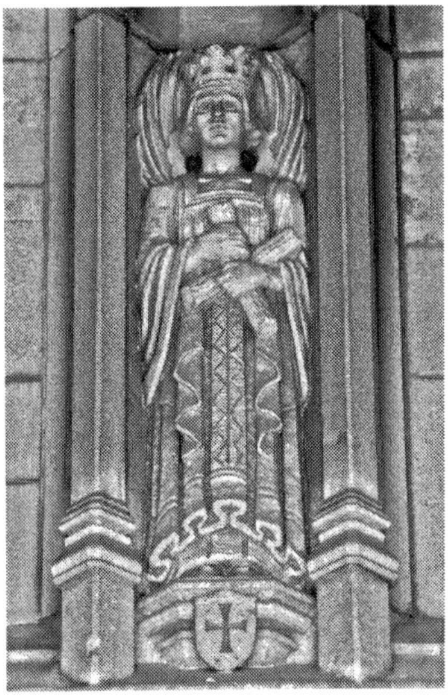

47. Jefferson Avenue Presbyterian Church
(1925-1926; Wirt Rowland of Smith, Hinchman & Grylls)
8625 E Jefferson Ave
Detroit, MI
[Speculative]
Ledger details: N/A

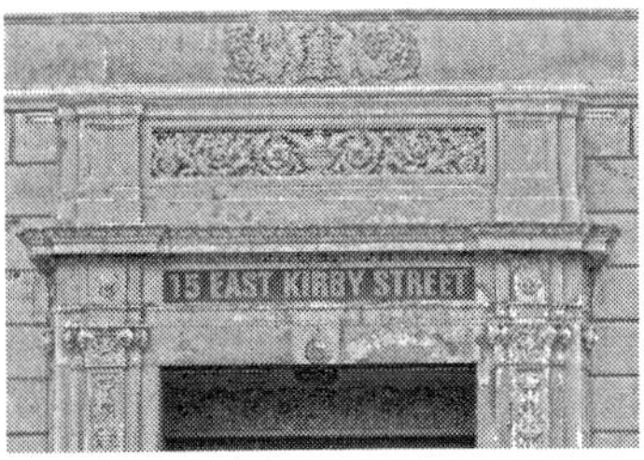

48. Park-Shelton Apartments
(1926; Weston & Ellington)
15 E Kirby St
Detroit, MI
[Speculative]
Ledger details: N/A

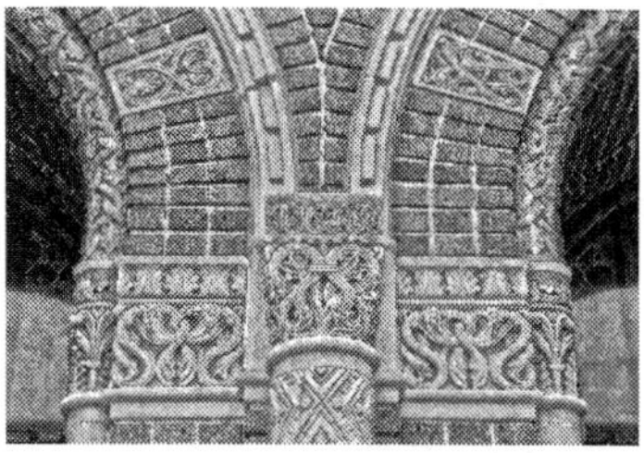

49. Chapel of St. Theresa the Little Flower also known as St. Patrick Catholic Church
(1926; Donaldson & Meier)
50 Parsons St
Detroit, MI
[Speculative]
Ledger details: N/A

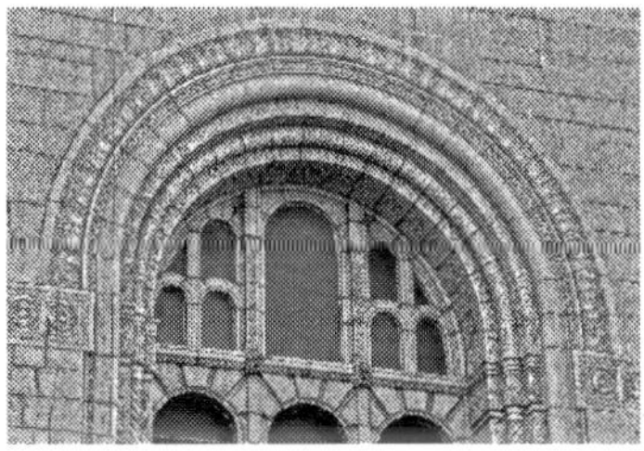

50. Grand Rapids Trust Company Building
(1926; Wirt Rowland of Smith, Hinchman & Grylls)
61-77 Monroe Center SW
Grand Rapids, MI
[L, SB, FH, WK]
Ledger details: Job #45; 1926
"Grand Rapids Trust Co"

The second gap in Parducci's record keeping appears between jobs #63 and #80 on the first of two 1927 ledger pages. We believe the following ten commissions (entries #51 through #60) fall within this gap. Entries #51 and #52 are confirmed by non-ledger sources. As with the 1926 ledger gap, the remaining attributions for these entries are supported primarily by nearly undeniable stylistic similarities to other Parducci works of the era, as well as his established and well documented professional relationships with both of the commissioning architectural firms. Parducci's close personal friendship with Wirt Rowland of Smith, Hinchman & Grylls is especially significant, as Rowland designed nearly all the Central Offices Michigan Bell erected statewide during their flurry of constructions between 1926 and 1930, five of which are included below. Incidentally, every Michigan Bell Central Office included in our list, save one, is now an AT&T Building. Petoskey's Bell Building now serves as the community's public library.

Also, in 1927 Parducci moved into new studio space at Tenth and Abbott in Detroit.

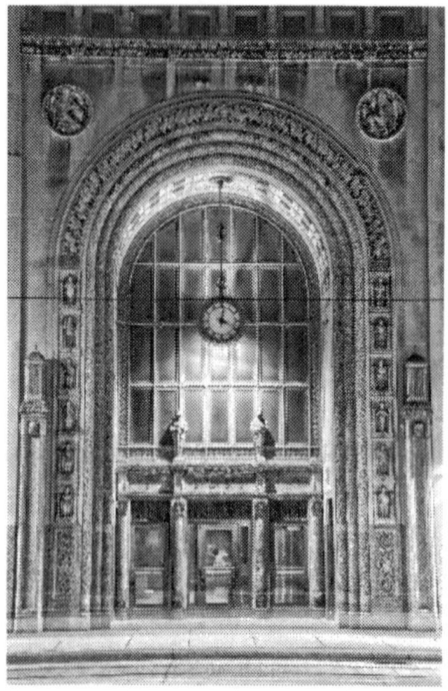

51. Maccabees Building
also known as
Detroit School Center Building
(1926-1927; Albert Kahn)
5057 Woodward Ave
Detroit, MI
[DB, WK]
Ledger details: N/A

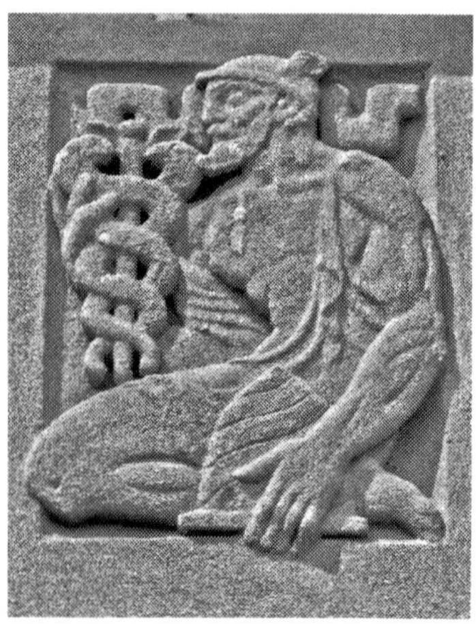

52. Nash-Kelvinator Plant Administration Building also known as American Motors Corporation Research and Design Center
(1927; Amadeo Leone of Smith, Hinchman & Grylls)
14250 Plymouth Rd
Detroit, MI
[SB]
Ledger details: N/A

53. Michigan Bell Central Office
(1927-1928; Wirt Rowland of Smith, Hinchman & Grylls)
142 E State St
Traverse City, MI
[Speculative]
Ledger details: N/A

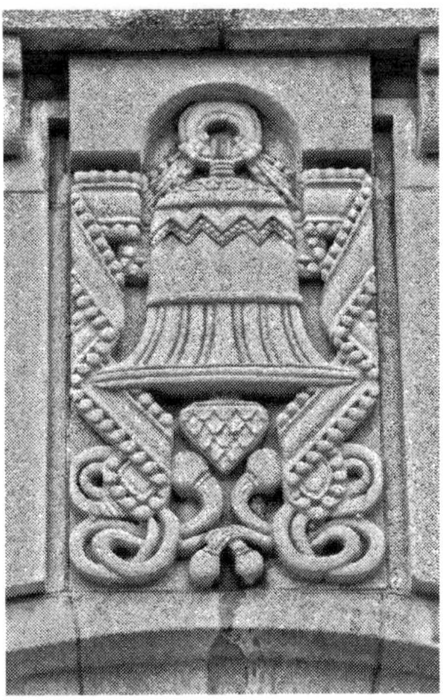

54. Michigan Bell Central Office
(1926; Wirt Rowland of Smith, Hinchman & Grylls)
300 S Jackson St
Jackson, MI
[Speculative]
Ledger details: N/A

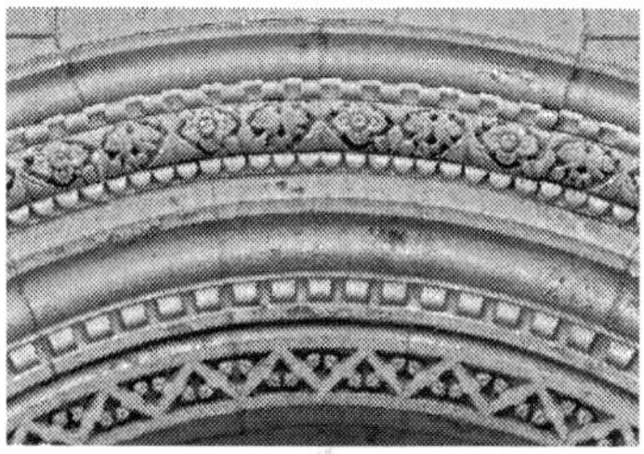

55. Michigan Bell "Hogarth" Central Office
(1926; Wirt Rowland of Smith, Hinchman & Grylls)
10515 Northlawn St
Detroit, MI
[Speculative]
Ledger details: N/A

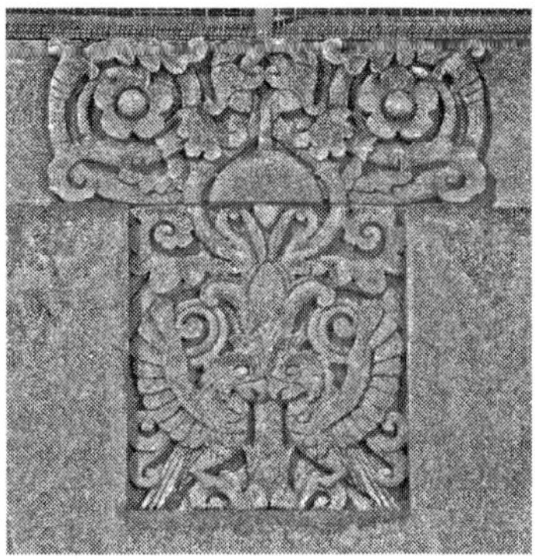

56. Michigan Bell "Columbia" Central Office
(1926; Wirt Rowland of Smith, Hinchman & Grylls)
52 Selden St
Detroit, MI
[Speculative]
Ledger details: N/A

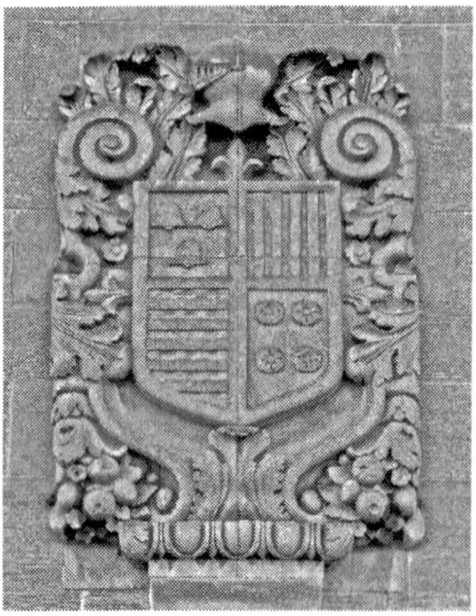

57. Michigan Bell "University" Central Office
(1926; Wirt Rowland of Smith, Hinchman & Grylls)
7000 W McNichols Rd
Detroit, MI
[Speculative]
Ledger details: N/A

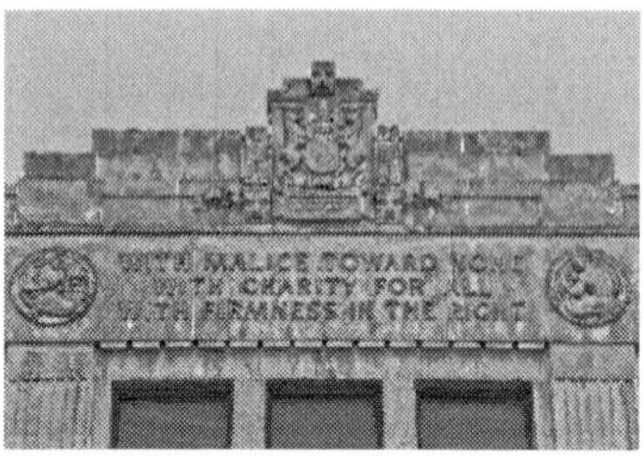

58. Jackson Citizen-Patriot Building
(1927; Albert Kahn)
214 S Jackson St
Jackson, MI
[Speculative]
Ledger details: N/A

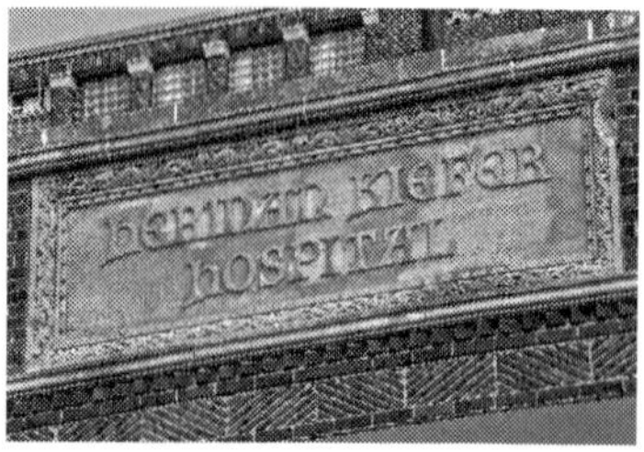

59. Herman Kiefer Hospital ~ Main Building
(1927-1928; Albert Kahn)
1151 Taylor St
Detroit, MI
[Speculative]
Ledger details: N/A

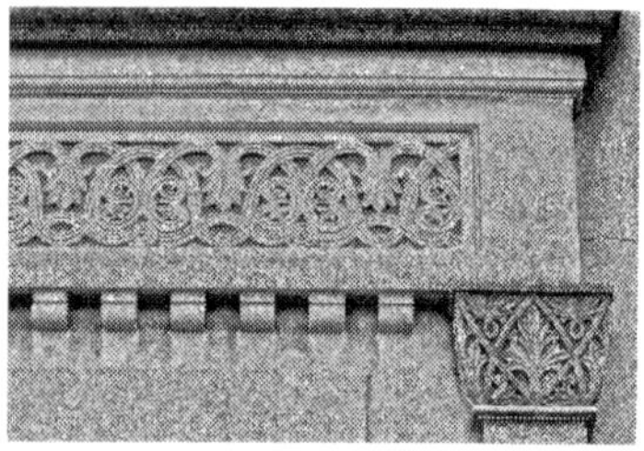

60. St. Brigid School now known as Flagship Charter Academy
(1927; architect undetermined)
13661 Wisconsin St
Detroit, MI
[Speculative]
Ledger details: N/A

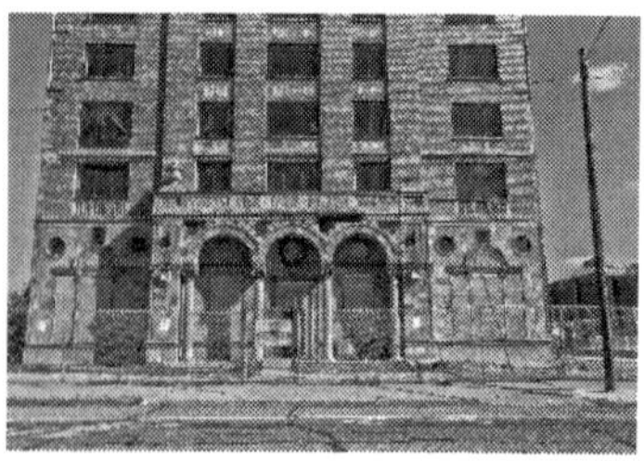

61. Lee Plaza
(1928; Charles Noble)
2240 W Grand Blvd
Detroit, MI
[L, DB]
Ledger details: Jobs #81/#325
1927/1932
"Lee Plaza Hotel Apts"

In the ledger margins Parducci erroneously attributes this building's design to Charles Agree.

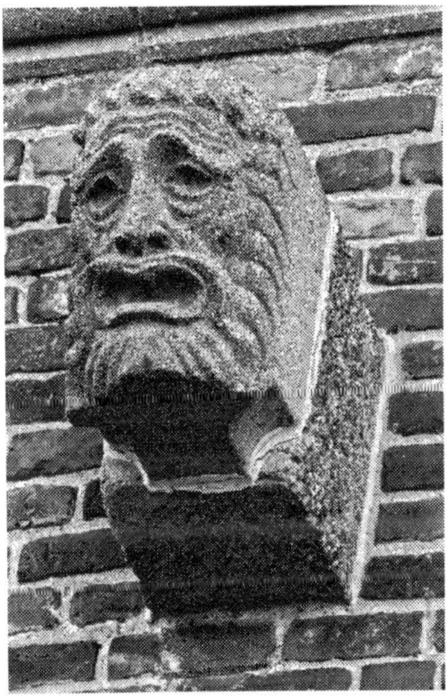

62. The Players Playhouse
(1925; William E. Kapp of Smith, Hinchman & Grylls)
3321 E Jefferson Ave
Detroit, MI
[L, DB, WK]
Ledger details: Jobs #82/#957
1927/1956
"Players Playhouse"

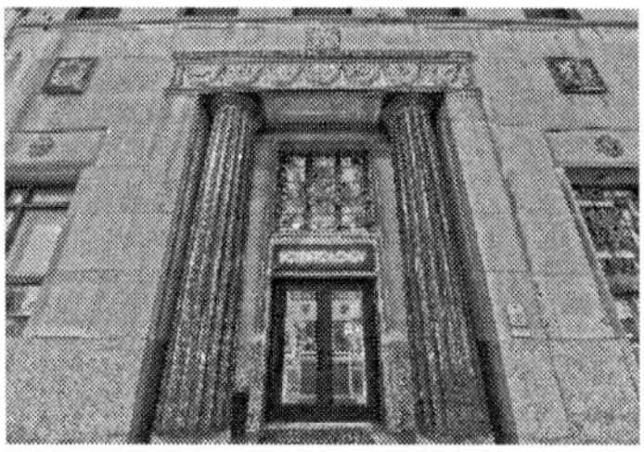

63. Standard Savings & Loan Building ~ Stone
(1927; George D. Mason)
1 Griswold St
Detroit, MI
[L, DB]
Ledger details: Job #83; 1927
"Standard Savings and Loan Bk"

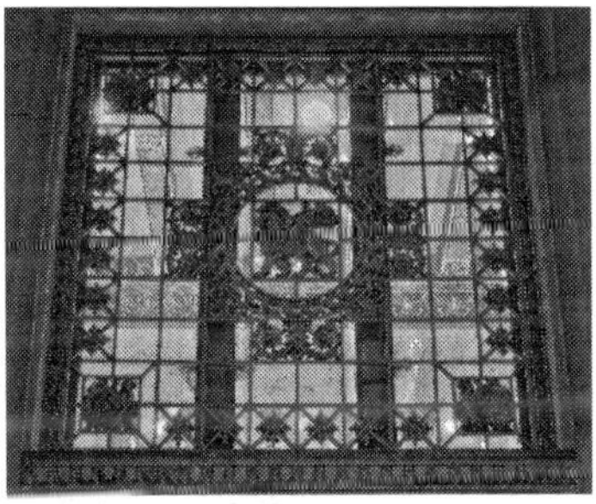

64. Standard Savings and Loan Building ~ Bronze
(1927; George D. Mason)
1 Griswold St
Detroit, MI
[L]
Ledger details: Job #83; 1927
"Standard Savings and Loan Bk"

Regarding this commission Parducci states in the 1975 Smithsonian interview: *"That bank building on the corner of Griswold and Jefferson, you know, that Standard Savings Bank, I think. If you look at that, there's very fine work in that. In fact, it won a medal in New York...And you go in that banking room, see some of the bronze and the screen between the hall and the banking room, and now the character of that work is different from any other character. It has a little touch of Greek, a little archaic touch to it. But it isn't a book style. You see what I mean?"*

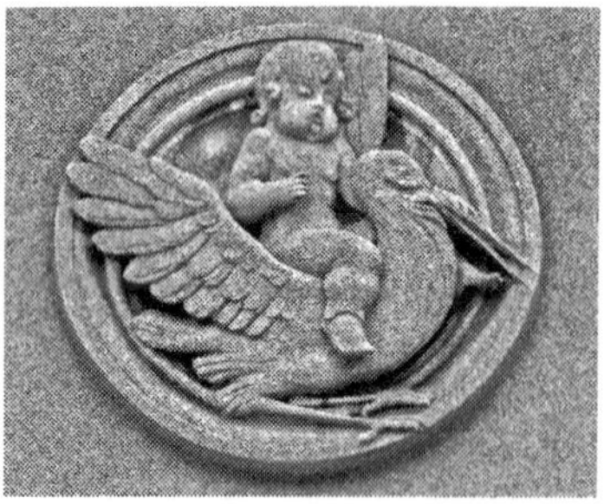

65. The Woman's Hospital
(1927-1929; Albert Kahn)
450 E Hancock St
Detroit, MI
[L]
Ledger details: Jobs #85/#166
1927/1928
"Womans Hospital"

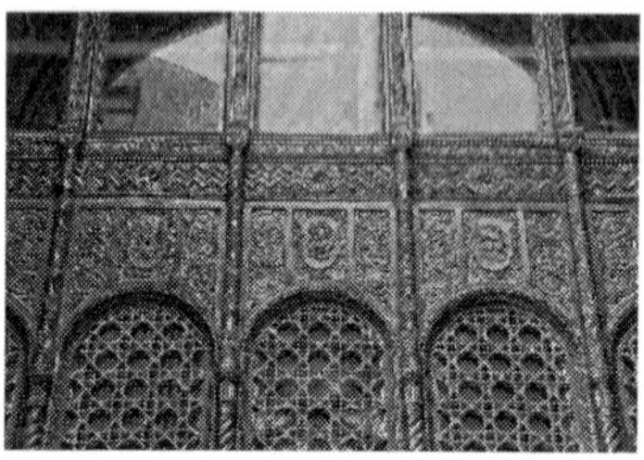

66. David Stott Building
(1929; Donaldson & Meier)
1150 Griswold St
Detroit, MI
[L]
Ledger details:
Jobs #87/#130, #150, #155
1927/1928
"David Stott Bldg"

67. University Museums Building at University of Michigan now known as Alexander G. Ruthven Building
(1926-1928; Albert Kahn)
1109 Geddes Ave
Ann Arbor, MI
[L]
Ledger details: Job #89; 1927
"University of Mich"

Other sources might lead one to believe that all exterior sculpture at this location was executed by Carleton Watson Angell, a former University of Michigan professor and museum director. We would beg to differ. Kahn, at this point in his career, often employed multiple architectural sculptors for a single structure and we believe this to be an example of such a division of labor. A 1955 accounting of Angell's lifetime output, published by the University Museums, lists only the "shield" portion of this structure's entrance surround and lintel. The stylistic tendencies of Parducci and Ricci are on full display throughout the many remaining elements. In our opinion there is very little doubt that Job #89 in Parducci's ledgers refers specifically to this building. Parducci's contributions might also include exterior bronze and interior plaster.

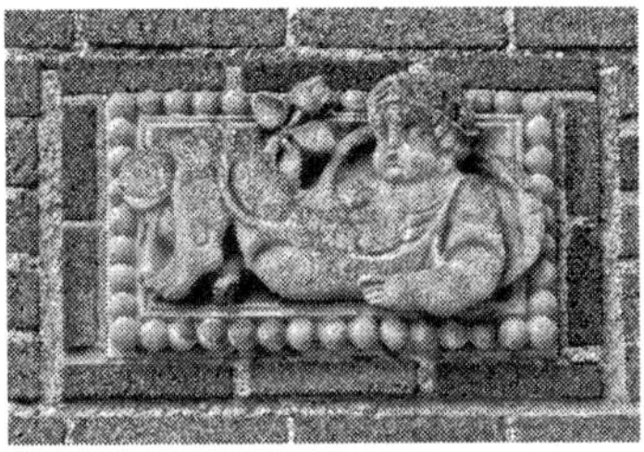

68. Brush Building ~
Harper Hospital at
Detroit Medical Center
(1928; Albert Kahn)
Approximately 3800 Brush St
Detroit Medical Center Mall
Detroit, MI
[L]
Ledger details: Job #90; 1927
"Harper Hospt"

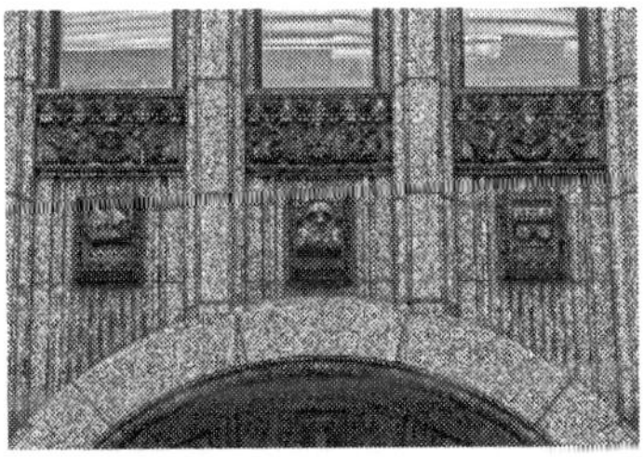

69. Fisher Building ~
Exterior Elements
(1928; Albert Kahn)
3011 W Grand Blvd
Detroit, MI
[L, DB, JB]
Ledger details: Jobs #91, #95/#311
1927/1931
"Fisher Building"

In her 1978 Master's Essay, 'Géza Maróti and the Decoration of the Fisher Building Lobby', Joan Boddie writes that Parducci "did much of the interior and exterior sculptural ornament under Maróti's guidance."

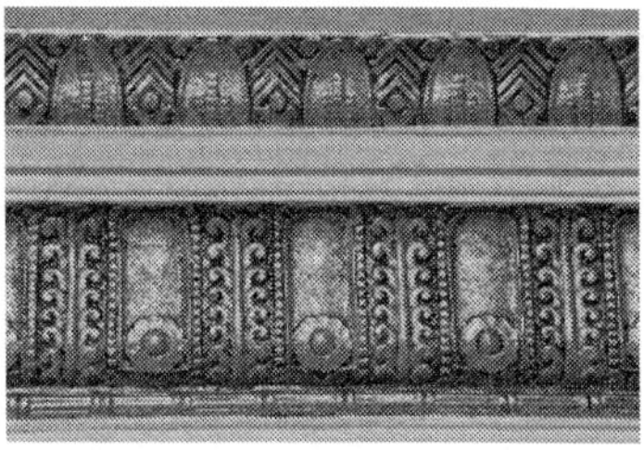

70. Fisher Building ~
Interior Plaster Elements
(1928; Albert Kahn)
3011 W Grand Blvd
Detroit, MI
[L, DB, JB]
Ledger details: Jobs #91, #95/#311
1927/1931
"Fisher Building"

Another excerpt from Boddie's Master's Essay, supporting our case for Parducci's contributions to the Fisher's plaster embellishments:

"Maróti designed nearly all of the decorations himself but employed numerous artisans to make full scale cartoons of some of his drawings, execute the painting, prepare three dimensional versions of his drawings for the sculpture and bronzework, and also execute it. The painting was done (in only two months' time) by Thomas DiLorenzo of Detroit; Ricci and Zari of New York modeled the exterior ornaments, excepting those of the main entrance doorway; Anthony DiLorenzo of New York prepared the models for most of the bronzework, and Corrado Parducci of Detroit also worked on the bronzework and created all the plaster ornaments."

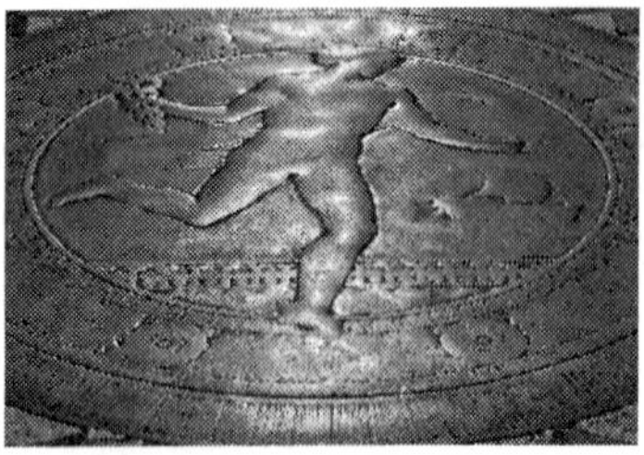

71. Fisher Building ~ Lobby Medallion
(1928; Albert Kahn)
3011 W Grand Blvd
Detroit, MI
[L, DB, JB]
Ledger details: Jobs #91, #95/#311 1927/1931
"Fisher Building"

An excerpt from Parducci's 1975 interview regarding the Fisher's many sculptural embellishments, including the lobby medallion:

"CORRADO PARDUCCI: *I did one third of the work, DiLorenzo made one third, and Ricci made one third. The building went up within twelve months, and the work was divided three ways. In fact, four ways: Géza Maróti had the, he did the murals and he also made sketches for some of the work which he…I finally had to finish, had to do…He just couldn't handle it, because the work, the pace of the work was too fast…I did a lot of miscellaneous for the interior bronze and the plaque on the floor.*
DENNIS BARRIE: *How did you divide up the work, with four of you working?*
CORRADO PARDUCCI: *Well, Kahn divided it. I mean, Albert Kahn divided the work. He decided where…*
DENNIS BARRIE: *Who would do work.*
CORRADO PARDUCCI: *Ricci did work you don't see; it's the marble up above. DiLorenzo did some work for the store fronts and the entrance bronze, you know, over the entrance?*
DENNIS BARRIE: *Um hmm.*
CORRADO PARDUCCI: *I didn't have anything to do with the division. Albert Kahn decided for himself who was better at what."*

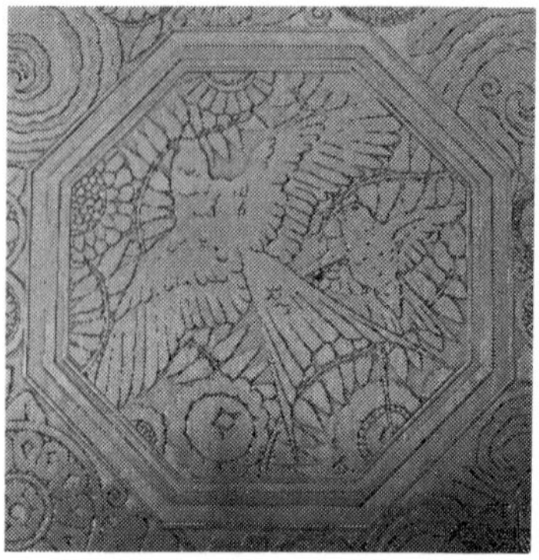

72. Fisher Building ~ Basement Elevator Doors
(1928; Albert Kahn)
3011 W Grand Blvd
Detroit, MI
[L, DB, JB]
Ledger details: Jobs #91, #95/#311 1927/1931
"Fisher Building"

A third excerpt from Boddie's Master's Essay, supporting our attribution for the Fisher's intaglio elevators doors found in its basement elevator bay:

"Other decorations are of perhaps questionable authorship. The *Michigan Manufacturer and Financial Record* credits the Parisian style Art Deco bronze intaglio doors, with their whimsical parrots, fish, and floating cogwheels, to Professor Maróti, while Corrado Parducci says the designs were his, just overseen by Maróti, and still possesses the drawings for them in his Detroit studio."

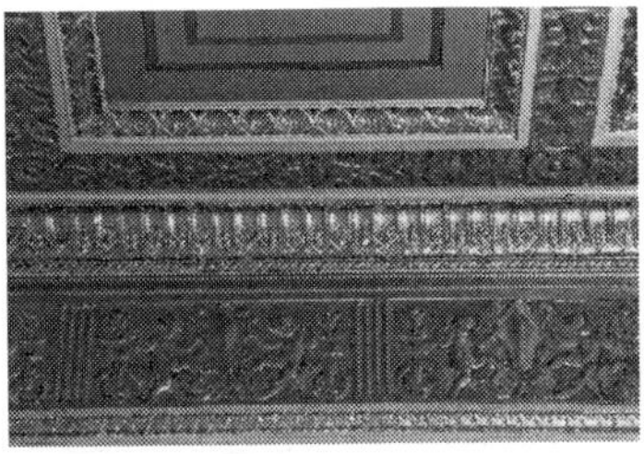

73. First National Bank Building Addition
(1928; Albert Kahn)
660 Woodward Ave
Detroit, MI
[L]
Ledger details: Jobs #92/#115 1927/1928
"First Nat Bk Bldg"

The First National Bank Building was built in two stages. The portions of the structure built in 1922 include all that faces Woodward Avenue and Campus Martius plus the length of the eleven westernmost dual window bays along Cadillac Square. The remaining portions, facing Cadillac Square, Bates Street and E. Congress, were built in 1928. Find Parducci's contributions inside the 1928 wing, in the vicinity of the first and second floor elevator bays and the connecting stairway.

Regarding entries #69 through #72, #74, #81 and #82, Parducci states in the 1975 Smithsonian interview: *"Now, besides making models, I also made scale models. Now I made a scale model of the Fisher Building. I made a scale of the Edsel Ford residence...I made two scale models of [the] Penobscot Building. Donaldson and Meier, they had the original contract for the architecture. And then the owners changed their minds and they had Smith, Hinchman & Grylls...And I made a scale model for both firms!"*

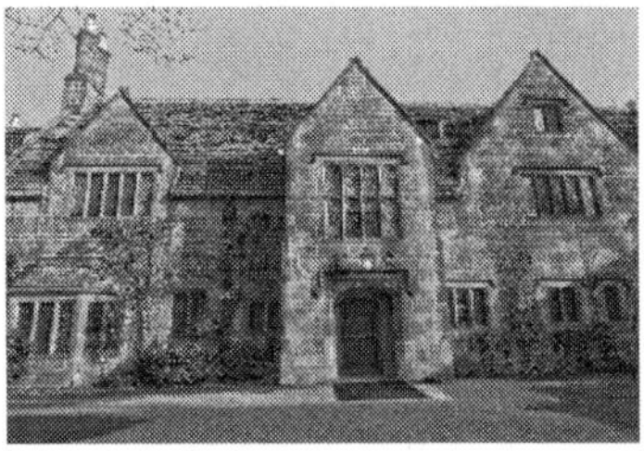

74. Ford House, Historic Estate of Edsel and Eleanor Ford ~ Scale Model
(1929; Albert Kahn)
1100 Lake Shore Dr
Grosse Pointe Shores, MI
[L, SB, DB]
Ledger details: Job #94; 1927
"Edsel Ford Res"

We also suspect Parducci of creating the residence's numerous plaster patterns but have yet to uncover incontrovertible proof.

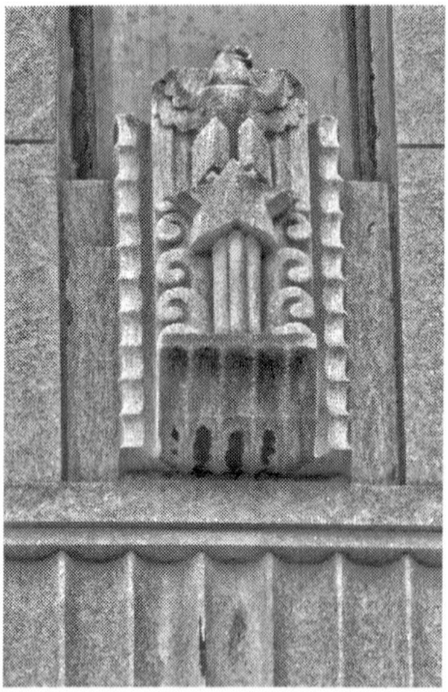

75. New Center Building now known as Albert Kahn Building
(1931; Albert Kahn)
7430 Second Ave
Detroit, MI
[L]
Ledger details: Job #96; 1927
"New Center Bldg"

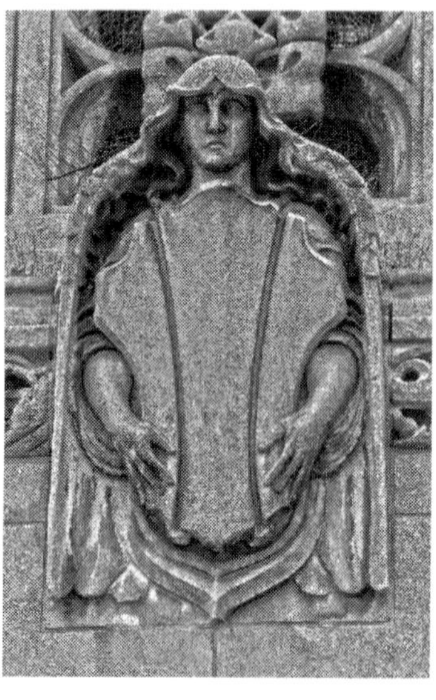

76. Central Woodward Christian Church now known as Little Rock Missionary Baptist church
(1926-1927; George D. Mason)
9000 Woodward Ave
Detroit, MI
[L]
Ledger details: Job #97; 1927
"Central Woodward Ch"

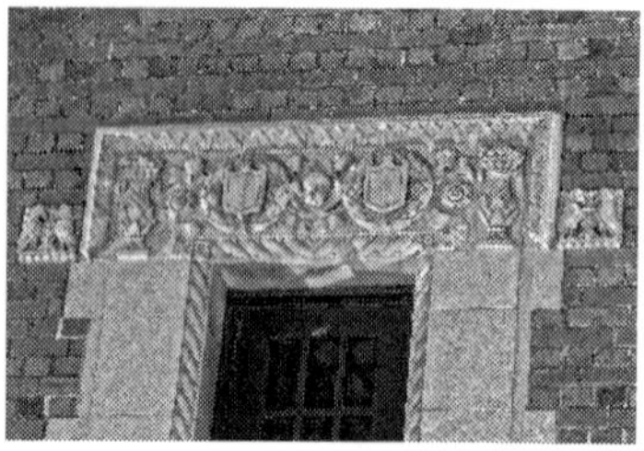

77. Gem Theatre
(1927; George D. Mason)
333 Madison Ave
Detroit, MI
[L]
Ledger details: Job #98; 1927
"20th Century Club"

78. Charles Lindbergh School
(1928, George D. Mason)
500 N Waverly St
Dearborn, MI
[L]
Ledger details: Job #105; 1927
"Dearborn Sch"

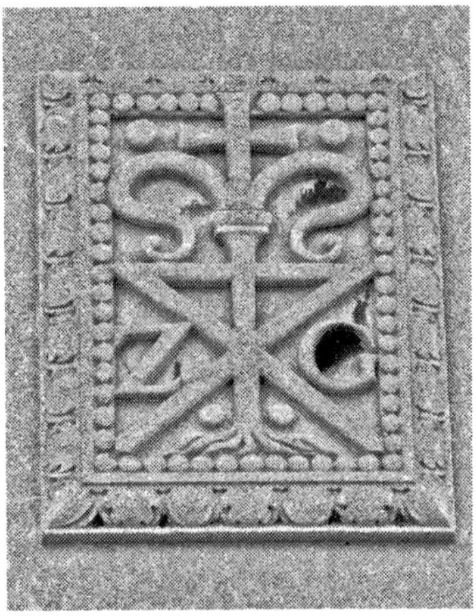

79. Muskegon Chronicle Building
(1927; Albert Kahn)
981 Third St
Muskegon, MI
[L]
Ledger details: Job #107; 1927
"Muskegon Chronicle"

80. Alpha Epsilon of Chi Psi Fraternity House
(c.1927; architect undetermined)
620 S State St
Ann Arbor, MI
[L]
Ledger details: Job #108; 1927
"Alpha Zhi (sic) Chi House"

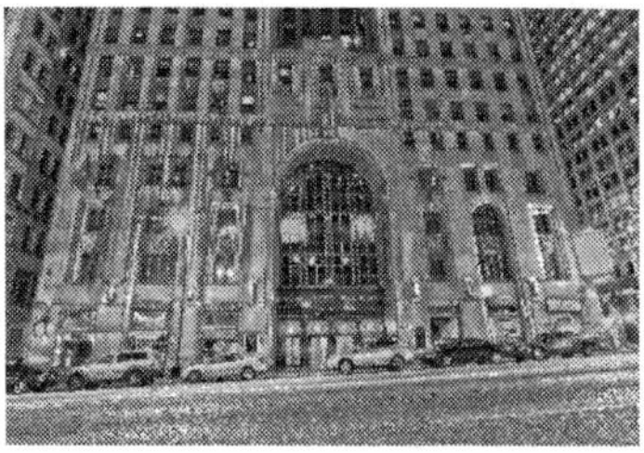

81. Greater Penobscot Building ~ Stone
(1928; Wirt Rowland of Smith, Hinchman & Grylls)
645 Griswold St
Detroit, MI
[L, SB, DB, WK]
Ledger details: Jobs #113/#169
1927/1929
"Greater Penobscot Bldg"

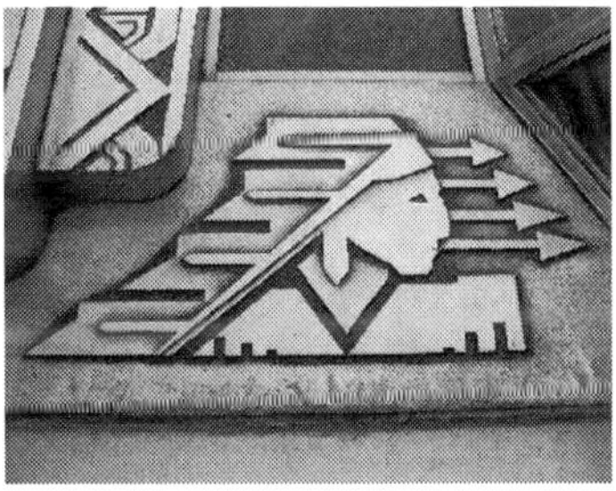

82. Greater Penobscot Building ~ Bronze
(1928; Wirt Rowland of Smith, Hinchman & Grylls)
645 Griswold St
Detroit, MI
[L, SB, DB]
Ledger details: Jobs #113/#169
1927/1929
"Greater Penobscot Bldg"

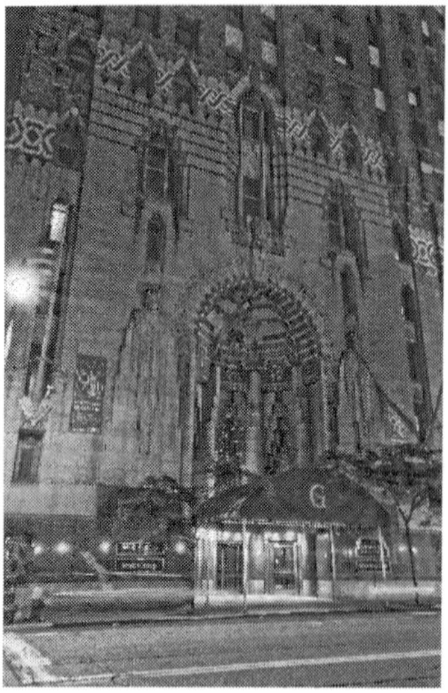

83. Guardian Building aka Union Trust Building
(1929; Wirt Rowland of Smith, Hinchman & Grylls)
500 Griswold St
Detroit, MI
[L, SB, DB, WK]
Ledger details: Job #114; 1927 "Union Trust Bldg"

Regarding this commission Parducci states in the 1975 Smithsonian interview: *"[T]hat's Wirt Rowland. I used to see a lot of him, and he drew there his dreams on the tablecloth. We used to have lunch together and... Of course, that building, it was an innovation in the sense that you had a thirty-degree angle on almost every detail... Which was different from the rectangular, circular lintel. And it has sort of an Aztec, Mayan, sort of a Mayan character to it. Well, I applied my work... You see, I made clay sketches, which met Wirt Roland's approval. But in making them... I always worked for fitness. In other words, I don't impose my will. I try to immerse myself in the character of the building, you see. Because the way I judge a piece of work is it doesn't scream. If you don't know it's there, and it's still functioning, that's good, see. Very few people know there's any carving there."*

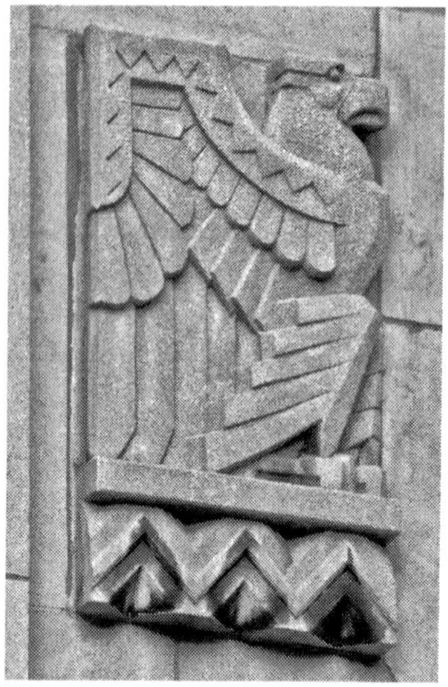

84. Griswold Building now known as "The Albert"
(1929: Albert Kahn)
1214 Griswold St
Detroit, MI
[L]
Ledger details: Job #117; 1928 "Griswold Bldg"

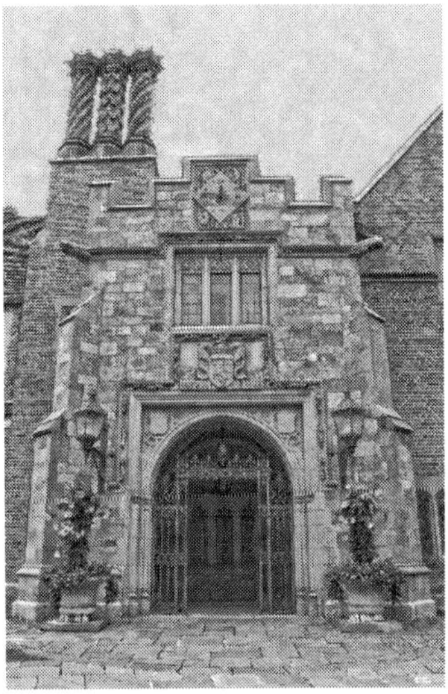

85. Meadow Brook Hall formerly known as Matilda Dodge Wilson Residence ~ Exterior Elements
(1926-1929; William E. Kapp of Smith, Hinchman & Grylls)
350 Estate Dr
Rochester Hills, MI
[L. SB, WK]
Ledger details: Jobs #118, #152
1928
"Wilson Res."

Parducci's contributions to the beauty of Meadow Brook Hall are legion, so much so that he could fairly be described as one of this construction's creative directors. Plaster works, woodwork and carved stone throughout bear his touch, as does the custom brick work of its unique triple chimneys. Parducci's personal scrapbook includes a photocopy of his well-deserved Meadow Brook Hall "Lifetime Pass".

86. Meadow Brook Hall formerly known as Matilda Dodge Wilson Residence ~ Interior Elements
(1926-1929; William E. Kapp of Smith, Hinchman & Grylls)
350 Estate Dr
Rochester Hills, MI
[L. SB, WK]
Ledger details: Jobs #118, #152
1928
"Wilson Res."

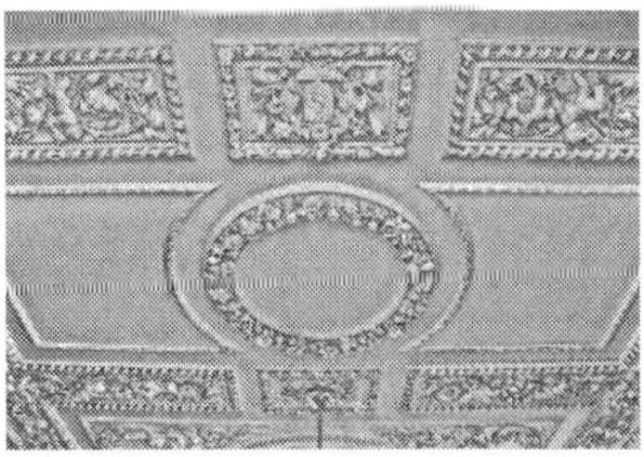

87. Meadow Brook Hall formerly known as Matilda Dodge Wilson Residence ~ Christopher Wren Dining Room Ceiling
(1926-1929; William E. Kapp of Smith, Hinchman & Grylls)
350 Estate Dr
Rochester Hills, MI
[L. SB, WK]
Ledger details: Jobs #118, #152
1928
"Wilson Res."

Parducci's masterwork and the Christopher Wren Dining Room are prominently featured in Michael Bay's 2011 film, "Transformers: Dark of the Moon".

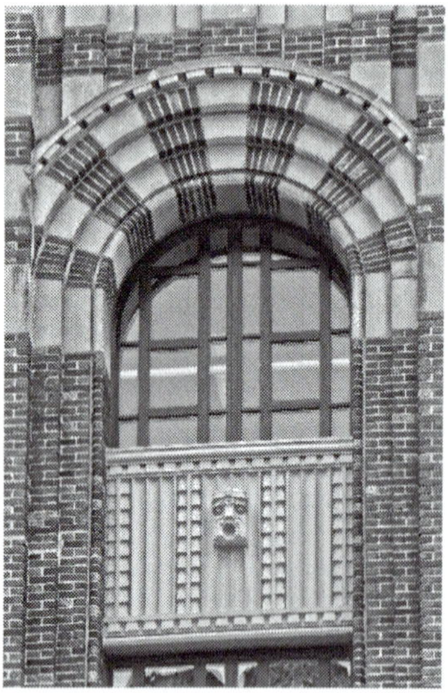

88. Argonaut Building
(1930; Albert Kahn)
425 W Milwaukee Ave
Detroit, MI
[L]
Ledger details: Job #120; 1928
"Argonaut Realty"

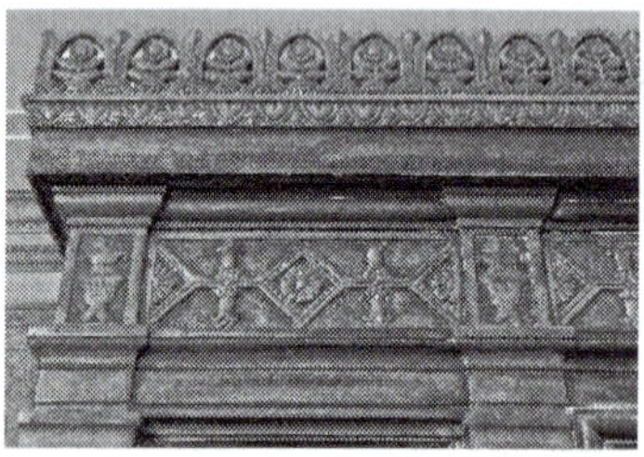

89. Youngstown Hospital
(1928-1929; Albert Kahn)
500 Gypsy Ln
Youngstown, OH
[L]
Ledger details: Jobs #123/#204
1928/1929
"Youngstown Hosp"

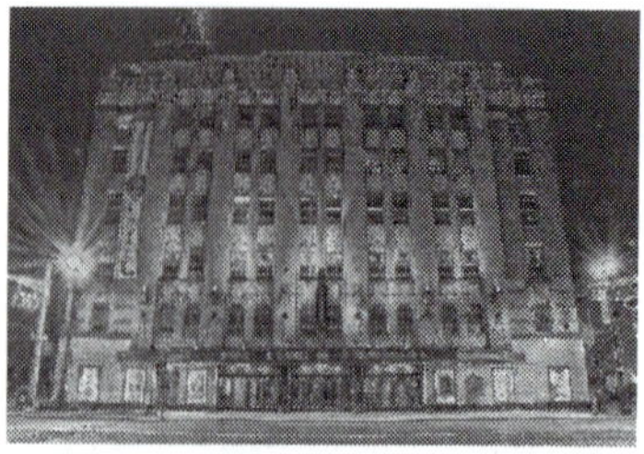

90. Wilson Theater now known as Music Hall Center for the Performing Arts
(1928, William E. Kapp of Smith, Hinchman & Grylls)
350 Madison Ave
Detroit, MI
[L, DB, WK]
Ledger details: Job #124; 1928
"Wilson Theatre"

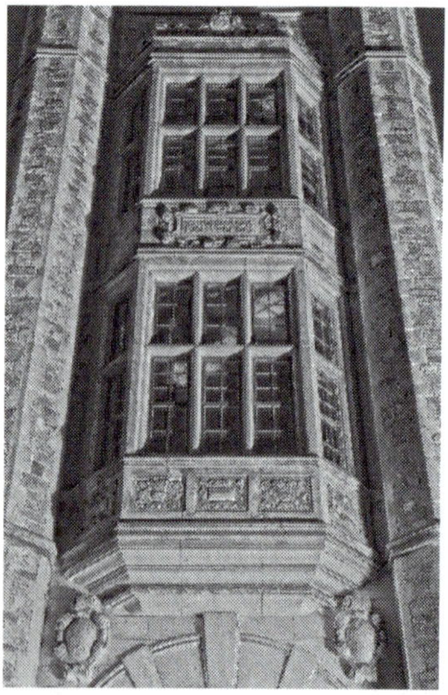

91. Dearborn Fordson High School
(1926-1928; Van Leyen, Schilling & Keough)
13800 Ford Rd
Dearborn, MI
[L]
Ledger details: Job #133; 1928
"Fordson Sch"

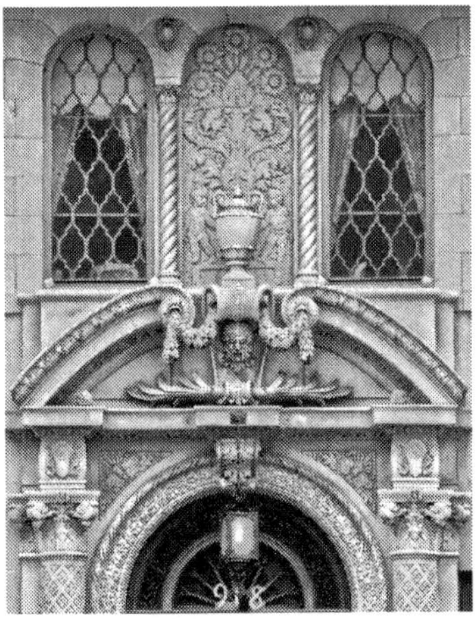

92. Leonard Augustus Young Residence formerly known as Nels Michelson Residence and Berry Gordy, Jr. Residence also known as "Motown Mansion"
(1926 renovation; Bingman & Davidson)
918 W Boston Blvd
Detroit, MI
[L]
Ledger details: Job #151; 1928
"LA Young"

The thorough 1926 renovation of L.A. Young's Boston Boulevard property included the addition of extensive architectural sculpture to the primary residence, originally built in 1917, and the construction of a detached "athletic building".

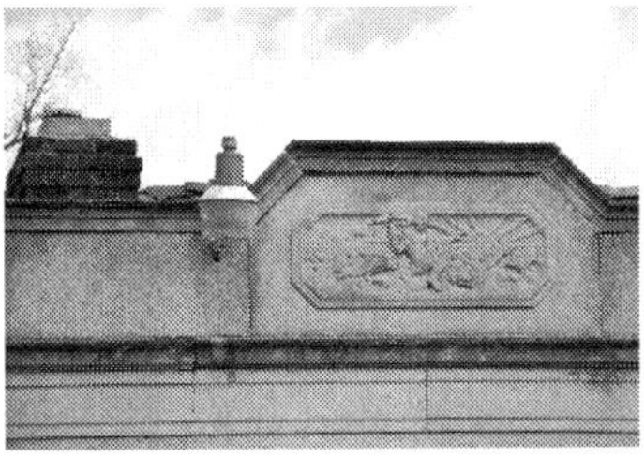

93. Leonard Augustus Young Residence ~ Athletic Building
(1926; Bingman & Davidson)
918 W Boston Blvd
Detroit, MI
[L]
Ledger details: Job #151; 1928
"LA Young"

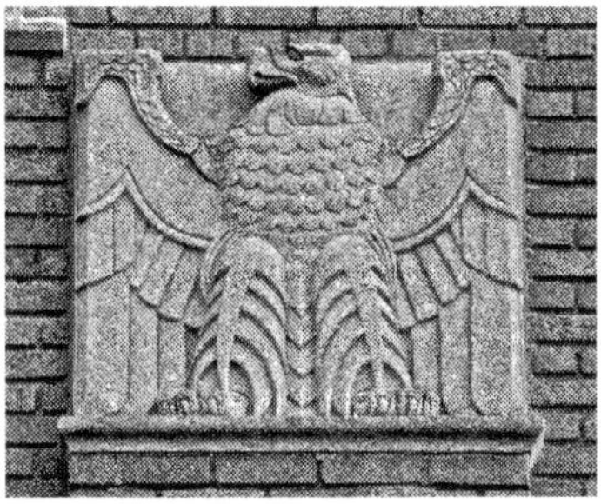

94. Gabriel Richard School
(1928; George D. Mason)
13840 Lappin St
Detroit, MI
[L]
Ledger details: Job #153; 1928
"Gabriel Richard Sch"

95. All Saints Episcopal Church
(1928; William E.N. Hunter)
3837 W Seven Mile Rd
Detroit, MI
[L]
Ledger details:
Jobs #154/#851, #867; 1928/1951
"All Saints Ch"

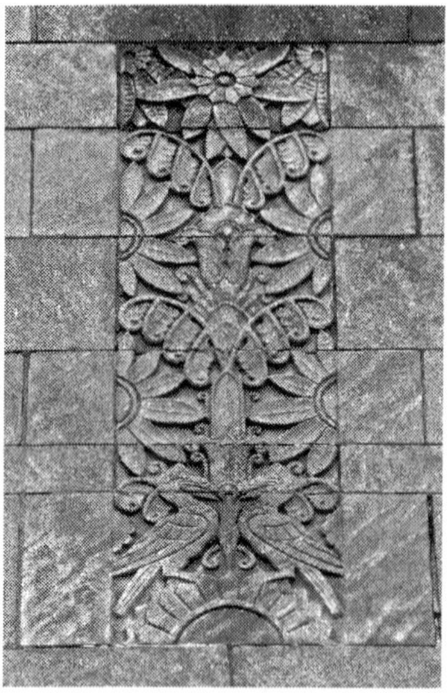

96. John C. Marshall Elementary School
(1928; McGrath, Dohmen & Page)
1255 E State Fair Ave
Detroit, MI
[L]
Ledger details: Job #162; 1928
"Marshal (sic) Sch"

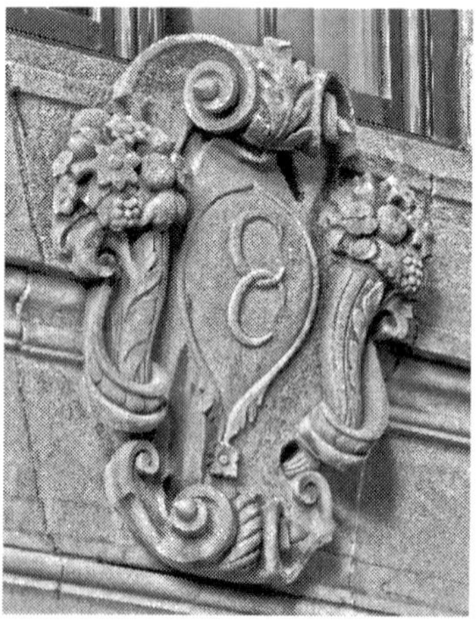

97. Colony Club ~ Exterior Elements
(1927-1929; Amadeo Leone of Smith, Hinchman & Grylls)
2310 Park Ave
Detroit, MI
[L, DB]
Ledger details: Jobs #163/#177
1928/1929
"Old Colony Club"

Regarding this commission Parducci states in the 1975 Smithsonian interview: *"See, now you take this building here, now Amadeo Leone's building here on Park? It used to be the Colony Club was it? You look at the entrance there, it's a very, you'd swear it was a seventeenth-century Italian cartouche over that...I'm very fond of that. Every time I pass it I say, 'Gee, that looks good.' After all these years."*

98. Colony Club ~ Interior Elements
(1927-1929; Amadeo Leone of Smith, Hinchman & Grylls)
2310 Park Ave
Detroit, MI
[L, DB]
Ledger details: Jobs #163/#177
1928/1929
"Old Colony Club"

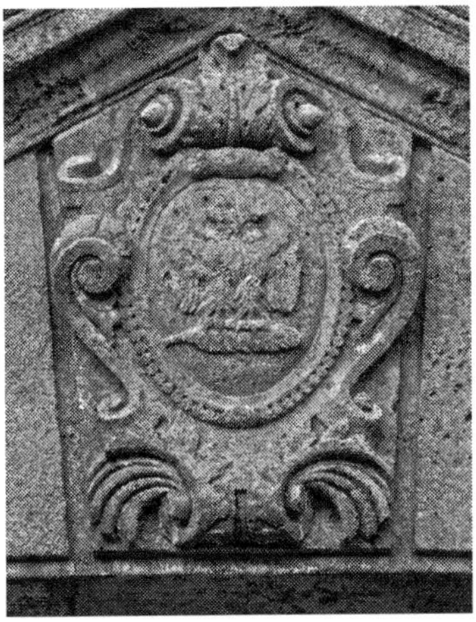

99. Charles Oakman School
(1929; Smith, Hinchman & Grylls)
12920 Wadsworth St
Detroit, MI
[L]
Ledger details: Jobs #171, #191
1929
"Charles Oakman Sch"
"Acme Cut Stone"

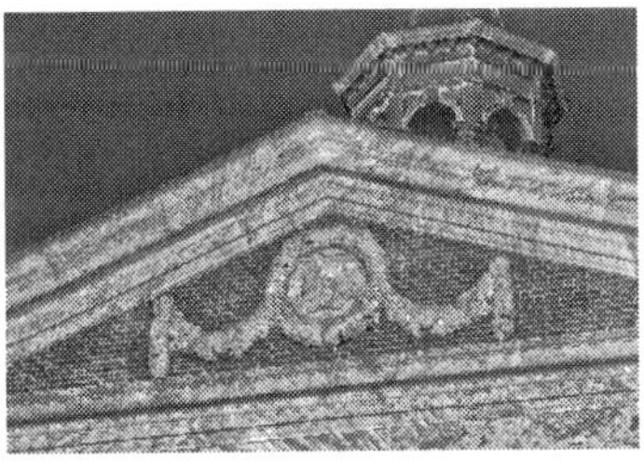

100. The Henry Ford Museum of American Innovation ~ Exterior Elements
(1929; Robert O. Derrick)
20900 Oakwood Blvd
Dearborn, MI
[L]
Ledger details: Jobs #172, #209
1929
"Ford Museum"

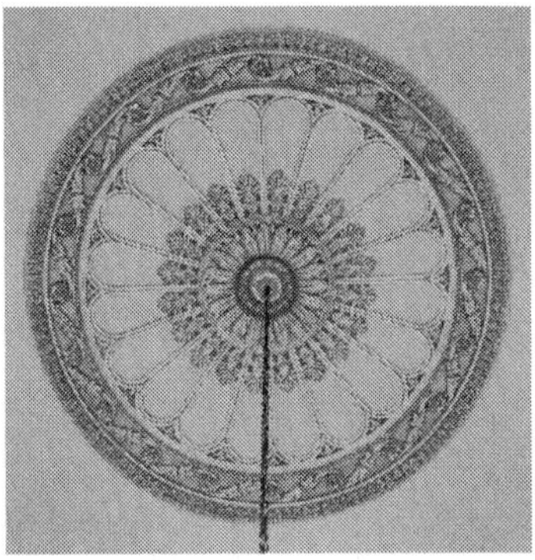

101. The Henry Ford Museum of American Innovation ~ Interior Plaster
(1929; Robert O. Derrick)
20900 Oakwood Blvd
Dearborn, MI
[L]
Ledger details: Jobs #172, #209
1929
"Ford Museum"

In addition to the ledger entries, the prior two commissions are also confirmed by the Edsel B. Ford Office Papers collection, held by the Benson Ford Research Center on the campus of The Henry Ford and Greenfield Village.

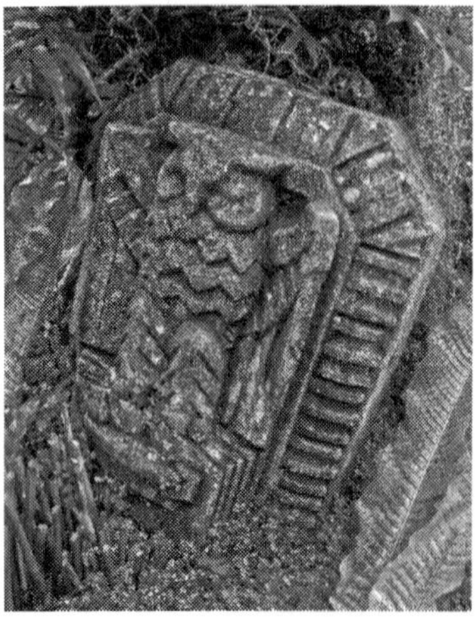

102. Detroit Times Building Sculpture at Anna Scripps Whitcomb Conservatory
(Detroit Times Building:
1929, demolished; Albert Kahn)
(Conservatory: 1904; Mason & Kahn and Nettleton & Kahn)
4 Inselruhe Ave
Belle Isle, Detroit, MI
[L, DB]
Ledger details: Job #184; 1929
"Detroit Times"

Local legend says that this piece of architectural sculpture, found in the fernery of the Anna Scripps Whitcomb Conservatory on Belle Isle, was salvaged from the rubble of the Albert Kahn designed Detroit Times Building when it was demolished decades ago. We know little else about how it ended up here. The Times Building formerly stood at 1370 Cass Avenue, on the corner of Times Square.

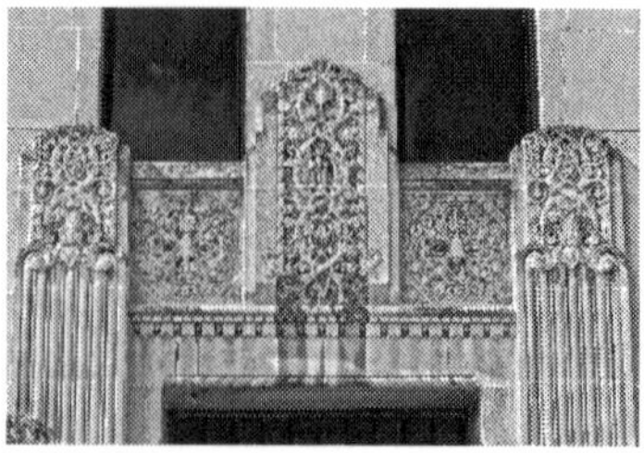

103. Ohio Bell Telephone Company Building
(c.1929; Mills, Rhines, Bellman & Nordhoff)
80 W Bowery St
Akron, OH
[L]
Ledger details: Jobs #186, #260
1929
"Akron Job"
"Ohio Bell Tel Co"

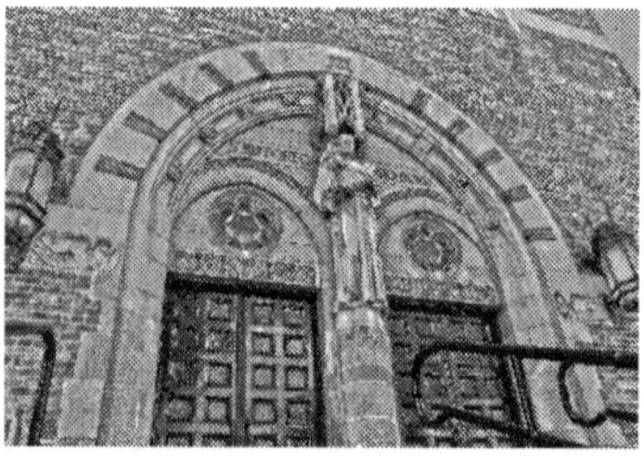

104. Duns Scotus College now known as Word of Life Church
(1929; Wilfrid B. Anthony)
20000 W Nine Mile Rd
Southfield, MI
[L, SB]
Ledger details:
Jobs #189, #190/#278; 1929/1930
"Duns Scotus"

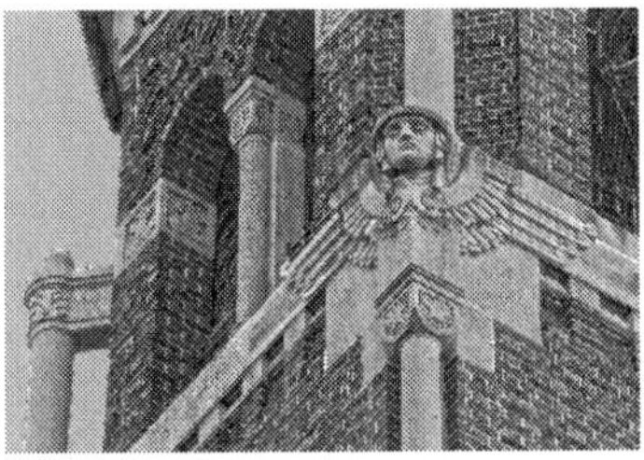

105. St. Catherine of Siena Catholic Church now known as St. Augustine & St. Monica Catholic Church
(1919-1920?, 1929-1930?; Donaldson & Meier)
4151 Seminole St
Detroit, MI
[L]
Ledger details:
Jobs #194/#950/#1005/#1016
1929/1955/1959/1960
"St. Catherine's Ch"

Detroit Free Press articles from both 1920 and 1930 relate the details of this Catholic church's dedication ceremonies. The National Registry of Historic Places reports its date of construction as 1929, but its cornerstone reports MCMXIX. A portion of this structure's history remains shadowy and elusive, but its sculpture is undeniably Parducci—and his ledgers also report 1929. We endeavor to discover and report in this book's second edition the full story of how Parducci sculpture was seemingly applied to this edifice a full decade after it was first erected. At press time it remains a mystery to us.

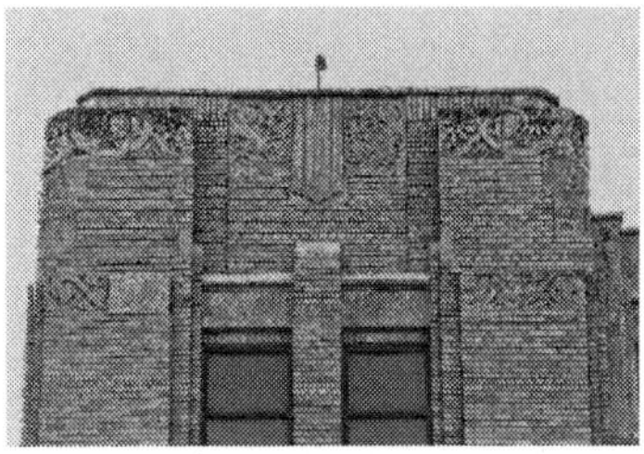

106. Detroit Press Building
(1929; George D. Mason)
2751 E Jefferson Ave
Detroit, MI
[L]
Ledger details: Job #200; 1929
"Detroit Press"

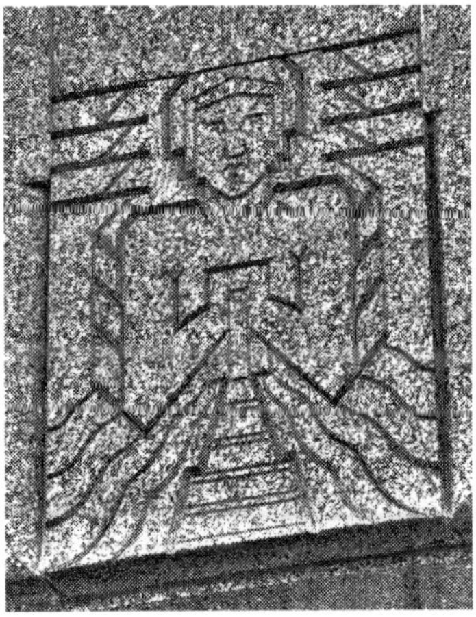

107. Michigan Bell Central Office
(1929; Wirt Rowland of Smith, Hinchman & Grylls)
919 Sixth St
Port Huron, MI
[L]
Ledger details: Job #201; 1929
"Port Huron Tele Bldg"

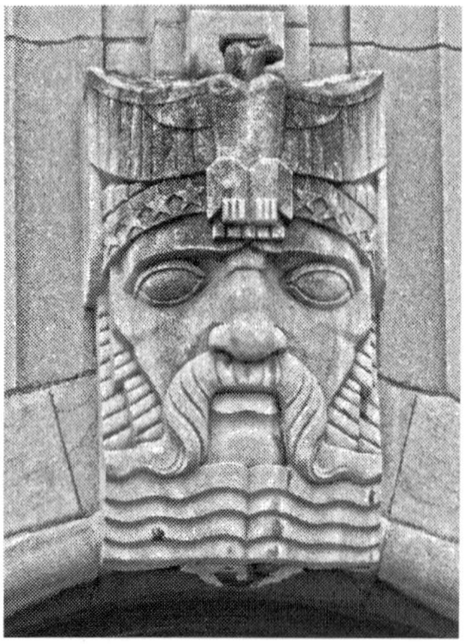

108. Union and Peoples National Bank Building now know as Jackson County Tower Building
(1929; Albert Kahn)
120 W Michigan Ave
Jackson, MI
[L]
Ledger details: Jobs #207, #238
1929
"Jackson Bank"

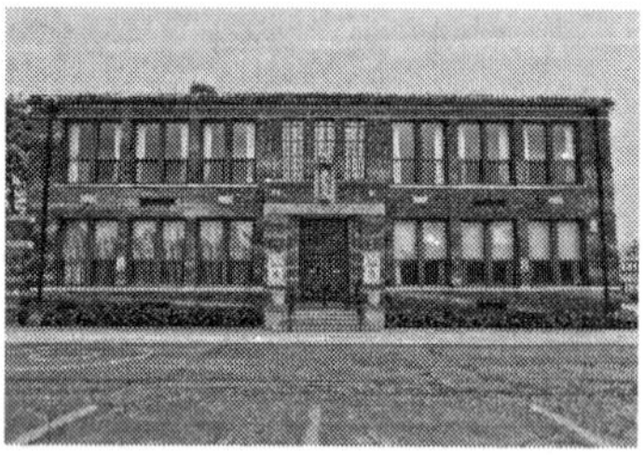

109. St. Clare of Montefalco School & Addition
(1926-1927; Van Leyen, Schilling & Keough / c.1963? addition; Diehl & Diehl)
16231 Charelvoix St
Grosse Pointe Park, MI
[L, SB]
Ledger details:
Jobs #210/#836/#1045/#1049
1929/1950/1963/1964
"St. Claire (sic) Sch"

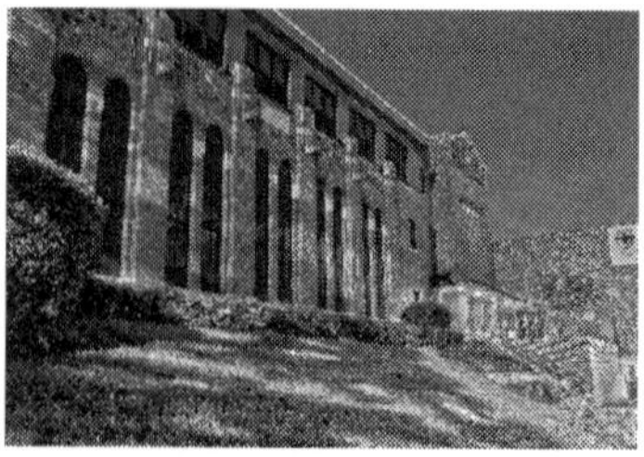

110. St. Thomas the Apostle School
(1930; Donaldson & Meier)
540 Elizabeth St
Ann Arbor, MI
[L]
Ledger details: Job #211; 1929
"St Thomas Sch"

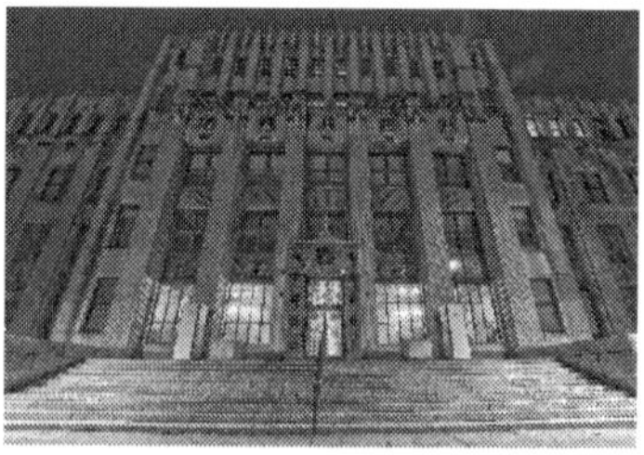

111. S.S. Kresge World Headquarters now known as Michigan Center for High Technology
(1929; Albert Kahn)
2727 Second Ave
Detroit, MI
[L, JB]
Ledger details: Jobs #218, #239
1929
"Kresge Bldg"

A second commission for which Albert Kahn secured the services of the Fisher Building's primary sculptor, Géza Maróti.

Regarding this building's sculptural embellishments, Joan Boddie writes in her 1978 Master's Essay:

"Shortly after the opening of the Fisher Building in the fall of 1928,

Maróti returned to Budapest for several months…Corrado Parducci, who did much of the interior and exterior ornament for the Fisher Building under Maróti's guidance, recalls that when Maróti came back to Detroit, he rented a floor on the Marquette Building, where Albert Kahn's offices were at that time, for his studio and residence. He did some decorative work on the Livingston Lighthouse on Belle Isle, and then, Parducci says, worked again for Albert Kahn on the decoration of the Kresge Building. At this point, it seems that Maróti began to experience a sort of American 'culture shock' which he must have been to some extent spared in the exceptional working conditions of the Fisher commission. After being permitted unlimited expenditures on the lobby, and receiving, according to Parducci, the staggering sum for 1928 of $40,000 for three months' work, Maróti began to chafe in his profession (sic) relationship to Kahn. Parducci says that Maróti felt that his fee, like the architects', should have been a percentage of the total cost of the building. He felt underpaid. He then quarreled with Kahn over the Kresge commission because he was insulted to be required to submit cost estimates for his contributions. Apparently he found the usual, practical American building procedures demeaning to his accustomed prima donna status.

"Parducci relates that despite the tensions in his relationship to Kahn, Maróti did get as far as doing the small granite sculptures around the Kresge Building entrance. Then his aggravation with Kahn seems to have exploded and he quit abruptly. He vehemently admonished Parducci, then a young man in his twenties, not to work for Albert Kahn anymore, and he departed Detroit for Budapest forthwith, never to return. Parducci finished the Kresge Building decorating job. He heard from Maróti occasionally for several years thereafter."

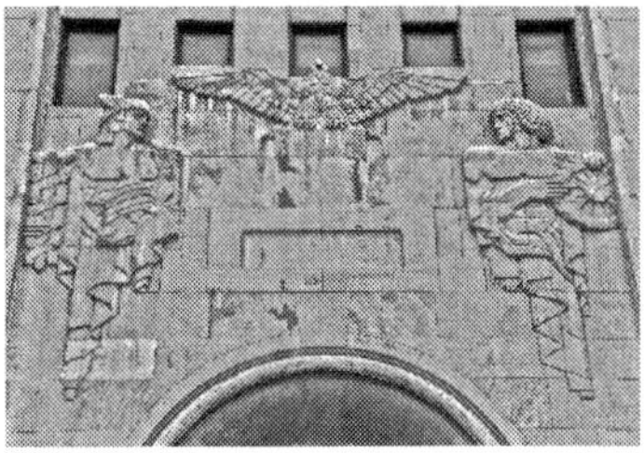

112. PNC Bank Building formerly known as National City Bank Building and Owens-Illinois (O-I) Building
(1929-1930; Mills, Rhines, Bellman & Nordhoff)
405 Madison Ave
Toledo, OH
[L]
Ledger details: Job #227; 1929
"Boody Bldg Toledo"

Built on the former site of the famed Boody House Hotel.

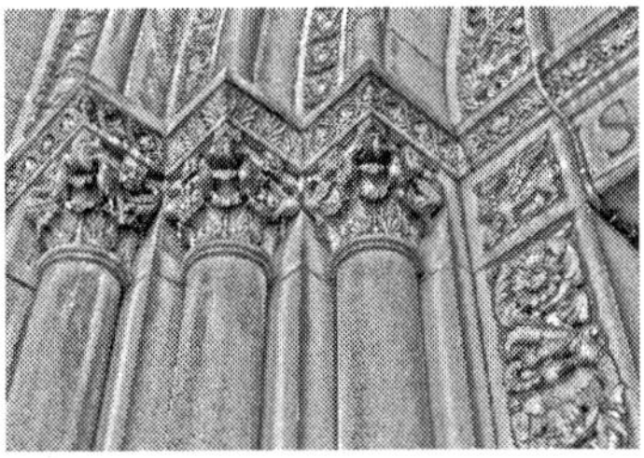

113. St. Cecilia Catholic Church now known as St. Charles Lwanga Catholic Church
(1929-1930; Antonio DiNardo)
10400 Stoepel St
Detroit, MI
[L]
Ledger details:
Jobs #230, #258/#279; 1929/1930
"St Cecelia (sic) Ch"

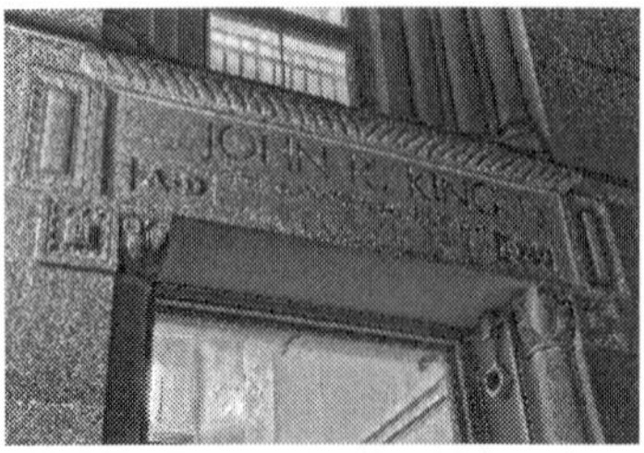

114. Edward Cerveny Middle School now known as John R. King Academic and Performing Arts Academy
(1929-1931; George D. Mason)
15850 Strathmoor St
Detroit, MI
[L]
Ledger details: Job #231; 1929
"Cervaney (sic) Sch"

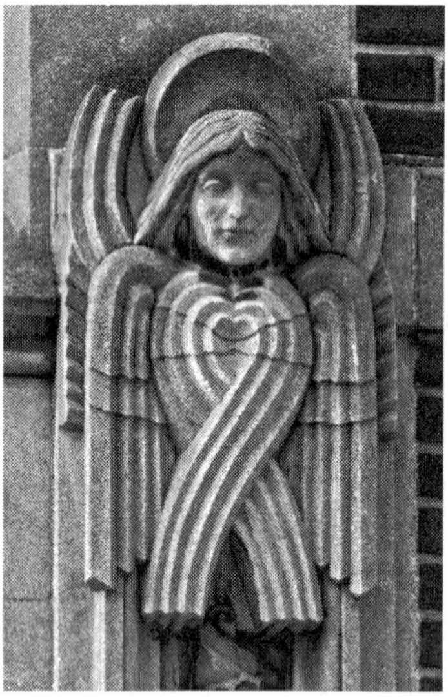

115. Guardian Angel Parish Convent now known as Capstone Academy North
(c. 1929; architect undetermined)
15255 Mayfield St
Detroit, MI
[L]
Ledger details: Job #236; 1929
"Guardian Angel Sch"

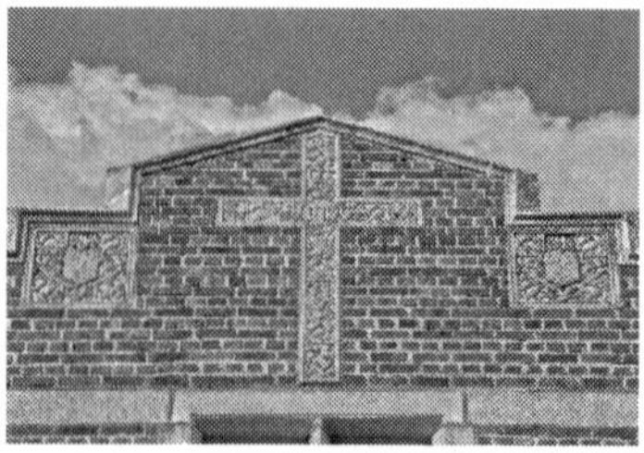

116. St. Peter's Episcopal Church
(1929, architect undetermined)
1950 Trumbull Ave
Detroit, MI
[L]
Ledger details: Job #240; 1929
"St Peters Ch"

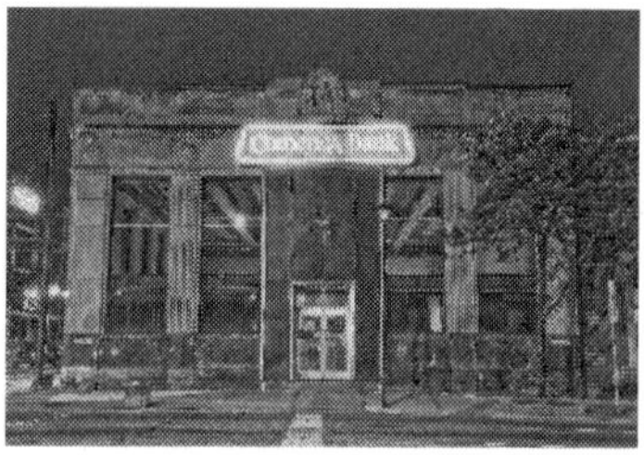

117. Dearborn State Bank Addition
(c.1929; Albert Kahn)
22101 Michigan Ave
Dearborn, MI
[L]
Ledger details: Jobs #249, #251
1929
"Dearborn State Bk"

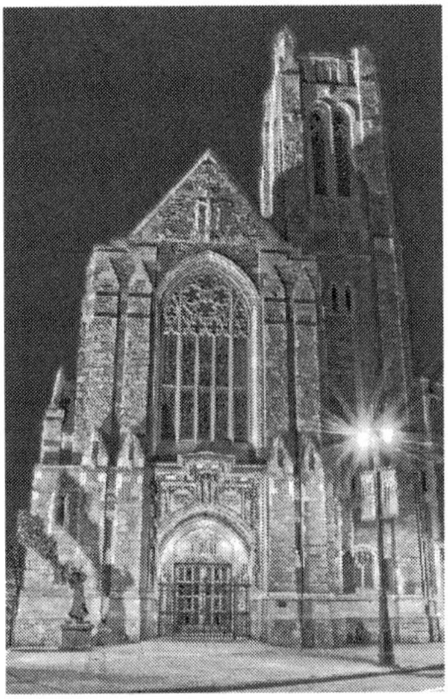

118. Historic Trinity Lutheran Church ~ Exterior Elements
(1929-1931; William E.N. Hunter)
1345 Gratiot Ave
Detroit, MI
[L, SB]
Ledger details: Job #252; 1929
"Trinity Lutheran Ch"

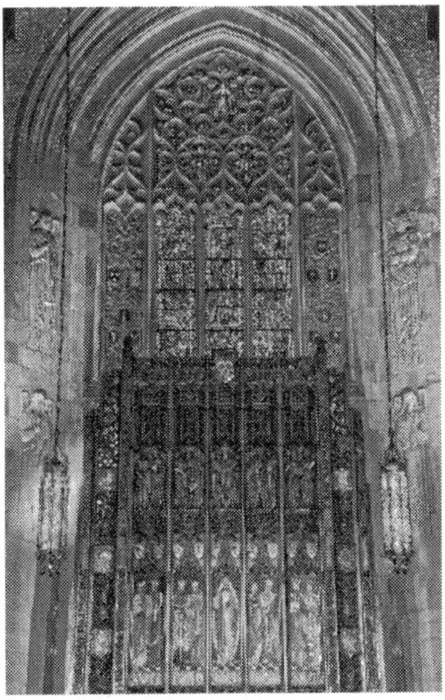

119. Historic Trinity Lutheran Church ~ Interior Elements
(1929-1931; William E.N. Hunter)
1345 Gratiot Ave
Detroit, MI
[L, SB]
Ledger details: Job #252; 1929
"Trinity Lutheran Ch"

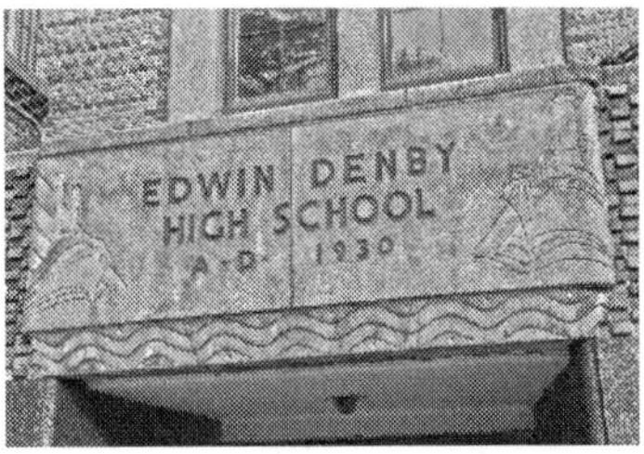

120. Edward Denby High School
(c.1930; Wirt Rowland of Smith, Hinchman & Grylls)
12800 Kelly Rd
Detroit, MI
[L]
Ledger details: Jobs #254/#563
1929/1938
"Denby School"

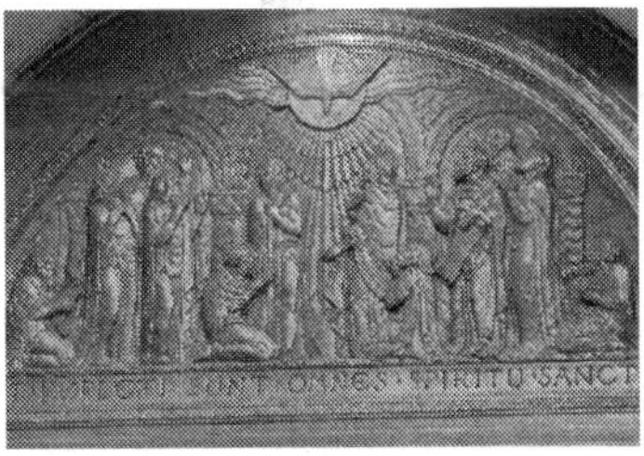

121. St. Aloysius Catholic Church
(1930; Walter Meier of Donaldson & Meier)
1232 Washington Blvd
Detroit, MI
[L, SB, DB, WK]
Ledger details: Jobs #259/#928
1929/1955
"St Aloysious (sic)"

Regarding this commission Parducci states in the 1975 Smithsonian interview: *"He [Samuel Cashwan] made, you know, on the St. Aloysius Church, he made those Apostles. You know, those twelve figures in the niches?...I did all the rest of the work: the bronze and the rest of the interior."*

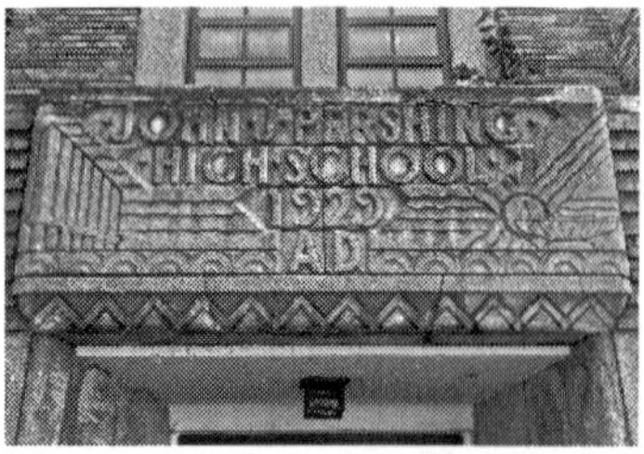

122. John J. Pershing High School
(c.1930; Wirt Rowland of Smith, Hinchman & Grylls)
18875 Ryan Rd
Detroit, MI
[L]
Ledger details: Job #261; 1930
"Pershing Sch"

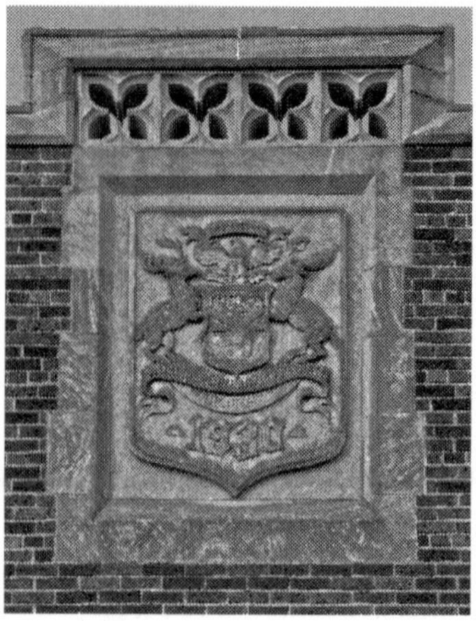

123. Ella Fitzgerald School Addition
(1930; McGrath, Dohmen & Page?)
8145 Puritan St
Detroit, MI
[L]
Ledger details: Job #262; 1930
"Fitzgerald Sch"

Find the 1930 addition on the far east side of the structure, along Cloverlawn Avenue.

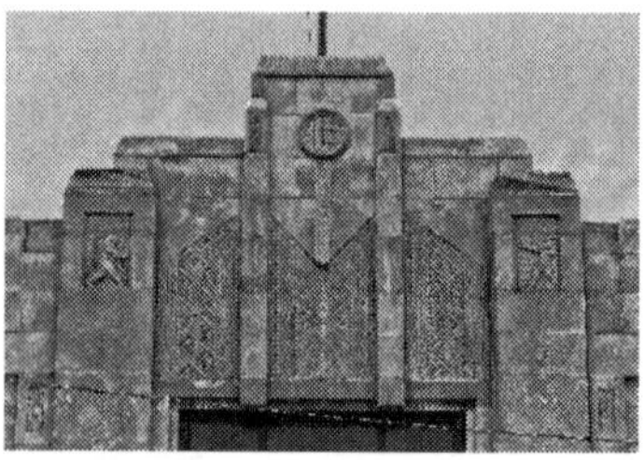

124. Electrograph Building now known as Latino Family Services
(c.1930; architect undetermined)
3815 W Fort St
Detroit, MI
[L]
Ledger details: Job #271; 1930
"Electrograph Bldg"

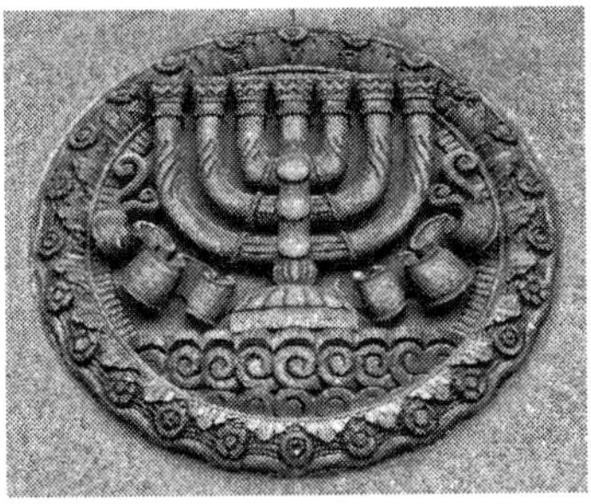

125. Congregation Shaarey Zedek Synagogue now known as Greater Bethlehem Temple
(1930; Albert Kahn)
2900 Chicago Blvd
Detroit, MI
[L]
Ledger details: Job #276; 1930
"Sharey Zedic Syague (sic)"

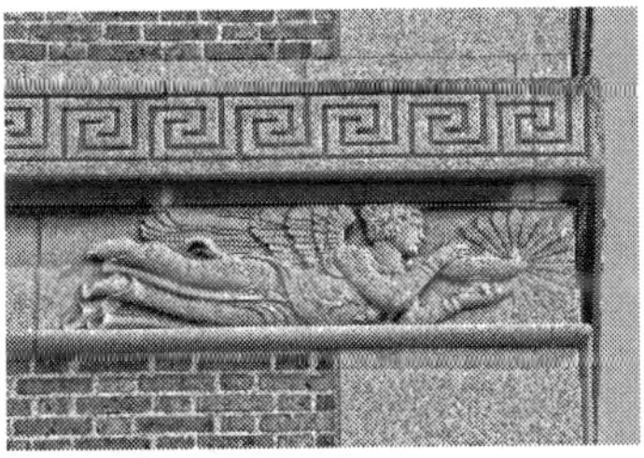

126. Highland Park Y.W.C.A.
(1930; George D. Mason)
13130 Woodward Ave
Highland Park, MI
[L]
Ledger details: Job #281; 1930
"Y.M.C.A."

Parducci erroneously identifies Robert O. Derrick as the architect in the ledger's notes for job #281. Parducci-esque features of the work in question convince us beyond any doubt that this ledger entry refers to Mason's Highland Park Y.W.C.A. and not the Derrick designed Hannan Memorial Y.M.C.A. at 10401 E. Jefferson Ave (entry #42).

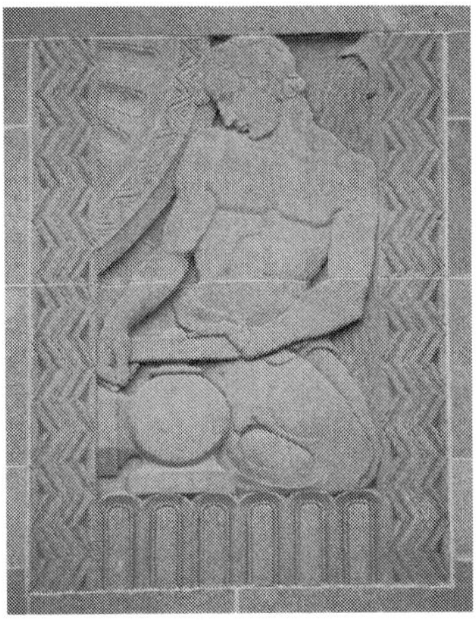

127. Springwells Water Treatment Plant
(c.1925-1935; architect undetermined)
8300 W Warren Ave
Dearborn, MI
[L]
Ledger details: Job #284; 1930
"Springwell Pumping Station"

Photo by Einar Kvaran

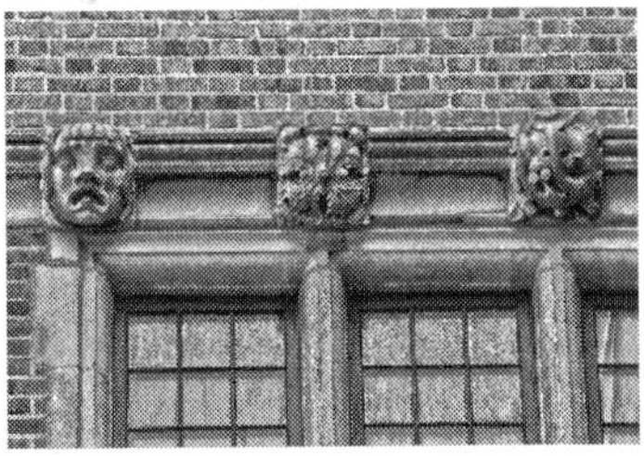

128. University Hall at University of Toledo
(1931; Mills, Rhines, Bellman & Nordhoff)
Bancroft St at Drummond Rd
Toledo, OH
[L]
Ledger details: Job #285; 1930
"Toledo University"

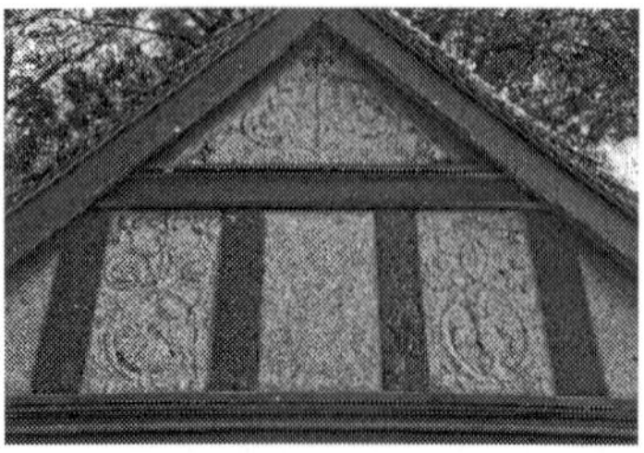

129. Children's Playhouse, Historic Estate of Edsel and Eleanor Ford
(c.1931; Robert O. Derrick)
1100 Lake Shore Dr
Grosse Pointe Shores, MI
[L, DB]
Ledger details: Job #287; 1930
"Ford Children's Playhouse"

Regarding this commission Parducci states in the 1975 Smithsonian interview: *"You know, Henry Ford, the Senior, as a gift to his grandchildren, he built a playhouse on Grosse Pointe. And the playhouse was a miniature Tudor building with pargetting. Are you familiar with English parget work?...It's modeling done directly in cement with a spatula...Now in order to do that work, I made clay models first, and I cast them. And then I went to the building. The building is a miniature home. The doorways are about four feet high and the rooms are all low ceilings. The children were young. I went to the job...I copied the modeling that I had made, Mother Goose rhymes, right in cement directly. And that's one of the very few occasions I had to work directly on a building."*

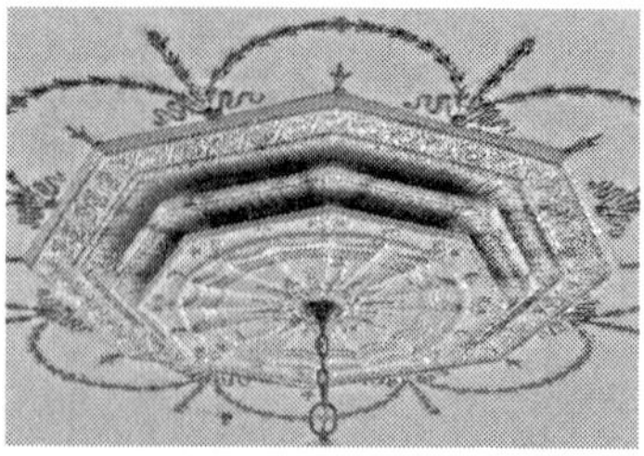

130. Dearborn Inn
(1931; Albert Kahn)
20301 Oakwood Blvd
Dearborn, MI
[L]
Ledger details:
Jobs #289/#324/#1009
1930/1932/1960
"Ford Hotel"

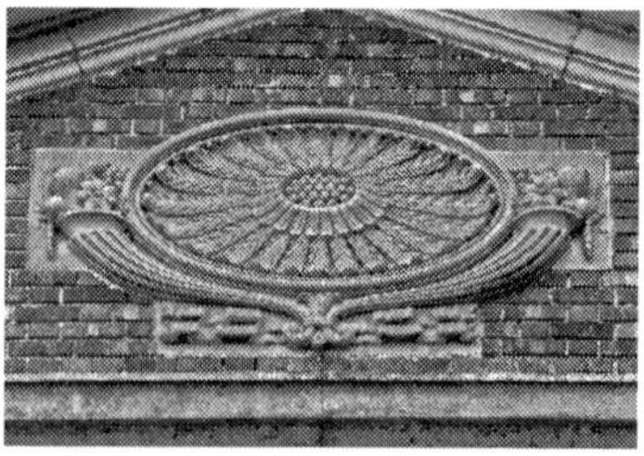

131. Grosse Pointe Farms Water Pumping and Filtration Station
(1929; Robert O. Derrick)
29 Moross Rd
Grosse Pointe Farms, MI
[L]
Ledger details: Job #292; 1930
"Grosse Pointe Pumping Station"

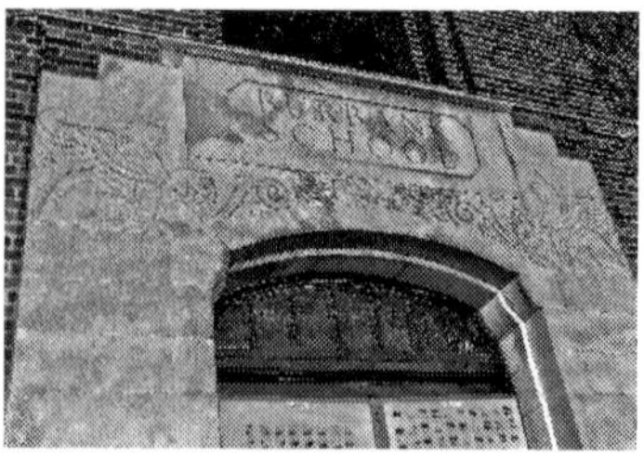

132. Luther Burbank School
(1930; McGrath, Dohmen & Page)
15600 E State Fair Ave
Detroit, MI
[L]
Ledger details: Jobs #302/#792
1931/1948
"Burbank Sch"

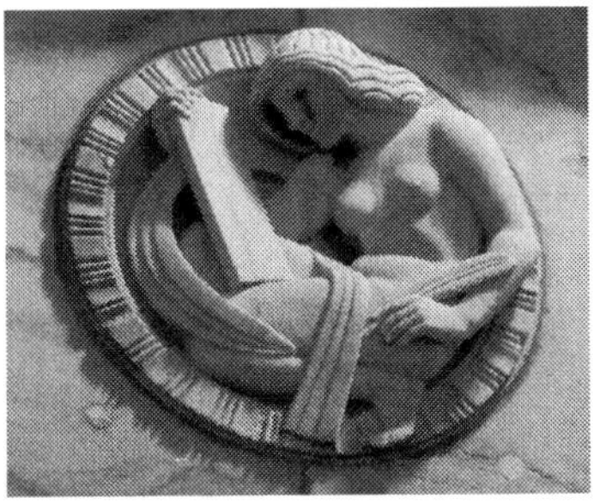

133. New York Times Brooklyn Printing Plant
(1929; Albert Kahn)
59 Third Ave
Brooklyn, NY
[L]
Ledger details: Job #303; 1931
"N.Y. Times Bldg"

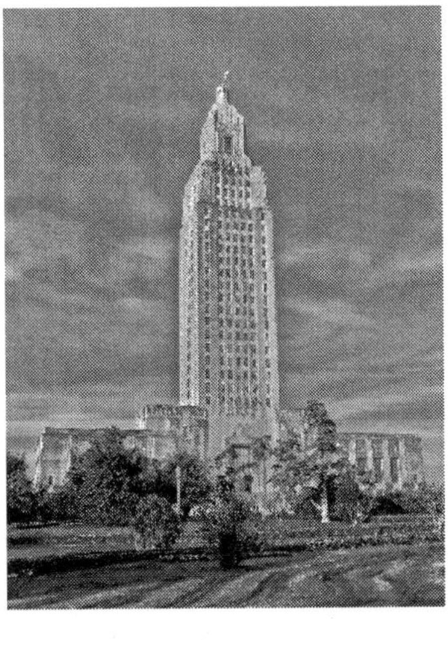

134. Louisiana State Capitol
(1930-1932; Weiss, Dreyfous & Seiferth)
900 N Third St
Baton Rouge, LA
[L, SB, DB]
Ledger details: Jobs #308/#326
1931/1932
"Louisiana State Cap"

(*See Figure G, page 135*)

"The Pelican Guide to the Louisiana Capitol" is, in our opinion, the most authoritative volume where attributions for the Capitol's extensive sculpture are concerned; but it is not without flaws. Within it, the only Parducci credited with creating sculpture for this site is Corrado's brother, Rudolph. The ledgers tell a broader story, however, and value the Parduccis' collective effort towards Huey Long's legacy at a healthy $9,000, a not at all modest sum in the year it is recorded, 1931. Therefore, we believe it highly likely that Parducci modeled at least a portion of what may be seen there, and he says as much in the 1975 interview, though no specific works thereupon are cited:

"[D]uring the thirties, I had the Federal Building, I had the Coughlin's Shrine [of the Little Flower], I had Louisiana ... There was some work I did on Louisiana's State Capitol for Huey Long. And other out of town work."

RUDOLPH PARDUCCI

At this point we diverge from our roster of commissions to succinctly examine the life of Parducci's brother, Rudolph, who first appears within Corrado's work history in 1930, at the time of the Louisiana State Capitol job. Despite a dearth of biographical information, Rudolph's well documented contributions to a handful of Corrado's most significant, Depression-era commissions warrant his inclusion in this book. We present below the merest of facts we have gathered about Rudolph from a limited breadth of resources.

Rudolph was born January 11th, 1899, in Italy, presumably like Corrado, in the small mountain town of Buti, just east of Pisa. He immigrated to the U.S. in 1906, most likely accompanied by his mother Zelinda, and died in Los Angeles on June 25, 1973.

U.S. Census records from 1920 show him living in New York City, and, along with Corrado, working as a "model maker" at a "statue factory" (*See Figures B and C, pages 130-131*). A 1923 issue of *The American Magazine of Art* suggests he remained in New York City through at least October of 1922. Nephew Allen Parducci places him in New Orleans, Louisiana for a large portion of the 1920s, and based on numerous listings in *Polk's Detroit City Directory*, we estimate Rudolph's time in the Detroit area to span the years of approximately 1929 to 1935. The remainder of Rudolph's life was lived out in Metropolitan Los Angeles, California.

In the 1979 interview with Fay Hendry, Corrado states that he employed his brother from 1927 to 1936. In our opinion, this suggests that Rudolph, in 1927 and 1928, may have been developing the New Orleans area business contacts that would lead to at least three Louisiana commissions for Corrado in the following decades. There is little evidence, however, with which to build a stronger case supporting this theory.

To the best of our knowledge, the complete extant works of architectural sculpture executed by Rudolph Parducci, are limited to five sites, four of which are included in our list of commissions and were modeled in tandem with Corrado during the time in which Rudolph lived in Metro Detroit. They are:

#134: Louisiana State Capitol
(1930-1932; Weiss, Dreyfous & Seiferth)
Baton Rouge, LA

#138: Theodore Levin U.S. Courthouse
(1932-1934; Robert O. Derrick & Branson V. Gamber)
Detroit, MI

#140: George W. Welsh Civic Auditorium now known as Grand Rapids Civic Auditorium
(1932; Smith, Hinchman & Grylls with Robinson & Campau)
Grand Rapids, MI

#141: National Shrine of the Little Flower ~ Stations of the Cross
(1931-1936; Henry J. McGill)
Royal Oak, MI

Rudolph's involvement in three of these four commissions is confirmed independent of Corrado's records by reputable published accounts, while the story of his work on the Stations of the Cross at the National Shrine of the Little Flower is related to us by Allen. Though undocumented, it is also a near certainty that Rudolph contributed at least in part to numerous other Parducci commissions executed during the early 1930s.

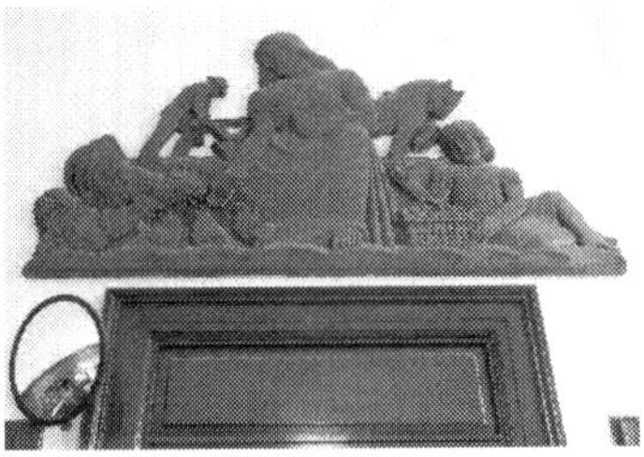

[Photo by Jimmy S. Emerson, DVM]

"Rural Life" (above), a 1941 relief in mahogany, is the fifth extant example of architectural sculpture designed by Rudolph. Find this remnant of his participation in the Federal Arts Project of the Works Progress Administration inside the post office at 1103 West Gardena Boulevard in Gardena, California.

Rudolph is also known to have worked for both Disney and Metro-Goldwyn-Mayer in the 1950s. His modeling of the elephants for the original "Dumbo" ride at Disneyland in Anaheim is well documented, as is his work for the film "Creature from the Black Lagoon". According to Allen, he also modeled set pieces for MGM's Biblical epic, "Ben Hur".

We are also told by Allen that in addition to Rudolph's skill as a sculptor, exemplified by the works enumerated above, he excelled as a designer of jewelry.

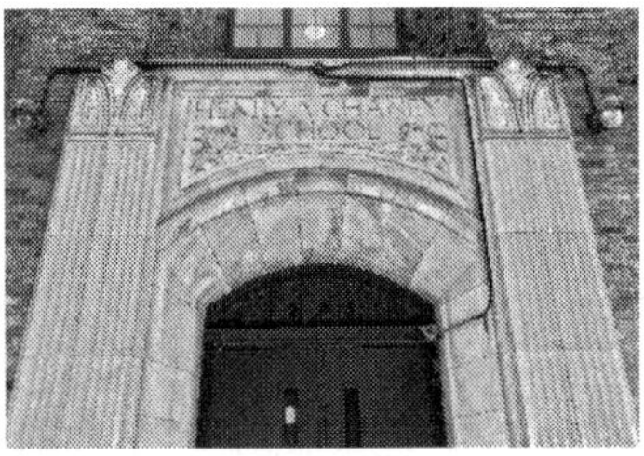

135. Henry A. Chaney School
(1931; Van Leyen, Schilling & Keough)
2750 Selden St
Detroit, MI
[L]
Ledger details: Job #314; 1931 "Chaney Sch"

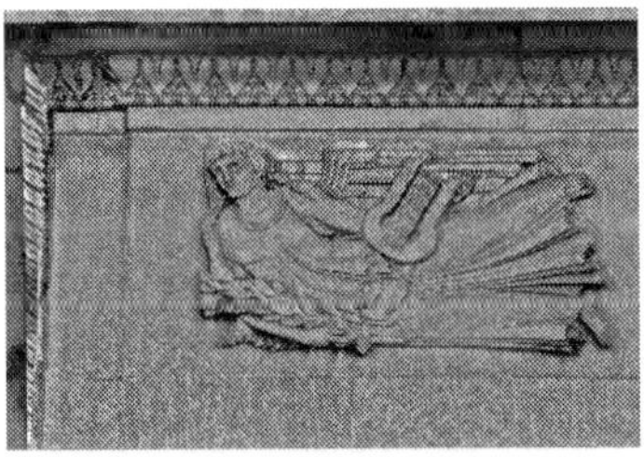

136. Detroit Public Library ~ Skillman Branch
(1932; William E. Kapp of Smith, Hinchman & Grylls)
121 Gratiot Ave
Detroit, MI
[L, DB, WK]
Ledger details: Job #317; 1931 "Library downtown Branch"

Regarding this commission Parducci states in his 1975 Smithsonian interview: *"[T]he Greek on the downtown library is not Greek—it's Parducci Greek. If you know what I mean."*

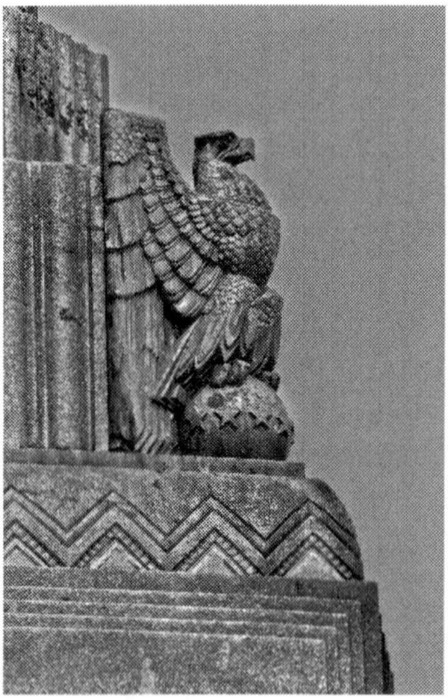

137. Samuel Francis Smith Memorial Flagpole
(1931; Albert Kahn)
Approximately 1400 Vista Dr
Belle Isle, Detroit, MI
[L, DB]
Ledger details: Job #321; 1931 "Smith Mem"

An excerpt from Parducci's 1975 interview, regarding this commission:

"CORRADO PARDUCCI: *You know, that flagpole on Belle Isle, Sam Cashwan...The committee in charge of that flagpole gave the job to Sam Cashwan. You know Sam Cashwan?*
DENNIS BARRIE: *Yes.*
CORRADO PARDUCCI: *Very talented. And Albert Kahn was on the art commission, and he didn't like his design. So he asked me if I would make a sketch of that flagpole. And Sam Cashwan had a rectangular base. At one side he had a figure, see? So I made the sketch of what that thing is; I made a clay, a rough clay model, while Kahn was in the place. I just did it very fast. And they gave Cashwan the medallion of a portrait on it—that's all he did—to pay him for his...But the work actually drifted to me, you see. Albert Kahn, who was on the art commission, he had the, just didn't accept the scheme that Cashwan had, see."*

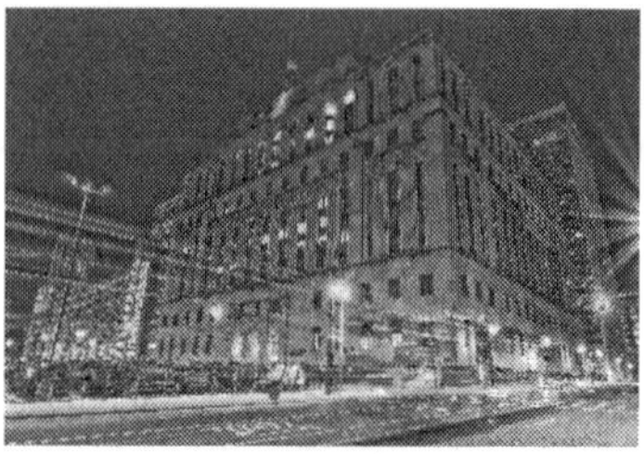

138. Theodore Levin U.S. Courthouse also known as Detroit Federal Building
(1932-1934; Robert O. Derrick & Branson V. Gamber)
231 W Lafayette Blvd
Detroit, MI
[L, SB, DB, DFP]
Ledger details: Job #323; 1932 "US Government Fed Bldg"

An excerpt from Parducci's 1975 Smithsonian interview regarding this commission:

"CORRADO PARDUCCI: *[T]hese are some of the details on the Federal Building.*
DENNIS BARRIE: *In Detroit.*
CORRADO PARDUCCI: *Yeah, now those panels were forty feet long, eight foot high. Eight foot in height. They have eight different ones. They had seven tons of clay on each model.*
DENNIS BARRIE: *Didn't you have some great difficulty with the Federal Building?*
CORRADO PARDUCCI: *Yeah. I didn't have any change or any . . . The difficulty was that I had to wait a long time for approval. I'd mail*

the photographs to Washington. See, they had some architectural politicians there, and the paperwork was bad, see."

A 1932 *Detroit News* article by H.C.L. Jackson confirms that the sculpture of the Levin Courthouse was rendered in tandem with Parducci's brother, Rudolph.

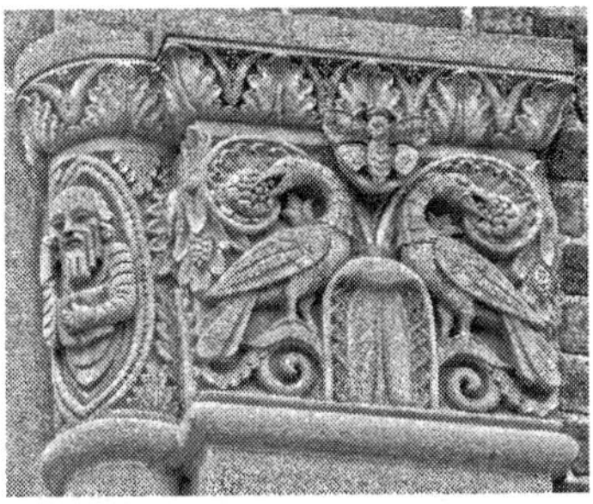

139. St. John the Baptist Catholic Church
(1932; McGrath & Dohmen)
411 Florence St
Ypsilanti, MI
[L]
Ledger details: Jobs #330/#514
1932/1937
"St. John's Church"

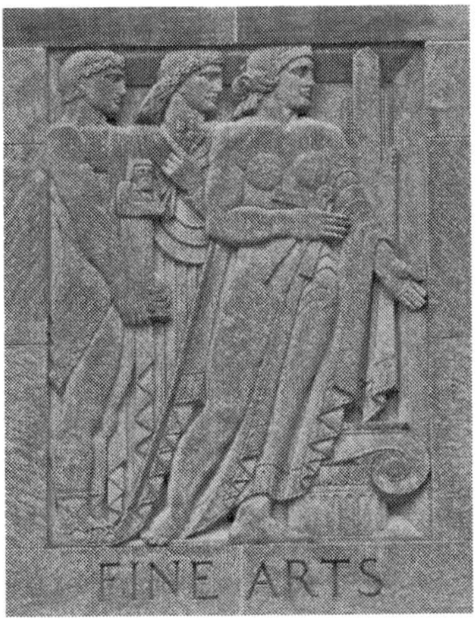

140. George W. Welsh Civic Auditorium now known as Grand Rapids Civic Auditorium
(1932; Smith, Hinchman & Grylls with Robinson & Campau)
255 Lyon St NW
Grand Rapids, MI
[L, DB, FH]
Ledger details: Job #335; 1932
"Grand Rapids Auditorium"

Regarding this commission Parducci states in the 1975 Smithsonian interview: *"[D]uring the Depression, the city of Grand Rapids, they built an auditorium with scrip. And at the time I wasn't doing very much and they called me in on a job and I had to do the work on condition that I do it in Grand Rapids, and I was the only one that got paid in dollars...And I had to do the work in a stoneyard! I made models in a stoneyard...And that's the auditorium. It has a lot of sculptural panels, music and drama, and the arts."*

Sadly, much of the work Parducci references has been removed or covered up over the course of numerous remodelings and modernizations.

A *Grand Rapids Press* article from June 21st, 1932 confirms that the sculpture of the Welsh Auditorium was rendered in tandem with Parducci's brother, Rudolph.

The third gap in Parducci's ledgers is substantial and complex. It stretches a full four years, from September of 1932 to August of 1936. In our opinion, the following twenty-one entries, #141 through #161, fall within this gap. Of these twenty-one, seventeen are confirmed by varying combinations of sources including scrapbook images, stylistic elements nearly identical to other Parducci works of the era, well established professional relationships with the commissioning architects, interview statements, and most importantly, ledger entries in subsequent years. We remind our readers that generally we have found if a commission site appears in the ledgers, regardless of the year it is first recorded, it is also very likely that Parducci produced the architectural sculpture for its original construction.

Additionally, a list of nine commissions completed by Parducci during this gap in record keeping, sans job numbers, is included on the 1932 ledger page. Four of these nine un-numbered commissions are included among the following twenty-one entries with their ledger year reported as "1932-1936". Three of these four commissions are again reported on ledger pages of subsequent years. The fourth, The National Shrine of the Little Flower, is broken up into three individual entries to accurately reflect the abundance of work Parducci produced for this structure.

In the 1975 Smithsonian interview, Parducci speaks at length regarding his contributions to The National Shrine of the Little Flower and his relationship with its most famous priest, Father Charles Coughlin.

It should be also be noted that Parducci was the secondary sculptor at The Shrine. The ornately carved sculpture upon the tower was modeled by the site's primary, Rene Paul Chambellan.

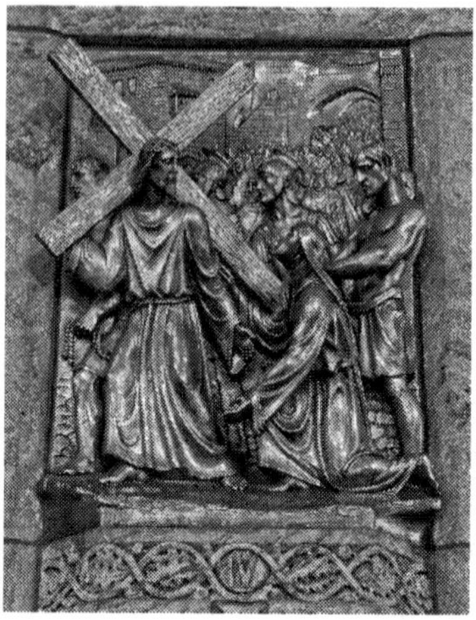

141. National Shrine of the Little Flower ~ Stations of the Cross
(1931-1936; Henry J. McGill)
1621 Linwood Ave
Royal Oak, MI
[L, SB, DB, AP]
Ledger details: No Job #; 1932-1936
"Shrine of the Little Flower"

According to Parducci's son, Allen, the Shrine's Stations of the Cross were rendered in tandem with Parducci's brother, Rudolph.

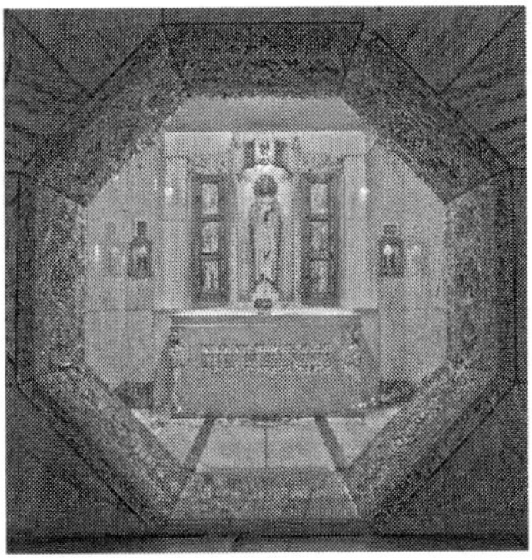

142. National Shrine of the Little Flower ~ Interior Elements
(1931-1936; Henry J. McGill)
1621 Linwood Ave
Royal Oak, MI
[L, SB, DB]
Ledger details: No Job #; 1932-1936 "Shrine of the Little Flower"

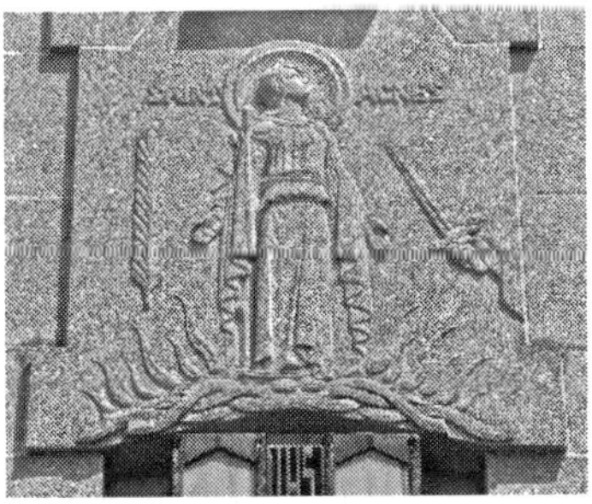

143. National Shrine of the Little Flower ~ Exterior Elements
(1931-1936; Henry J. McGill)
1621 Linwood Ave
Royal Oak, MI
[L, SB, DB]
Ledger details: No Job #; 1932-1936 "Shrine of the Little Flower"

144. St. Hugo of the Hills
(1931-1934; Arthur DesRosiers)
2215 Opdyke Rd
Bloomfield Hills, MI
[Speculative]
Ledger details: N/A

In a mid-1990s interview with Father Livius Paoli of St. Scholastica Parish Detroit, an accomplished mosaicist with whom Parducci had extensive contact over the course of his career, co-author Einar Kvaran was told of Parducci's alleged contribution to this church's exterior. A complete lack of any further substantiating evidence, however, compels us to categorize this commission as "speculative".

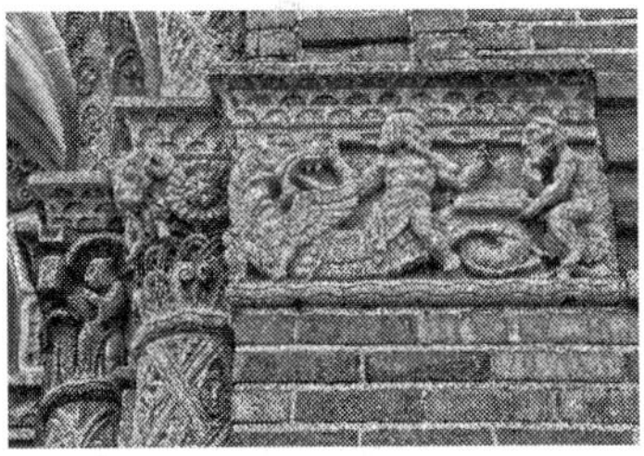

145. Toledo Y.M.C.A. now known as Lucas County Common Pleas Court and Correctional Treatment Facility
(1934; Mills, Rhines, Bellman & Nordhoff)
1100 Jefferson Ave
Toledo, OH
[Speculative]
Ledger details: N/A

Conspicuous stylistic similarities to other Parducci works of this era and Parducci's longstanding professional relationship with the commissioning architects form the basis of our attribution case for both entry #145 and #149.

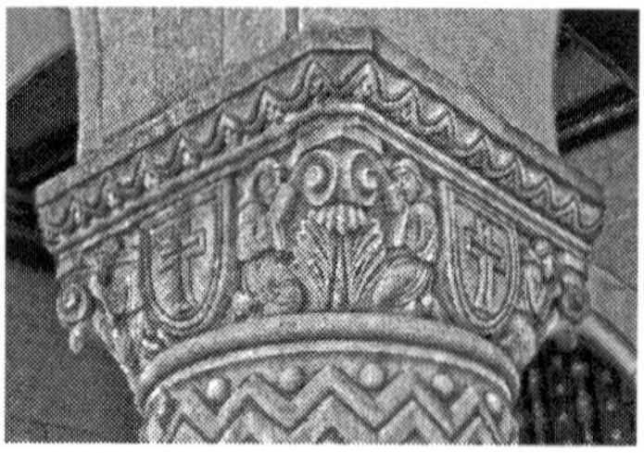

146. Gesu Catholic Church
(1935; Diehl & Diehl)
17180 Oak Dr
Detroit, MI
[L]
Ledger details: Jobs #877/#948
1952/1955
"Gesu Ch"

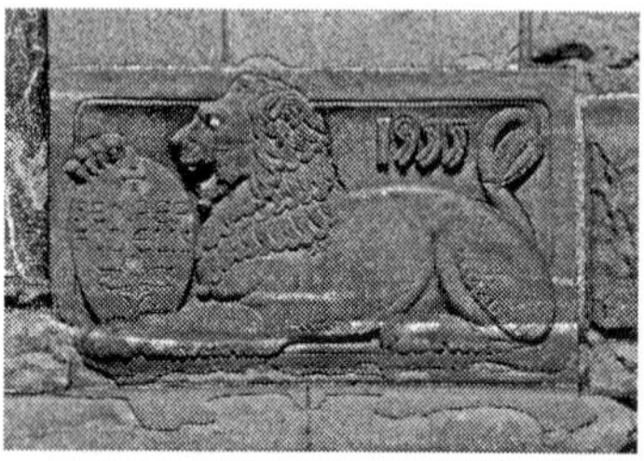

147. First Presbyterian Church now known as Ecumenical Theological Seminary
(1889; Mason & Rice / 1935 remodel; George D. Mason)
2930 Woodward Ave
Detroit, MI
[L]
Ledger details: Job #897; 1953
"First Presbyterian Ch"

In the late 1990s architectural historian Dr. Thomas Brunk (1949-2018) of Detroit related to co-author Kvaran the legend of how, around 1935, Woodward Avenue was widened and the congregation of First Presbyterian was forced to foreshorten its building's original footprint to accommodate new lanes. Once the remodel was complete, fresh architectural sculpture was required for the new façade and Parducci was enlisted to create it. Far from a flawless case for attribution, but plausible, and surely worthy of inclusion in this guide, given Brunk's well known and impressive breadth of Detroit architectural history knowledge.

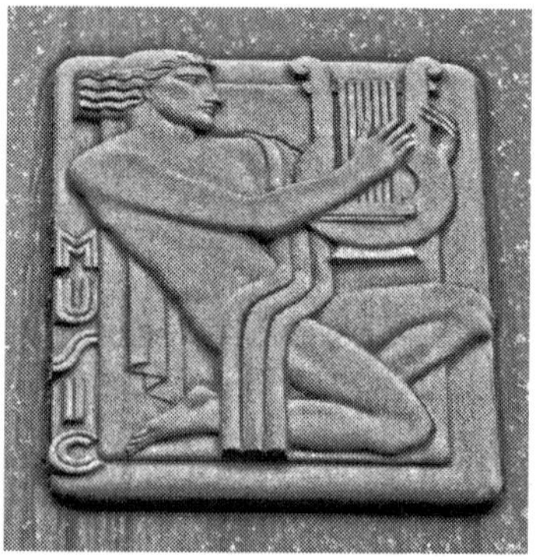

148. Ann Arbor News Building now known as University of Michigan Credit Union ~ Administrative Office
(1936; Albert Kahn)
340 E Huron St
Ann Arbor, MI
[SB]
Ledger details: N/A

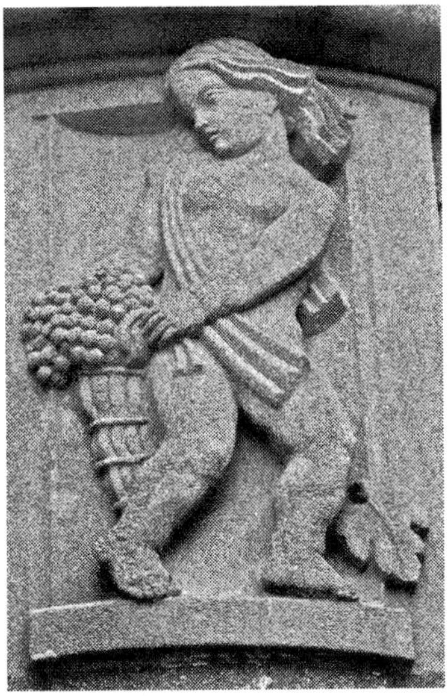

149. Earhart Manor at Concordia University
(1936; Smith, Hinchman & Grylls)
4090 Geddes Rd
Ann Arbor, MI
[Speculative]
Ledger details: N/A

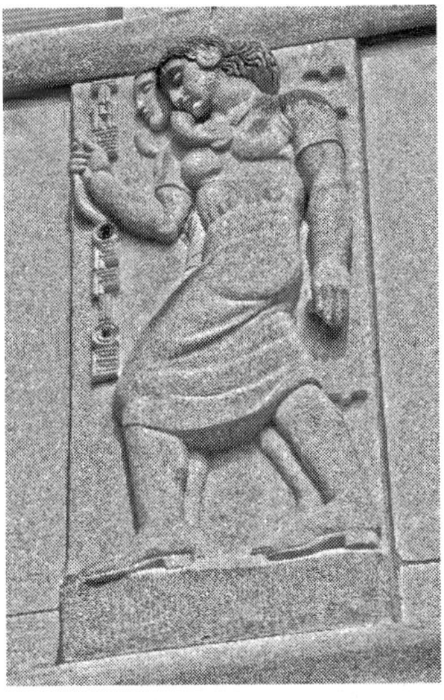

150. Michigan Bell Central Office
(North wing: 1924 / south wing: c.1936;
Smith, Hinchman & Grylls)
220 N Capitol Ave
Lansing, MI
[L, FH]
Ledger details: Job #639; 1941 "Telephone Bldg Lansing Mich"

Currently we theorize that when the south wing of this building was added around 1936, to unify the old and new, a renovation was applied to the north wing's first floor façade that included Parducci sculpture. The full story of this building's construction history remains somewhat unclear to us.

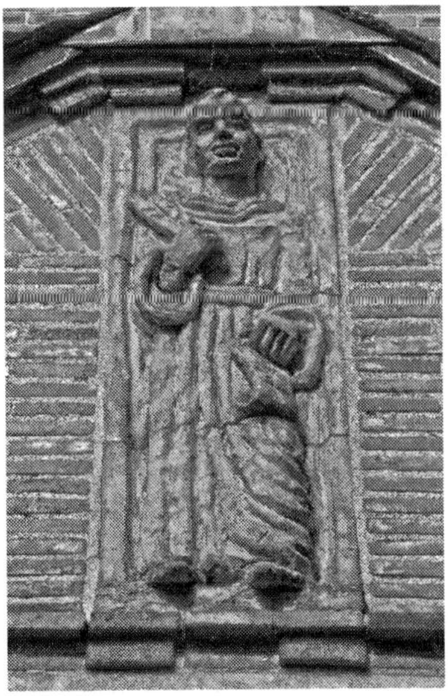

151. Lewis Maire Elementary School
(1936; O'Dell & Rowland)
740 Cadieux Rd
Grosse Pointe, MI
[Speculative]
Ledger details: N/A

To our knowledge there are very few, if any buildings designed or co-designed by Wirt Rowland after 1922 featuring architectural sculpture created by someone other than Parducci. This well established professional relationship plus their life-long friendship form the basis of our case supporting this attribution for sculpture that, admittedly, bears only the slightest stylistic similarity to other Parducci works.

152. St. Peter's Cathedral also known as Marquette Cathedral
(1880-1890; Henry G. Koch & Son / Rebuilt 1935-1938; Edward A. Schilling)
311 W Baraga Ave
Marquette, MI
[L]
Ledger details:
No Job #; 1932-1936 + #503; 1936
"St Peter's Cathedral Marquette"

After a November 1935 fire that left only the walls standing, this Upper Peninsula cathedral was fully reconstructed between 1935 and 1938.

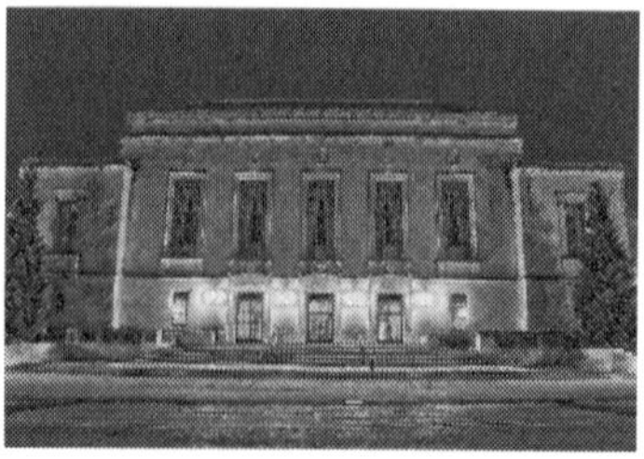

153. Horace H. Rackham School of Graduate Studies at University of Michigan ~ Stone
(1936-1938; William E. Kapp of Smith, Hinchman & Grylls)
915 E Washington St
Ann Arbor, MI
[L, SB, DB, WK]
Leder details: No Job #; 1932-1936 + Jobs #505/#540/#629
1936/1938/1941
"H.H. Rackham
Sch. of Grad Studies"

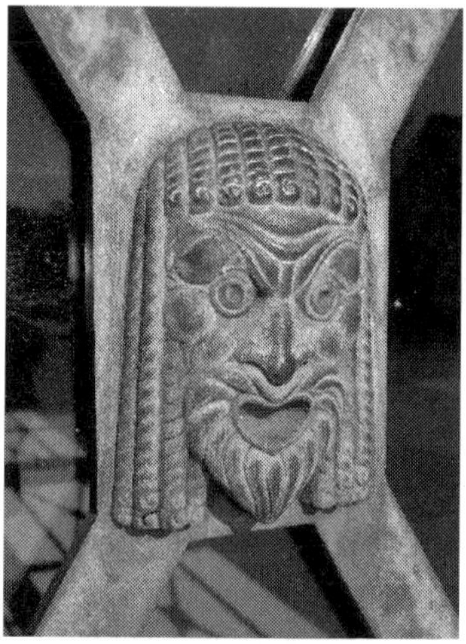

154. Horace H. Rackham School of Graduate Studies at University of Michigan ~ Bronze
(1936-1938; William E. Kapp of Smith, Hinchman & Grylls)
915 E Washington St
Ann Arbor, MI
[L, SB, DB, WK]
Ledger details: No Job #; 1932-1936 + Jobs #505/#540/#629
1936/1938/1941
"H.H. Rackham Sch. of Grad Studies"

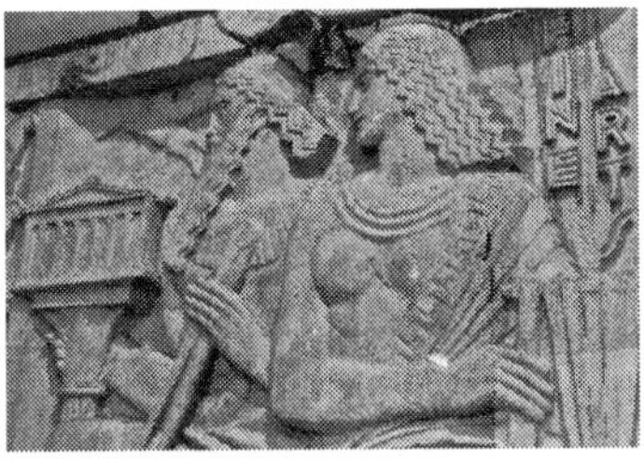

155. Tappan Hall at University of Michigan ~ Original Plaster Model for Horace H. Rackham School of Graduate Studies
(Tappan Hall: 1893-1894;
Spier & Rohns)
855 S University Ave
Ann Arbor, MI
[L, SB, DB, WK]
Ledger details: No Job #; 1932-1936
+ Jobs #505/#540/#629
1936/1938/1941
"H.H. Rackham Sch. of Grad Studies"

Regarding this commission Parducci states in the 1975 Smithsonian interview: *"This thing with the Greek work on the Rackham Building in Ann Arbor. That's my personal interpretation of Greek. I couldn't make book Greek."*

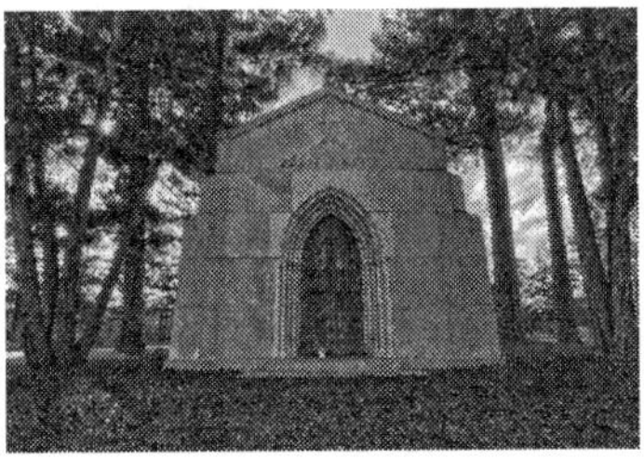

156. Frank Navin Mausoleum at Holy Sepulchre Catholic Cemetery
(1935; architect undetermined)
25800 W 10 Mile Rd
Southfield, MI
[L]
Ledger details: No Job #; 1932-1936
+ Job #509; 1936
"Navin Mausoleum"

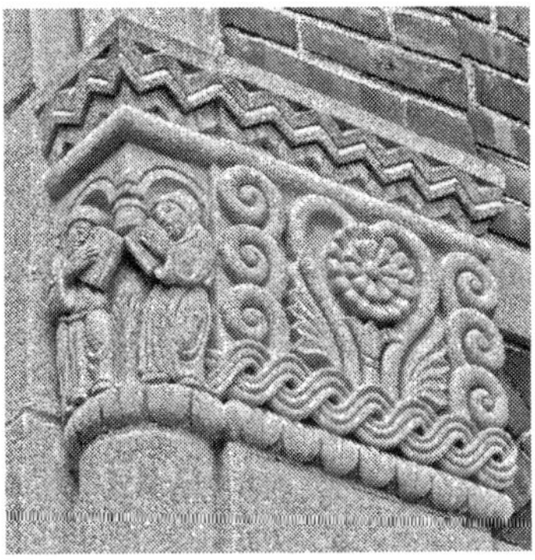

157. Felician Sisters Motherhouse aka Villa St. Felix ~ Chapel
(1936; architect undetermined)
36800 Schoolcraft Rd
Livonia, MI
[L, SB]
Ledger details: Job #644; 1941
"Provincial House Sisters of Mercy"

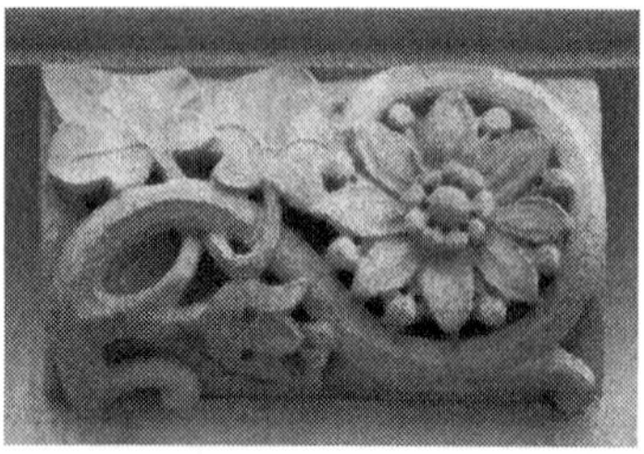

158. First Presbyterian Church ~ Exterior Elements
(1937; Mayers, Murray & Phillip)
1432 Washtenaw Ave
Ann Arbor, MI
[L]
Ledger details: Job #693/1943
"First Presbyterian Ch"

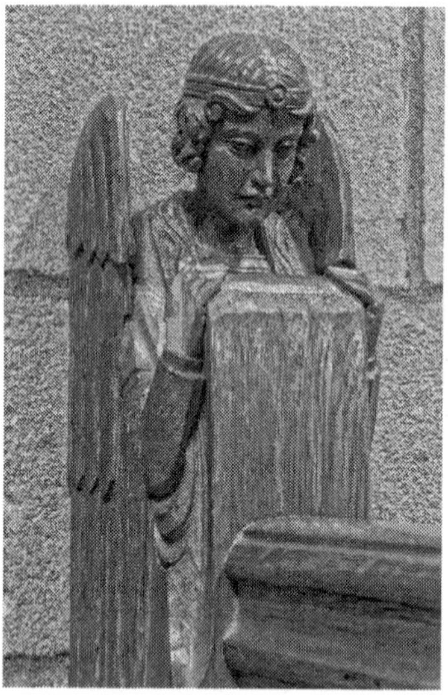

159. First Presbyterian Church ~ Interior Elements
(1937; Mayers, Murray & Phillip)
1432 Washtenaw Ave
Ann Arbor, MI
[L]
Ledger details: Job #693/1943
"First Presbyterian Ch"

First Presbyterian's written history credits an immigrant from Oberammergau, Germany by way of Grand Rapids, Michigan as the party responsible for this sanctuary's beautifully carved reredos and Latin cross. Glaring stylistic similarities to other Parducci works of the era convince us that this unnamed woodworker was almost certainly duplicating models created by Parducci.

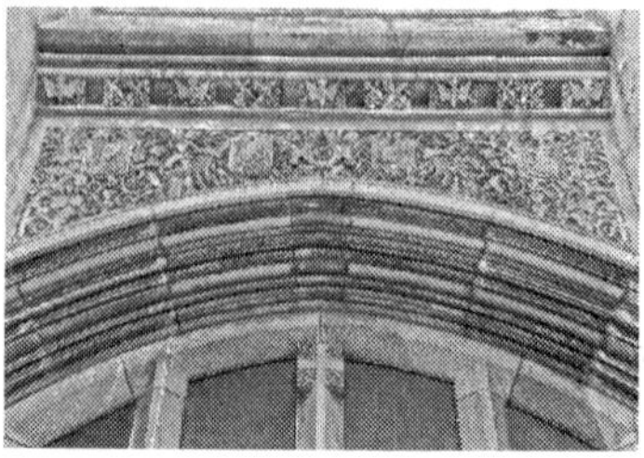

160. Queen of Angels Catholic Church
(1938; McCarthy, Smith & Eppig?)
2330 W Sunnyside Ave
Chicago, IL
[L]
Ledger details: Jobs #981, #984
1958
"Queen of Angels"

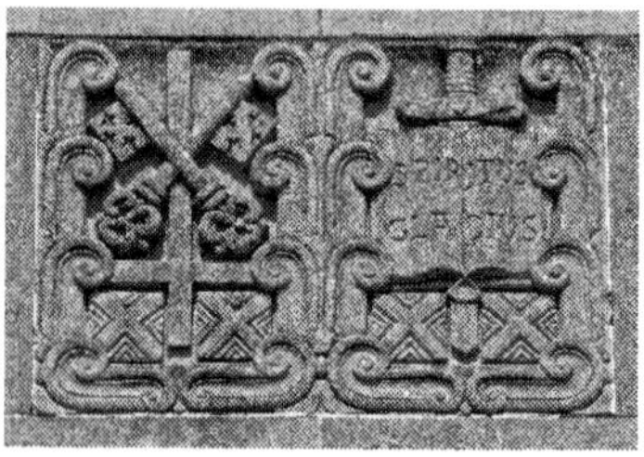

161. Saints Peter & Paul School
(1938; Donaldson & Meier)
19400 Sawyer St
Detroit, MI
[L]
Ledger details: Job #686; 1942
"Peter & Paul Ch"

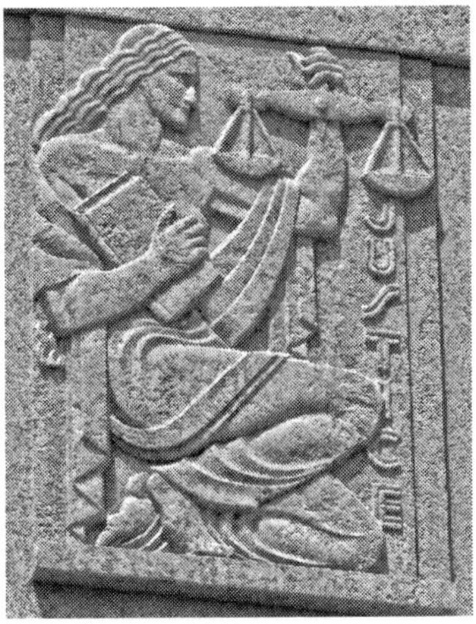

162. Kalamazoo County Building
(1937; Smith, Hinchman & Grylls with M.J.C. Billingham)
227 W Michigan Ave
Kalamazoo, MI
[L, SB, FH]
Ledger details: Job #500; 1936
"Kalamazoo County Bldg"

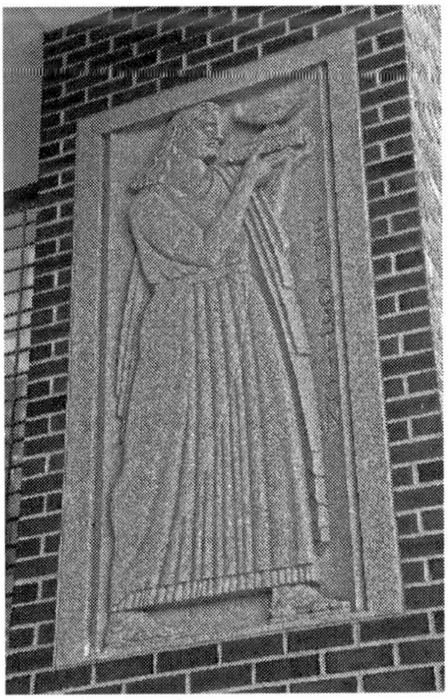

163. Detroit College of Law Sculpture at Michigan State University
(Detroit College of Law: 1936-1937, demolished; George D. Mason)
(Michigan State University College of Law: c.1997; architect undetermined)
648 N Shaw Ln
East Lansing, MI
[L]
Ledger details: Job #504; 1936
"Detroit College of Law"

This sculptural embellishment was transplanted from the original George D. Mason designed Detroit College of Law which formerly stood on E. Elizabeth Street. It was demolished in the late 1990s to make room for Comerica Park, the current home of the Detroit Tigers.

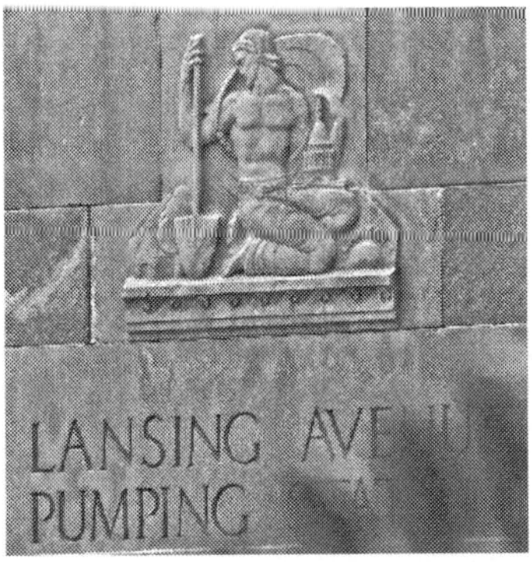

164. Lansing Board of Water and Light Pumping Station
(1937; Lee & Kenneth C. Black)
1711 Lansing Ave
Lansing, MI
[L, FH]
Ledger details: Job #524; 1937
"Lansing Pumping Station"

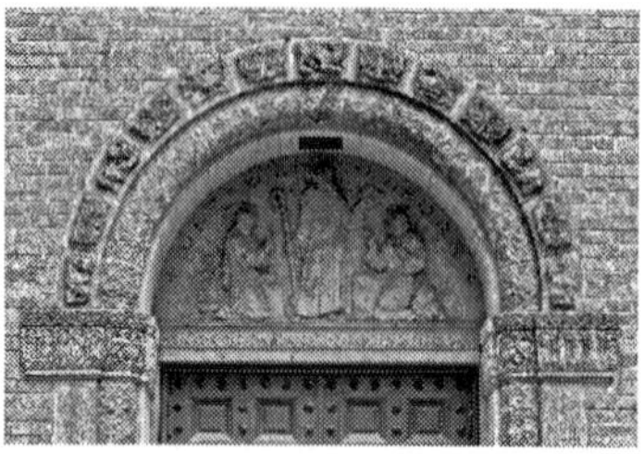

165. St. Sylvester
Benedictine Monastery
(1938; Diehl & Diehl)
17320 Rosemont Ave
Detroit, MI
[L, SB]
Ledger details:
Jobs #551, #564/#784; 1938/1948
"St Benedictine Monastery"
"St Sylvester Monastery"

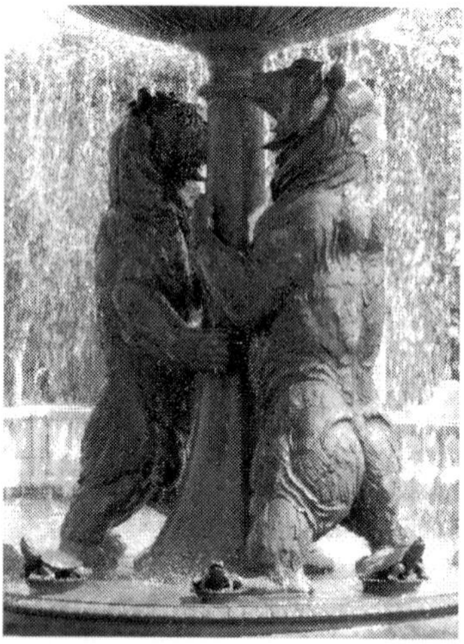

166. Horace H. Rackham
Memorial Fountain
at the Detroit Zoo
(1938; architect undetermined)
25425 Woodward Ave
Royal Oak, MI
[L, SB, DB]
Ledger details: Jobs #552, #560; 1938
"H.H. Rackham Fountain"

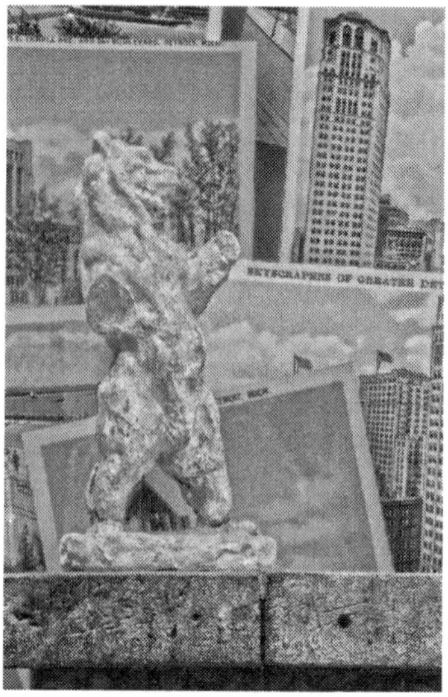

167. Horace H. Rackham
Memorial Fountain Maquette
at Detroit Historical Museum
(Maquette: c.1938; N/A)
5401 Woodward Ave
Detroit, MI
[L, SB, DB, DHM]
Ledger details: Jobs #552, #560; 1938
"H.H. Rackham Fountain"

Image courtesy Detroit Historical Museum

Dale A. Carlson, Photographer

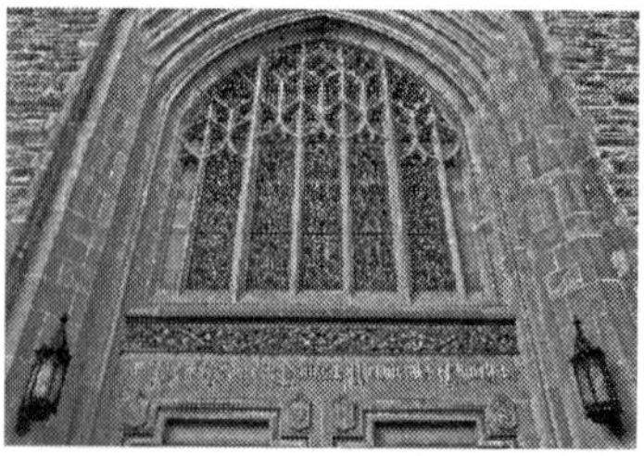

168. Grosse Pointe Memorial Presbyterian Church Additions
(c.1939; William E.N. Hunter / c.1958; George D. Mason, Inc? / c.1961; Herman & Simons?)
16 Lake Shore Rd
Grosse Pointe Farms, MI
[L, SB]
Ledger details:
Jobs #577/#980/#1023/#1034
1939/1958/1961/1962
"G.P.M. Ch"

We fell short of fully unravelling this structure's complex construction history and aim to improve upon this entry in the second edition.

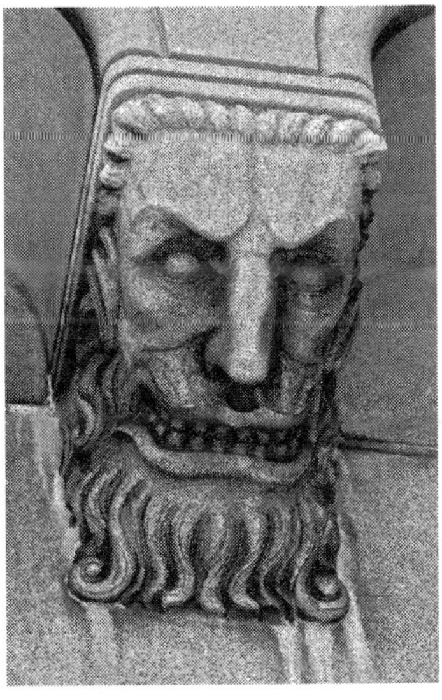

169. Kalamazoo State Hospital
(1939-1952; Knecht, McCarty & Thebaud)
1312 Oakland Dr
Kalamazoo, MI
[L, FH]
Ledger details: Job #579; 1939
"Kalamazoo State Hospt"

170. Pierce Junior High School
(1939; Robert O. Derrick & Branson V. Gamber)
15430 Kercheval Ave
Grosse Pointe Park, MI
[L]
Ledger details: Job #581; 1939
"Grosse Pointe Sch"

171. Motherhouse of the Immaculate Heart of Mary Sisters Chapel
(1940; D.A. Bohlen & Son)
610 W Elm Ave
Monroe, MI
[L]
Ledger details: Jobs #583, #597; 1939
"Immaculate Heart of Mary" "St. Mary's Acadamy (sic) Monroe Mich"

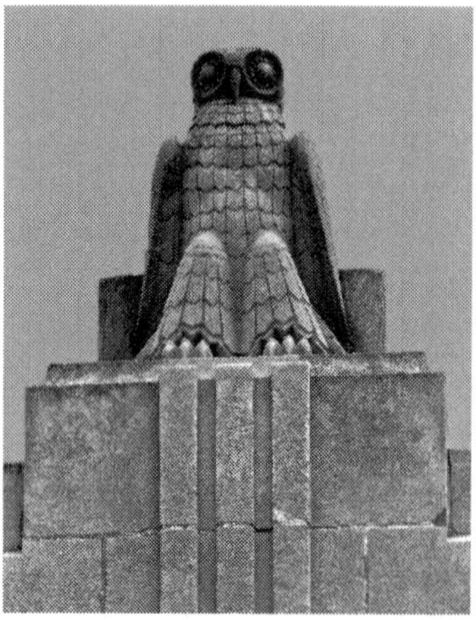

172. Isaac Crary Elementary School
(1939; McGrath & Dohmen)
16164 Asbury Park
Detroit, MI
[L]
Ledger details: Job #584; 1939
"Isaic (sic) Crary Sch."

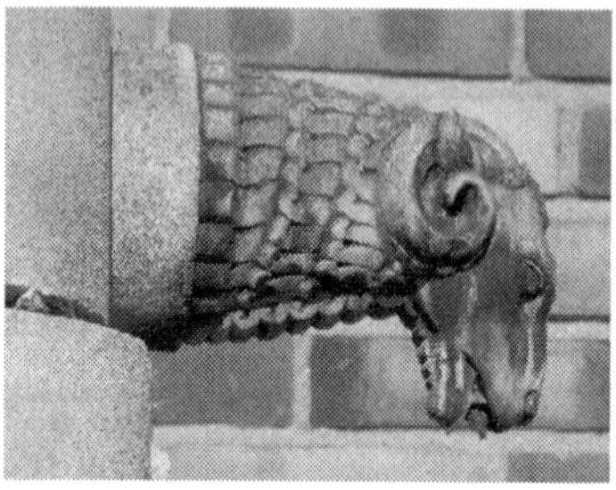

173. Fenton Community Center ~ Fountain
(1938; Eliel & Eero Saarinen)
150 S Leroy St
Fenton, MI
[L]
Ledger details: Job #589; 1939
"Fenton Comm. House"

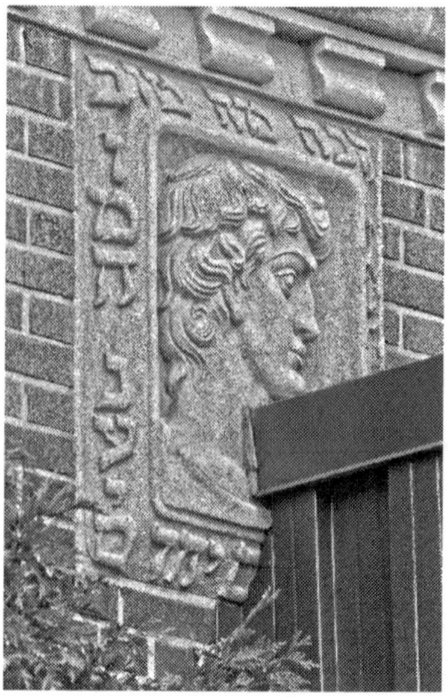

174. Aaron DeRoy Memorial Community Center now known as Cleary University
(1939; Charles Agree)
8904 Woodward Ave
Detroit, MI
[L]
Ledger details: Job #592; 1939
"Jewish Comm. Center"

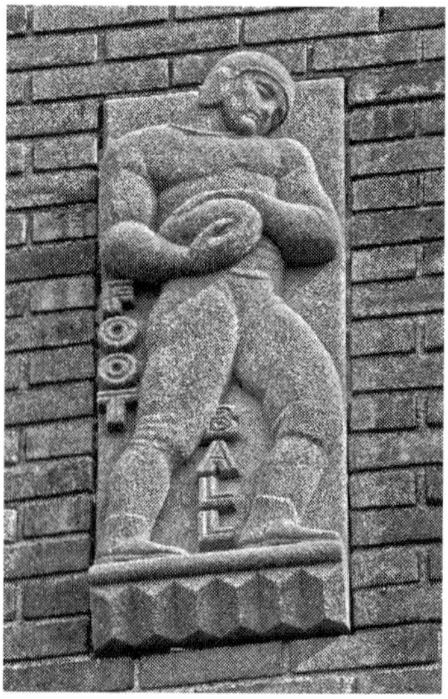

175. Blessed Sacrament Center
(1940; Diehl & Diehl)
150 Belmont St
Detroit, MI
[L]
Ledger details:
Jobs #596/#647/#66
1939/1941/1942
"Sacred Heart (sic) Cath"
"Bl. Sacr. Cath"
"Blessed Sacr. Cath"

Continuous interior renovations managed by Diehl & Diehl at the nearby Cathedral of the Most Blessed Sacrament (entry #258) between 1942 and 1951 render difficult the task of flawlessly separating these two commissions by job number. We present our best estimate.

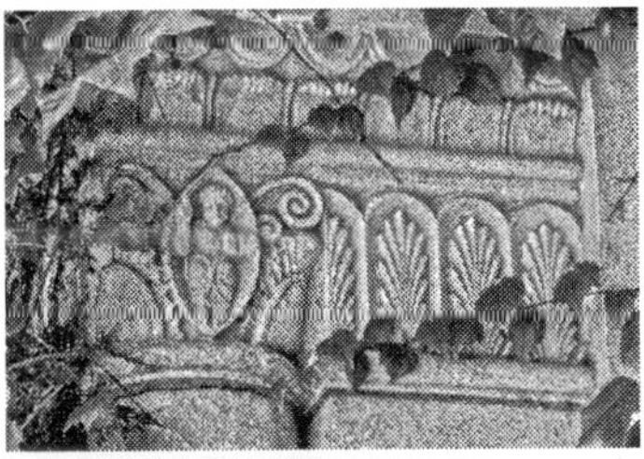

176. St. Mary High School
(1939; architect undetermined)
14751 Mansfield St
Detroit, MI
[L]
Ledger details:
Jobs #560, #561/#780; 1939/1948
"St Mary's High Sch"
"St Mary's Chapel"

For this commission Parducci erroneously duplicates job numbers 560 and 561, previously assigned to jobs recorded on the 1938 page.

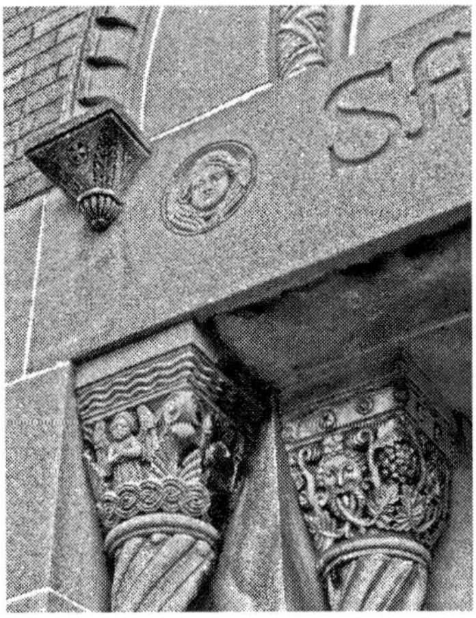

177. St. Michael the Archangel Catholic Church
(c.1940; architect undetermined)
420 Sandusky St
Toledo, OH
[L]
Ledger details: Jobs #599/#638
1939/1941
"St Michael's Ch Toledo Ohio"

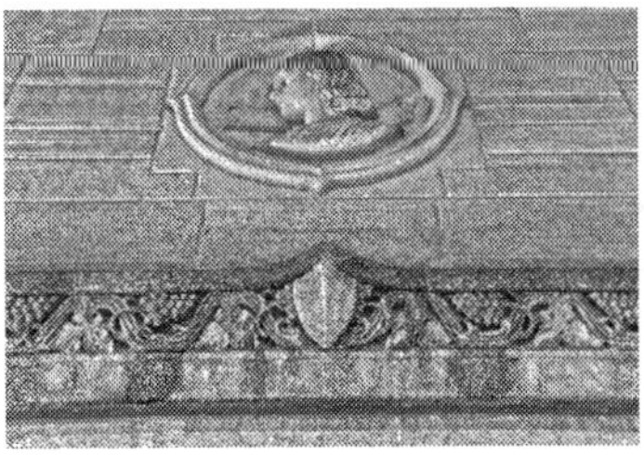

178. First United Methodist Church
(1939; architect undetermined)
120 S State St
Ann Arbor, MI
[L]
Ledger details: Job #600; 1940
"Ann Arbor Ch"

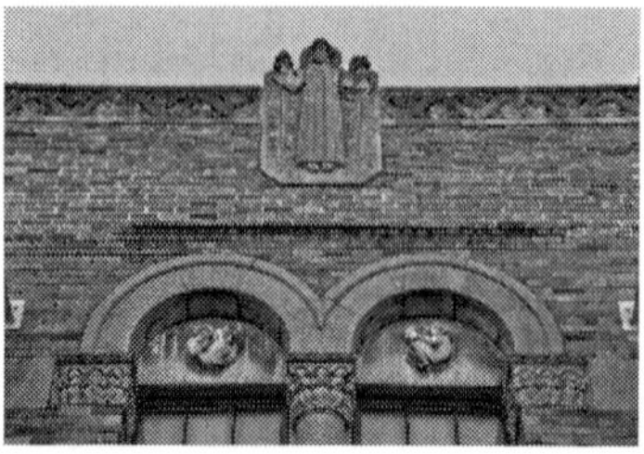

179. St. Scholastica School and Additions now known as Cornerstone Health + Technology High School
(1939/c.1940s; Diehl & Diehl)
17351 Southfield Fwy
Detroit, MI
[L]
Ledger details:
Jobs #726/#782/#902
1945/1948/1953
"St Scholastica Sch. add"

In our opinion there is little to no doubt that Parducci created the sculpture for this school's original 1939 construction. Why the ledgers lack a corresponding job number in an appropriate year remains unclear. It is possible but unlikely that the date of the original commission fell within the 1932 to 1936 ledger gap. Until a more plausible explanation emerges, we classify it as an inexplicable chronological misplacement supporting our theory that Parducci created his ledgers from less than flawless memories and incomplete records at some point late in his career.

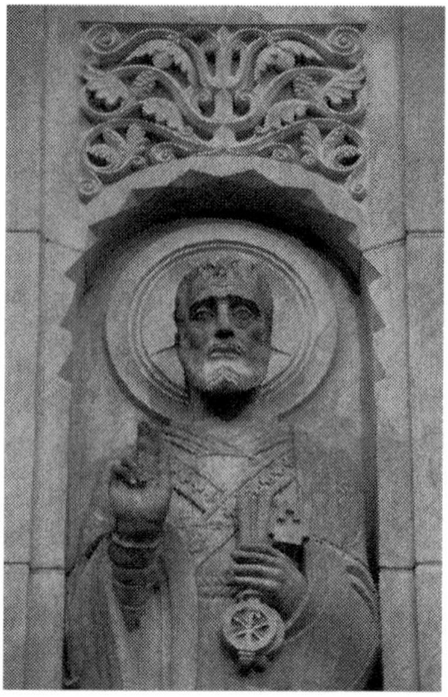

180. St. Peter Catholic Church
(1940; architect undetermined)
125 E Nineteenth Ave
Covington, LA
[L, SB]
Ledger details: Job #609; 1940
"St. Peters Statue Covington La"

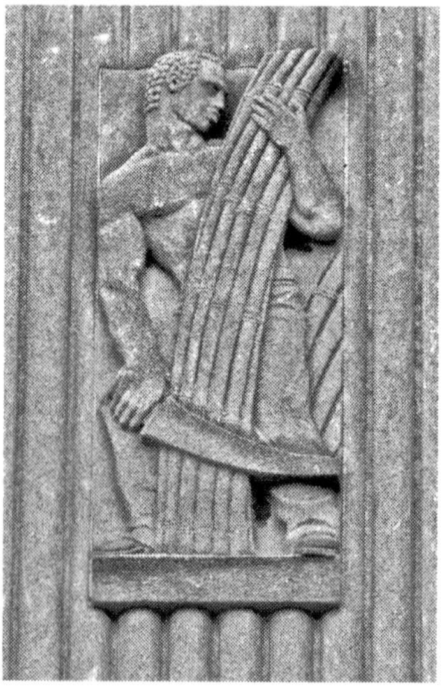

181. Sander's Candy Company Offices and Plant
(1941; architect undetermined)
100 Oakman Blvd
Highland Park, MI
[L]
Ledger details: Job #610; 1940
"Sanders Bakery"

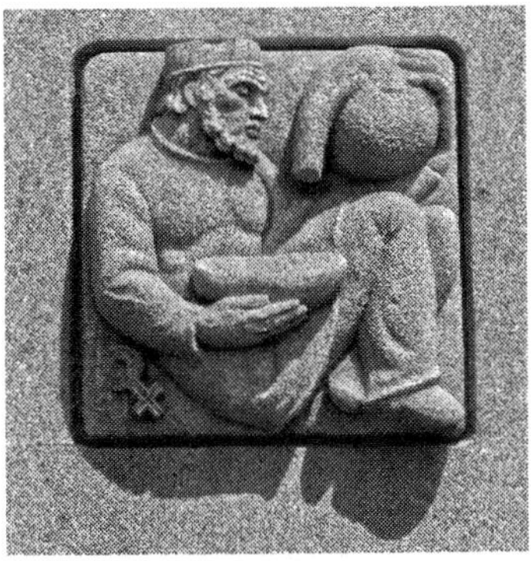

182. Old Grace Hospital Sculpture at Sinai-Grace Hospital
(Old Grace Hospital: c.1941; demolished; architect undetermined)
Ardmore St @ Santa Maria Ave
Detroit, MI
[L]
Ledger details: Job #613; 1940
"Grace Hospital"

Two pieces at the northeast corner of Ardmore and Santa Maria, on walls separating this hospital's small power plant from the surrounding residential properties, were originally created for the main entrance of Old Grace Hospital, formerly located at approximately 18700 Meyers Rd. How they ended up at their present location is unknown to us. We endeavor to present more of the story of this transplanted commission in our second edition.

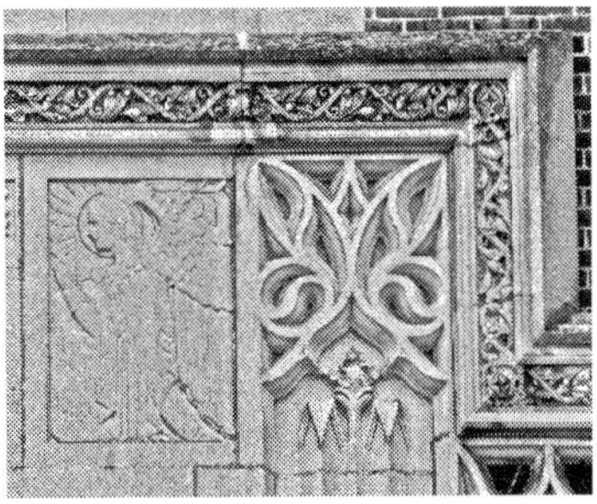

183. St. Joseph Catholic Church Façade Reconstruction
(c.1940; Herman & Simons)
36 Melmore St
Tiffin, OH
[L]
Ledger details: Job #618; 1940
"St. Joseph's Ch Tiffin Ohio"

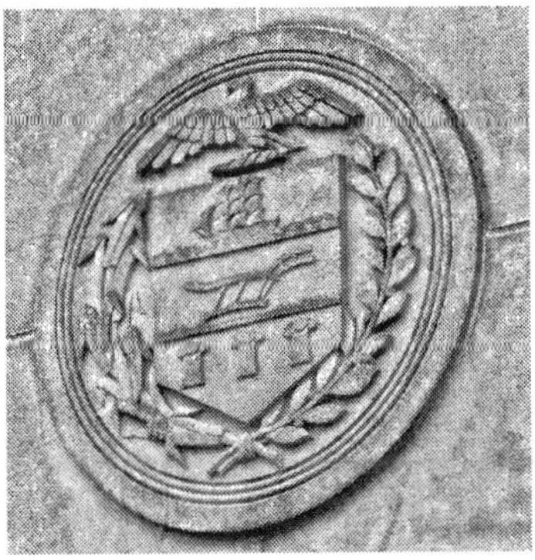

184. Employers Mutual Insurance Company Building now known as Wausau City Hall
(1940; Childs & Smith)
407 Grant St
Wausau, WI
[L]
Ledger details: Jobs #622/#843
1940/1950
"Employers Mutuals Wausau Wisc."

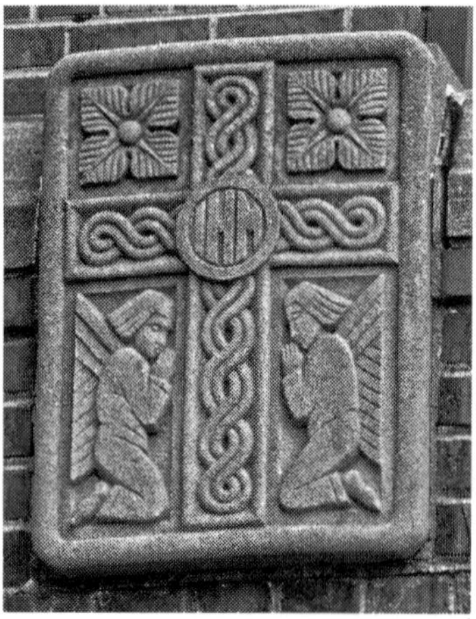

185. Our Lady of Good Counsel Parish ~ Rectory
(c.1941; Diehl & Diehl)
17200 Rowe St, Detroit
Detroit, MI
[L, SB]
Ledger details: Job #631; 1941
"Our Lady of Good Counsel"

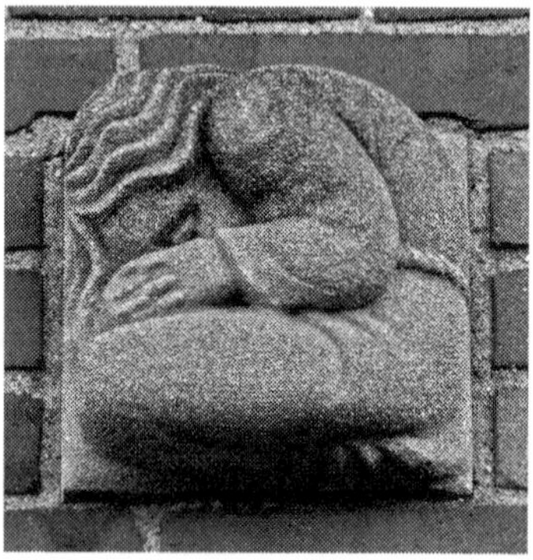

186. St. Brigid Parish ~ Rectory
(c.1941; Diehl & Diehl)
8809 Schoolcraft Rd
Detroit, MI
[L]
Ledger details: Job #632; 1941
"St Bridget (sic) Ch."

187. Michigan Bell Central Office now known as Petoskey District Library
(1940; Smith, Hinchman & Grylls)
500 E Mitchell St
Petoskey, MI
[L]
Ledger details: Job #633; 1941
"Mich. Bell Telephone
Petoskey Mich"

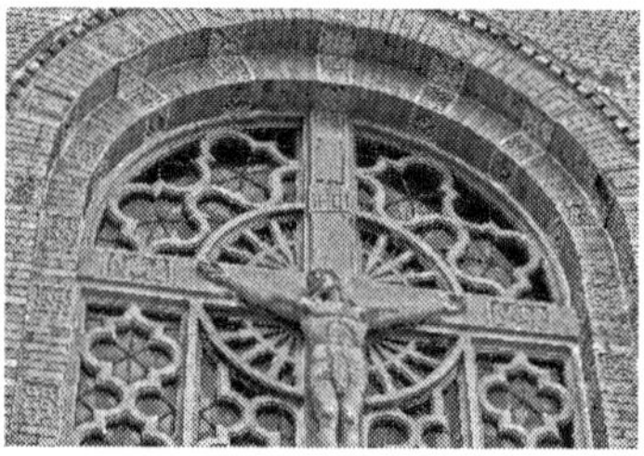

188. Immaculate Conception Ukrainian Catholic Church
(1941; Howard T. Simons of Herman & Simons)
11700 McDougall St
Hamtramck, MI
[L]
Ledger details:
Jobs #646, #651, #656; 1941
"Immaculate Conception Ukrainian"
"Ukrainian Cath Ch."

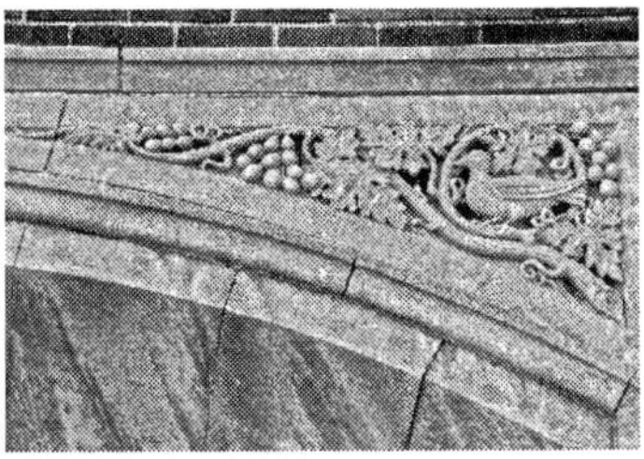

189. Bethany Lutheran Church
(1941; John C. Stahl)
11475 E Outer Drive
Detroit, MI
[L]
Ledger details: Job #648; 1941
"Bethany Lutheran Ch."

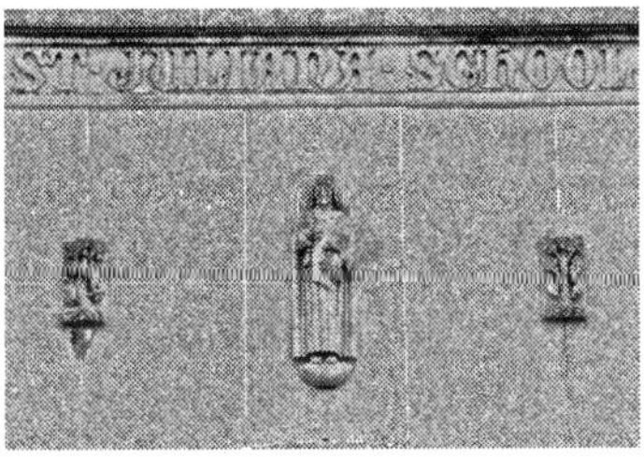

190. St. Juliana Elementary School Original Wing and Addition
(1941, 1946; Diehl & Diehl)
9755 Chalmers St
Detroit, MI
[L]
Ledger details: Jobs #649/#747
1941/1946
"St Juliana Sch."

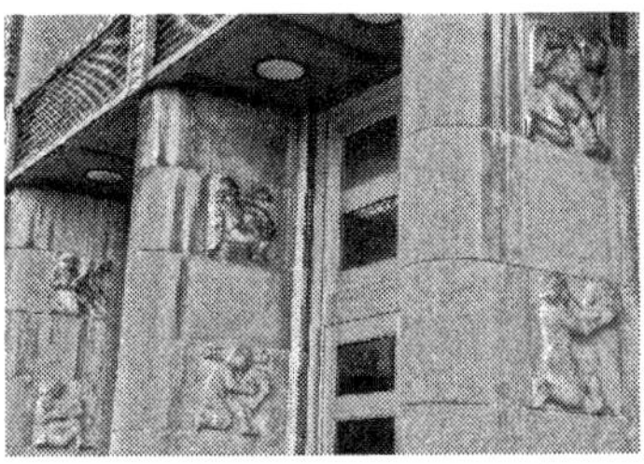

191. J.W. Sexton High School
(1942; Warren Holmes Co.)
102 McPherson Ave
Lansing, MI
[L, SB, FH]
Ledger details: Job #650; 1941
"Western High Sch Lansing Mich"

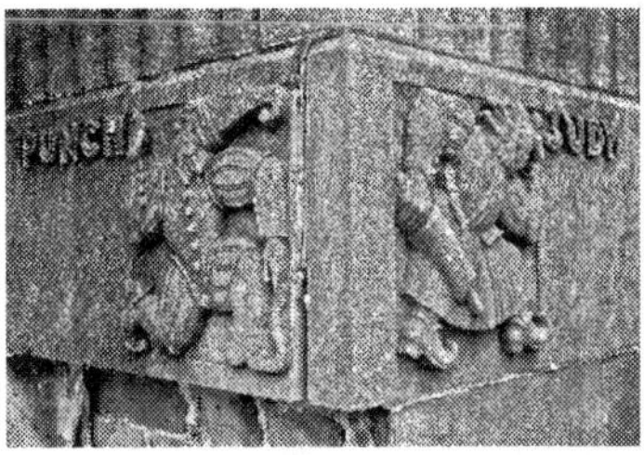

192. J.W. Sexton High School Auditorium
(1942; Warren Holmes Co.)
102 McPherson Ave
Lansing, MI
[L, SB, FH]
Ledger details: Job #650; 1941
"Western High Sch Lansing Mich"

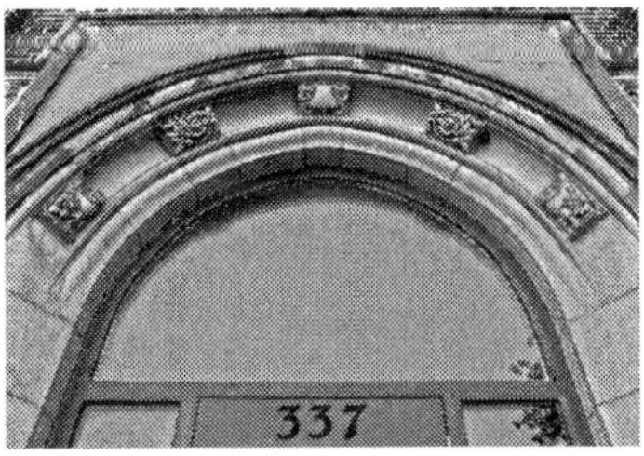

193. Michigan Bell Central Office
(1941; Smith, Hinchman & Grylls)
337 Abbot Rd
East Lansing, MI
[L]
Ledger details: Job #657; 1941
"East Lansing Telephone Bldg"

Regarding entries #194 and #195:

"Midland: The City of Modern Explorers", also known as The Midland Theatre History Mural, was created solely by Parducci's hand in the early 1940s for installation in the Midland Theatre on Ashman Circle. At some point in the building's history it was covered up during a remodeling. It was rediscovered during the building's late 1990s demolition at which point an impressive historical preservation effort was undertaken by a host of interested parties including the Midland County Historical Society and The Dow Corning Corporation. The preservation and restoration project spanned the years of 1998 to 2000, and the mural was installed at its current location, the Herbert D. Doan Midland County History Center, in 2003.

Over the course of the restoration project a bronze casting was created from the original plasterwork and placed in Ned S. Arbury Park.

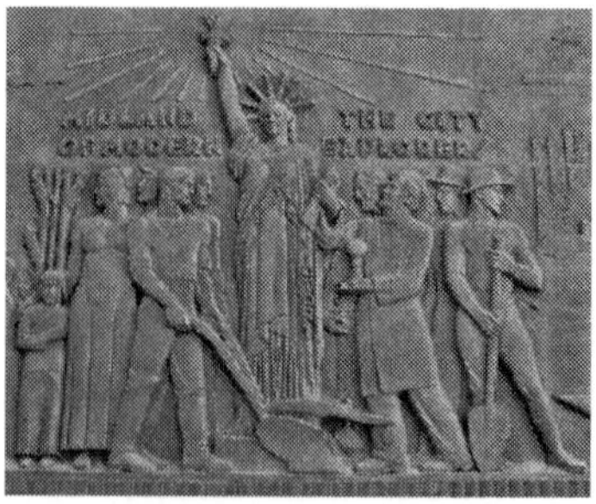

194. Midland Theatre History Mural at Herbert D. Doan Midland County History Center
(Midland Theatre: 1942; architect undetermined)
(Doan History Center: c.2003; architect undetermined)
3417 W Main St
Midland, MI
[L, SB]
Ledger details: Job #667; 1942 "Midland Mich Theatre"

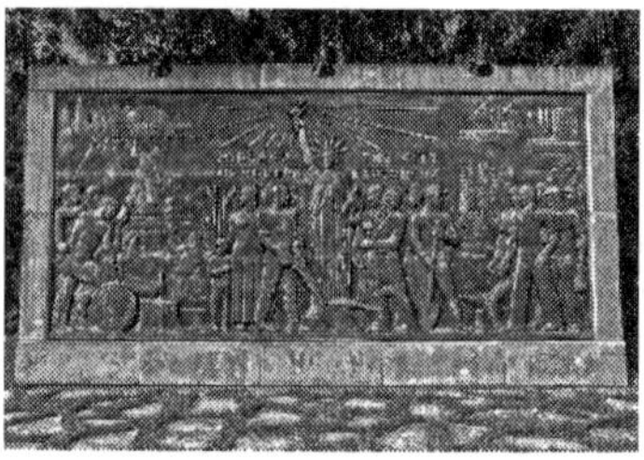

195. Midland Theatre History Mural Bronze Casting at Ned S. Arbury Centennial Park
(c.2000; N/A)
401 W Main St
Midland, MI
[L, SB]
Ledger details: Job #667; 1942 "Midland Mich Theatre"

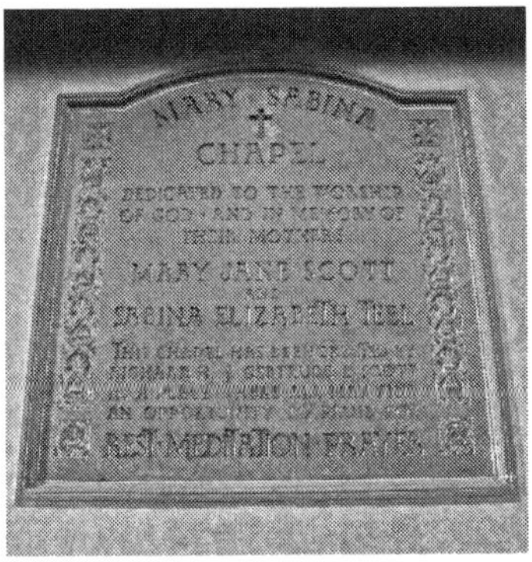

196. Central United Methodist Church ~ Mary-Sabina Chapel Addition
(1942; Lee & Kenneth C. Black)
215 N Capitol Ave
Lansing, MI
[L]
Ledger details: Job #670; 1942
"Chapel Mem Lansing"

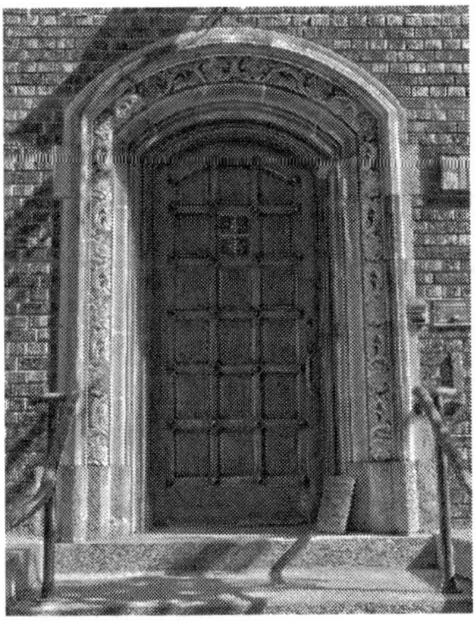

197. St. Ambrose Parish ~ Rectory
(c.1941; Diehl & Diehl)
15050 Hampton St
Grosse Pointe Park, MI
[L]
Ledger details: Job #671; 1942
"St. Ambrose Ch."

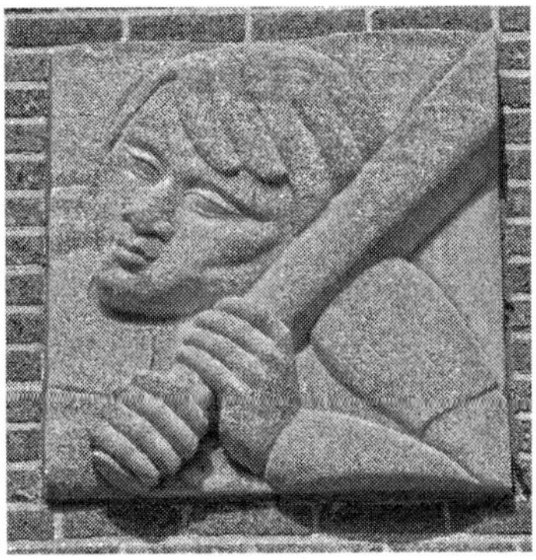

198. St. John Berchmans Servite High School Addition
(c.1941; Diehl & Diehl)
4800 Coplin St
Detroit, MI
[L, SB]
Ledger details:
Jobs #679, #682/#687, #690
1942/1943
"St John Berchman Ch"

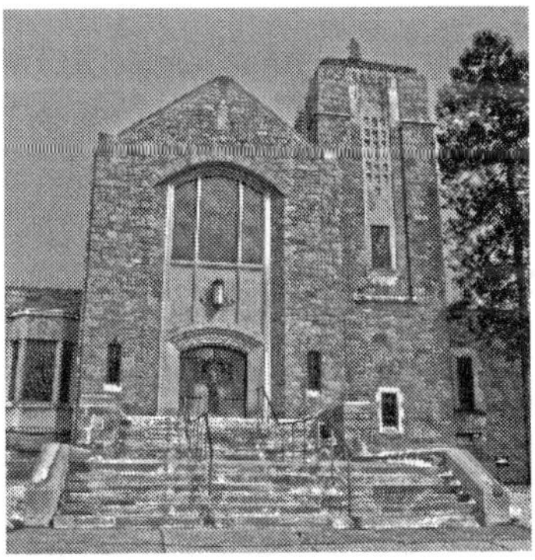

199. Woodlawn Cemetery Community Mausoleum
(1942; Harley, Ellington & Day)
19975 Woodward Ave
Detroit, MI
[L, SB]
Ledger details: Jobs #680/#969
1942/1967
"Woodlawn Cem"

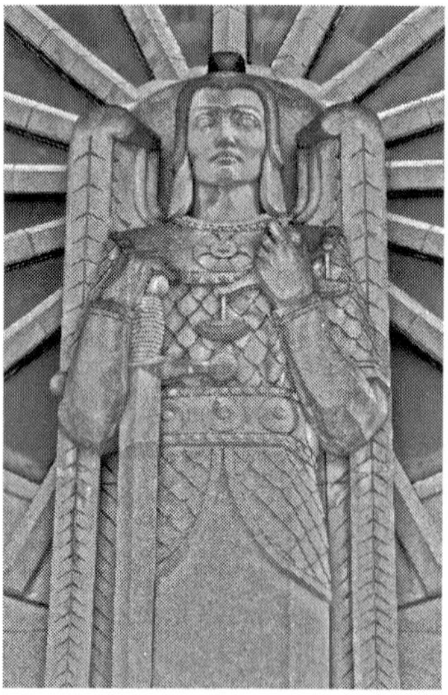

200. St. Michael the Archangel Catholic Church
(1942; McGrath & Dohmen?)
1716 Sixth St
Muskegon, MI
[L]
Ledger details: Job #684; 1942
"St. Michael's Ch. Muskegon Mich"

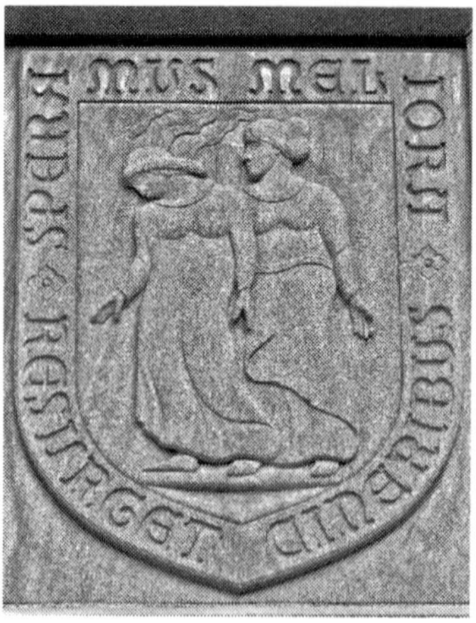

201. Marion Law School Addition
(1945; J. Ivan Dise)
19411 Cliff St
Detroit, MI
[L]
Ledger details: Job #719; 1945
"Marion Law Sch. add."

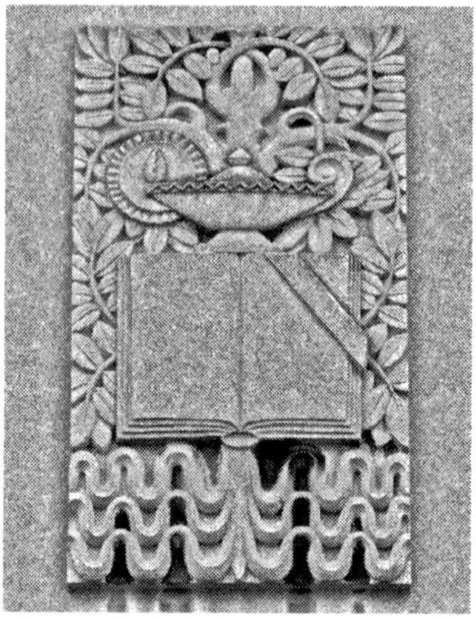

202. Our Lady of La Salette School
(1943, 1947; Diehl & Diehl)
2600 Harvard Rd
Berkley, MI
[L]
Ledger details: Job #727; 1945
"Our Lady of La Salette Sch"

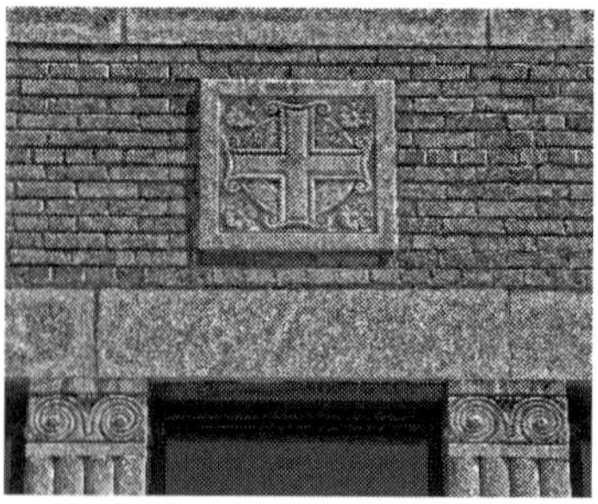

203. St. Joan of Arc School
(1946; Diehl & Diehl)
22415 Overlake St
St. Clair Shores, MI
[L]
Ledger details: Job #745; 1946
"Joan of Arch (sic) Ch"

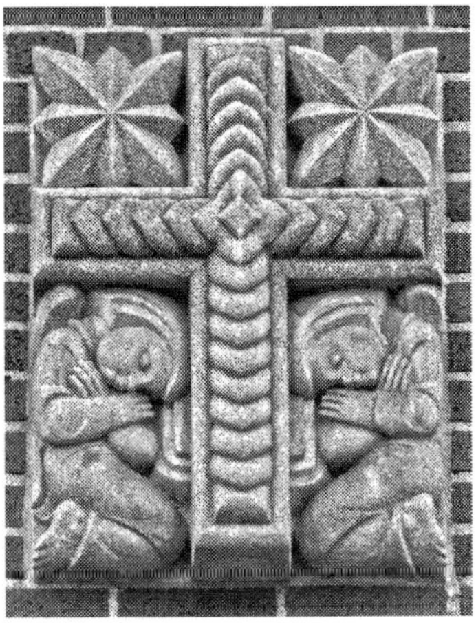

204. St. Rita Parish ~ Convent
(1949; Diehl & Diehl)
19675 Hawthorne St
Detroit, MI
[L]
Ledger details: Job #746; 1946
"St. Rita Ch."

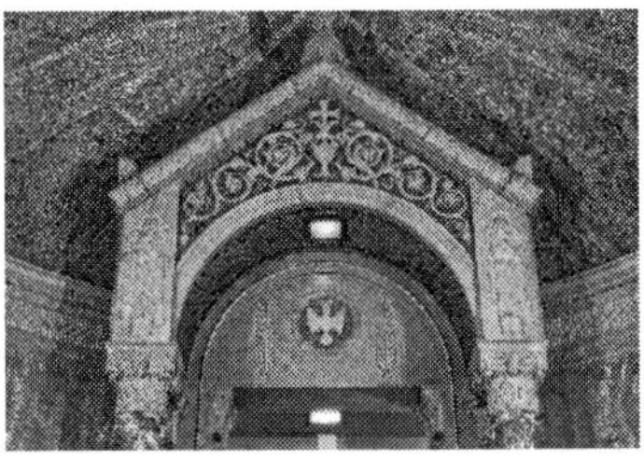

205. The Chapel of the Sorrowful Mother at Ascension Via Christi Regional Medical Center ~ St. Francis Campus
(1946; Maguolo & Quick)
929 St Francis N
Wichita, KS
[L]
Ledger details: Job #749; 1946
"St Francis Chapel"

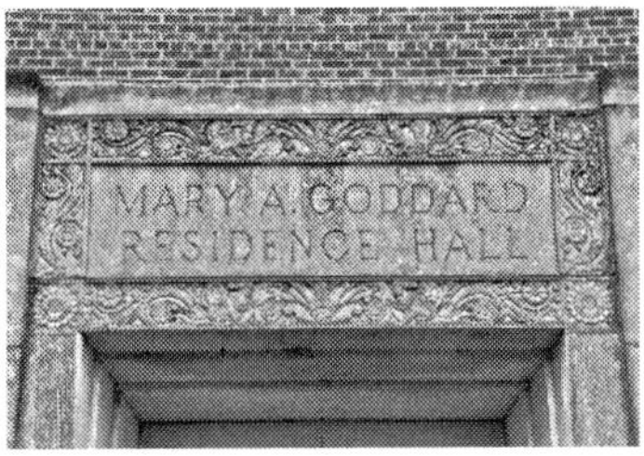

206. Jones-Goddard Residence Hall at Eastern Michigan University
(1948, 1955; Ralph Gerganoff)
649 Jones-Goddard
Ypsilanti, MI
[L]
Ledger details: Job #769; 1947
"Mich. Normal College"

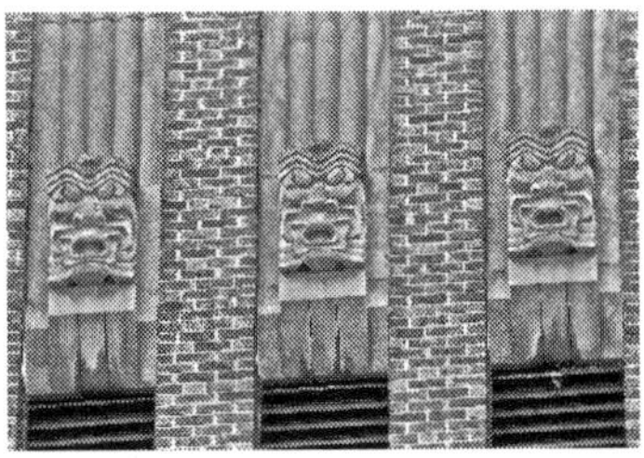

207. Pierce Hall at Eastern Michigan University
(1948; Ralph Gerganoff)
550 College Pl
Ypsilanti, MI
[L]
Ledger details: Job #769; 1947
"Mich. Normal College"

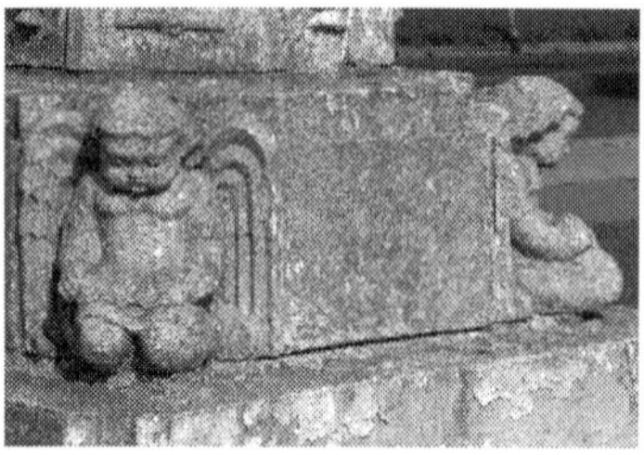

208. St. Juliana Elementary School Flagpole Base
(c.1948; Diehl & Diehl)
9755 Chalmers St
Detroit, MI
[L]
Ledger details: Job #776; 1948
"St Julian (sic) Flagpole Base"

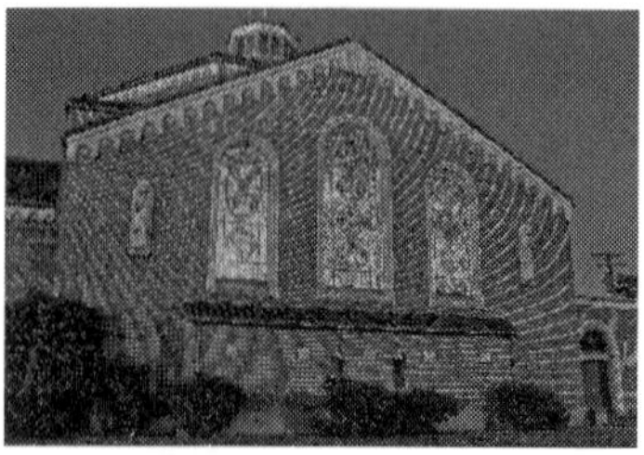

209. St. Brigid Catholic Church ~ Exterior
(1948-1949; Diehl & Diehl)
8809 Schoolcraft Rd
Detroit, MI
[L, WK]
Ledger details: Jobs #777/#946
1948/1955
"St Bridget (sic) Ch"

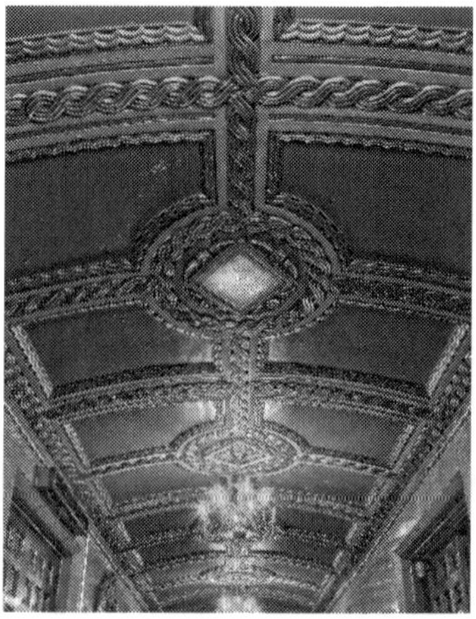

210. St. Brigid Catholic Church ~ Interior
(1948-1949; Diehl & Diehl)
8809 Schoolcraft Rd
Detroit, MI
[L, WK]
Ledger details: Jobs #777/#946
1948/1955
"St Bridget (sic) Ch"

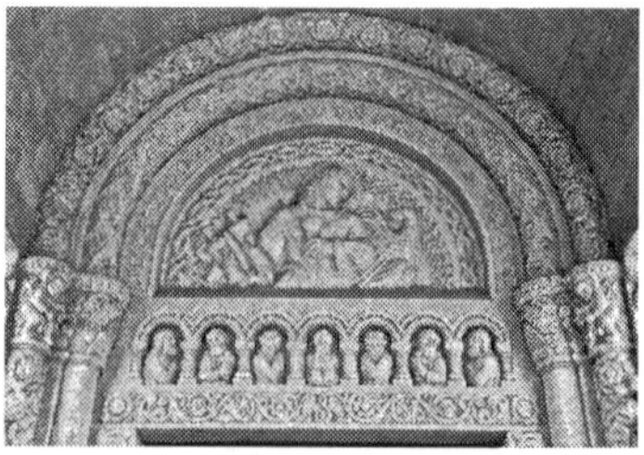

211. St. John's Provincial Seminary now known as The Inn at St. John's ~ Exterior Elements
(1948-1955; Diehl & Diehl)
44045 Five Mile Rd
Plymouth Township, MI
[L, SB, DB, WK]
Ledger details:
Jobs #778/#798/#908
1948/1949/1953
"St John's Provincial Ceminary (sic)"

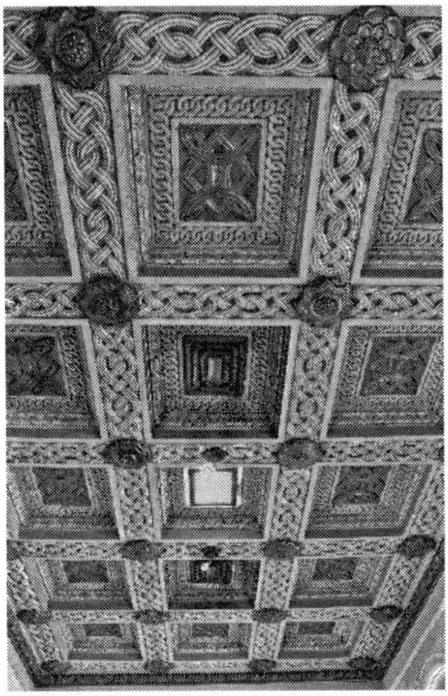

212. St. John's Provincial Seminary now known as The Inn at St. John's ~ Interior Elements
(1948-1955; Diehl & Diehl)
44045 Five Mile Rd
Plymouth Township, MI
[L, SB, DB, WK]
Ledger details:
Jobs #778/#798/#908
1948/1949/1953
"St John's Provincial Ceminary (sic)"

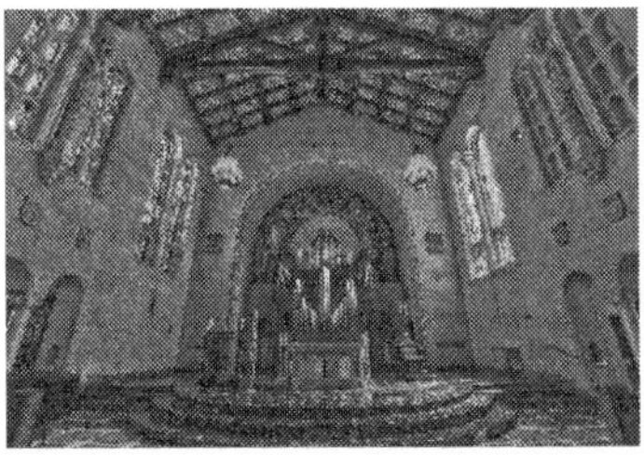

213. St. John's Provincial Seminary now known as The Inn at St. John's ~ Chapel
(1948-1955; Diehl & Diehl)
44045 Five Mile Rd
Plymouth Township, MI
[L, SB, DB, WK]
Ledger details:
Jobs #778/#798/#908
1948/1949/1953
"St John's Provincial Ceminary (sic)"

Regarding this commission Parducci states in the 1975 Smithsonian interview: *"St. John's Seminary in Northville. That has a lot of my work there. I must have had over $50,000 worth of work on that place—more than that."*

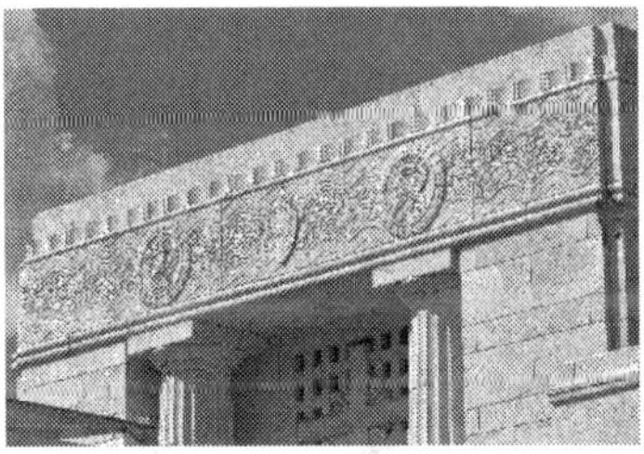

214. Holy Sepulchre Catholic Cemetery Mausoleum ~ Exterior Elements
(1948; Harley, Ellington & Day)
25800 W Ten Mile Rd
Southfield, MI
[L, SB]
Ledger details: Jobs #779/ #921/#935; 1948/1954/1955
"Holy Sepulchre Maus"

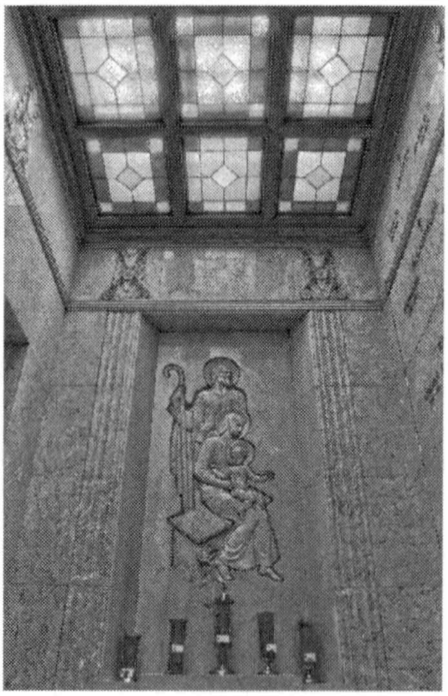

215. Holy Sepulchre Catholic Cemetery Mausoleum ~ Interior Elements
(1948; Harley, Ellington & Day)
25800 W Ten Mile Rd
Southfield, MI
[L, SB]
Ledger details: Jobs #779/ #921 #935; 1948/1954/1955
"Holy Sepulchre Maus"

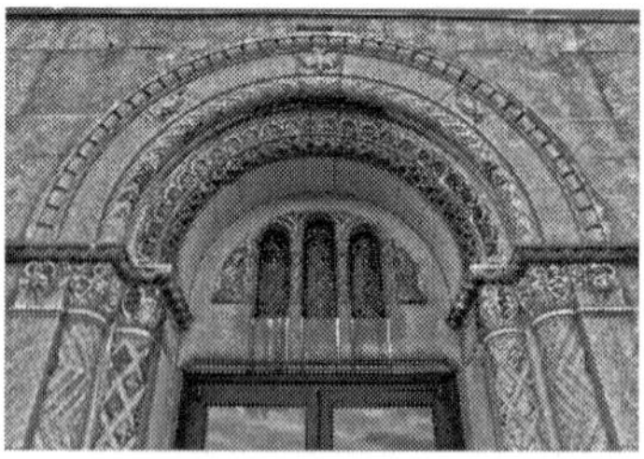

216. St. David Catholic Church
(1947; Herman & Simons)
8105 E Outer Drive
Detroit, MI
[L, SB, WK]
Ledger details: Jobs #781/#870 1948/1951
"St David's"

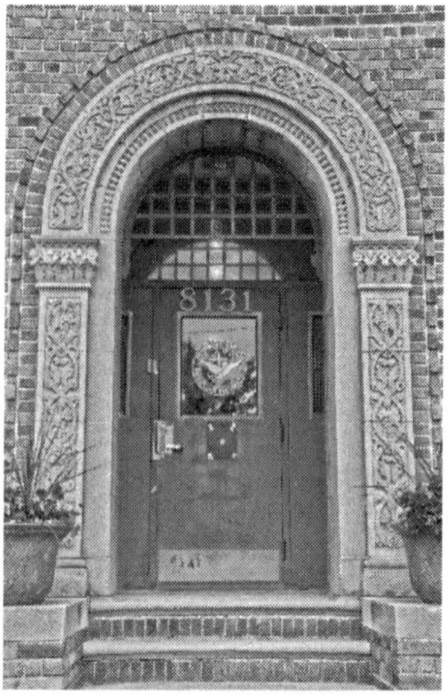

217. St. David Parish ~ Convent
(1947; Herman & Simons)
8131 E Outer Drive
Detroit, MI
[L, SB, WK]
Ledger details: Jobs #781/#870 1948/1951
"St David's"

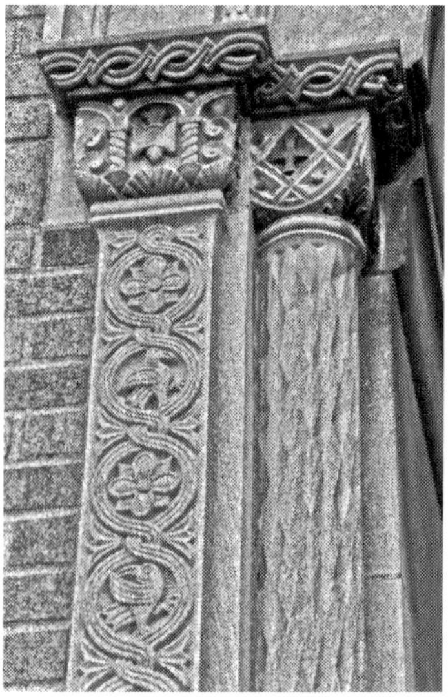

218. St. David Parish ~ Rectory
(1947; Herman & Simons)
8105 E Outer Drive
Detroit, MI
[L, SB, WK]
Ledger details: Jobs #781/#870
1948/1951
"St David's"

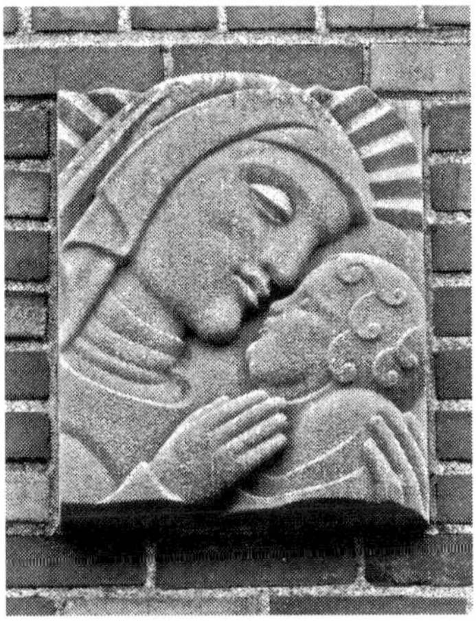

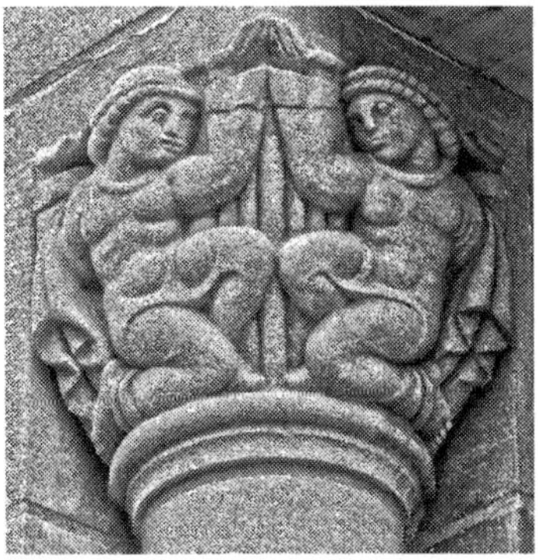

219. Our Lady of Good Counsel School Auditorium
(c.1947; Diehl & Diehl)
Sauer St at Annott Ave
Detroit, MI
[L]
Ledger details: Job #785; 1948
"Our Lady of Good Counsel"

220. Epiphany Parish ~ Rectory
(c.1948?; McGrath & Dohmen?)
Orangelawn St at Mendota St
Detroit, MI
[L]
Ledger details: Job #786; 1948
"Epiphany Parish"

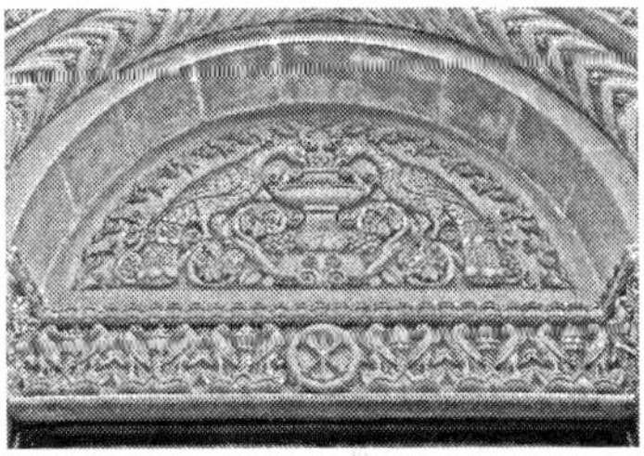

221. Queen of the Miraculous Medal Catholic Church
(1948; Diehl & Diehl)
1111 Carlton Blvd
Jackson, MI
[L, SB]
Ledger details: Job #789; 1948
"Our Lady Queen of the Medal
Jackson Mich"

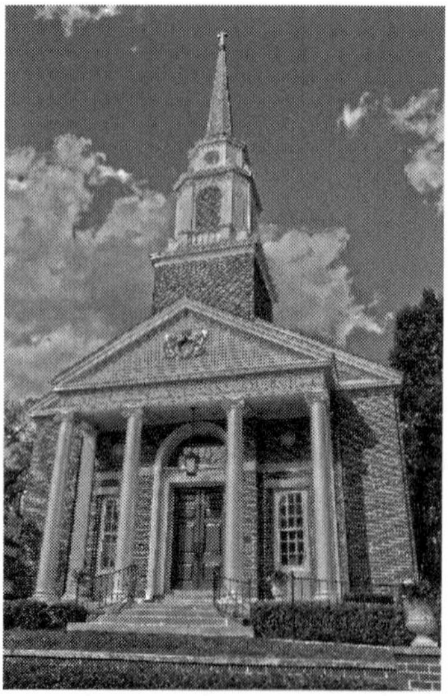

222. St. James Lutheran Church
(1948; David H. Williams of George D. Mason, Inc.)
170 McMillan Rd
Grosse Pointe Farms, MI
[L]
Ledger details: Job #791; 1948
"St James Lutheran Ch"

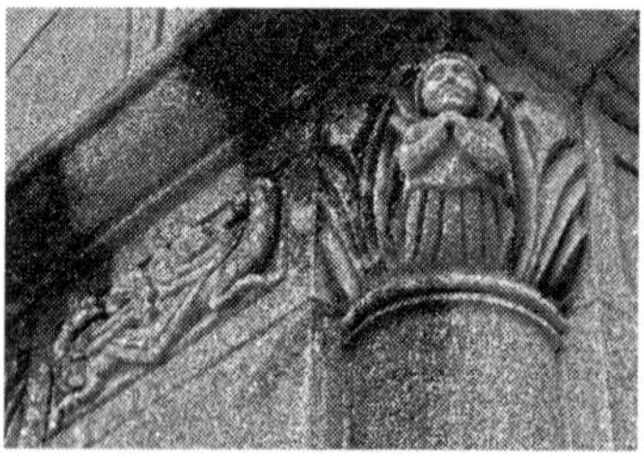

223. St. Augustine Catholic Church now known as Greater Concord Missionary Baptist Church
(1948; Herman & Simons)
4510 E Davison St
Detroit, MI
[L]
Ledger details: Job #793; 1948
"St Augustine Ch"

The last gap in Parducci's ledgers spans the last six months of 1947 and the first six months of 1948. In our opinion, the following six entries, #224 through #229, fall within this gap. All seven are confirmed by varying combinations of sources including scrapbook images, stylistic elements nearly identical to other Parducci works of the era, well established professional relationships with the commissioning architects, interview statements, and most importantly, ledger entries in subsequent years. Once again, we remind our readers that generally we have found if a commission site appears in the ledgers, regardless of the year it is first recorded, it is also very likely that Parducci produced the architectural sculpture for its original construction.

Additionally, in 1948 Parducci moved his operations into a new studio at 141 Sibley Street in Detroit, where they remained until his death in 1981. The address of this demolished structure is now encompassed by the footprint of Little Caesars Arena's open-air market and parking ramp.

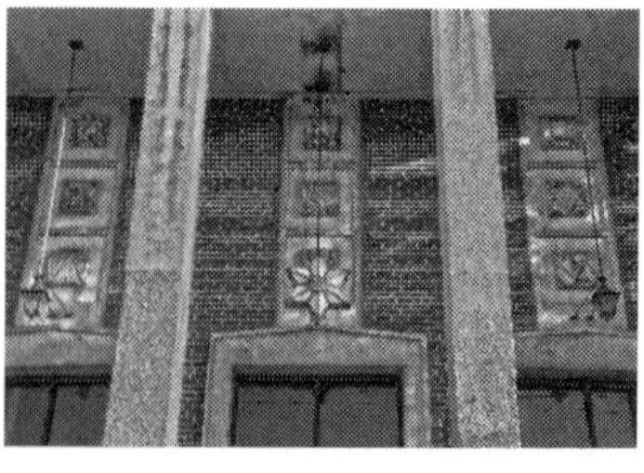

224. Northwest Hebrew Center aka Adat Shalom Temple now known as Bailey Cathedral Church of God
(1946; architect undetermined)
7045 Curtis St
Detroit, MI
[L]
Ledger details: Job #842; 1950
"Northwest Hebrew Center"

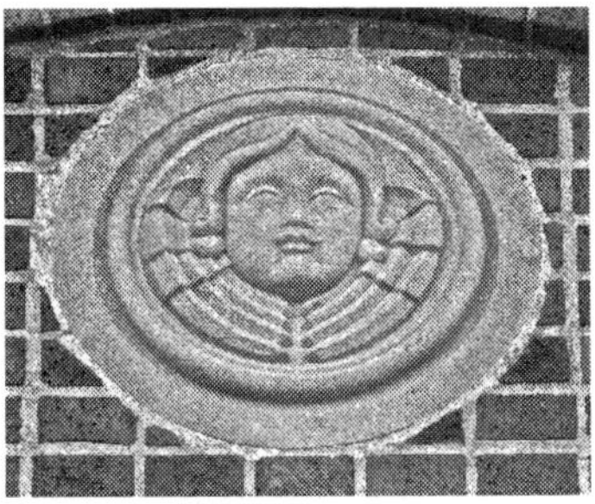

225. Our Lady Gate of Heaven School
(1946; McGrath & Dohmen?)
9600 Mettetal St
Detroit, MI
[L, SB]
Ledger details: Job #1043; 1964
"Our Lady Gate of Heaven"

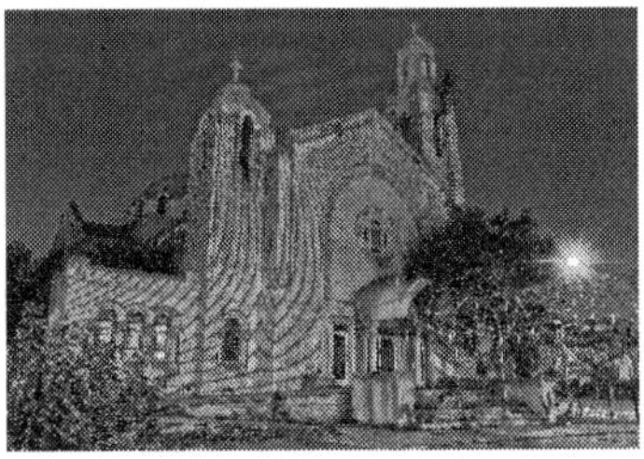

226. Saints Constantine & Helen Greek Orthodox Church
(1948; Arthur Grieg, Jr.)
4801 Oakman Blvd
Detroit, MI
[L]
Ledger details: Job #890; 1953
"Greek Orthodox Ch."

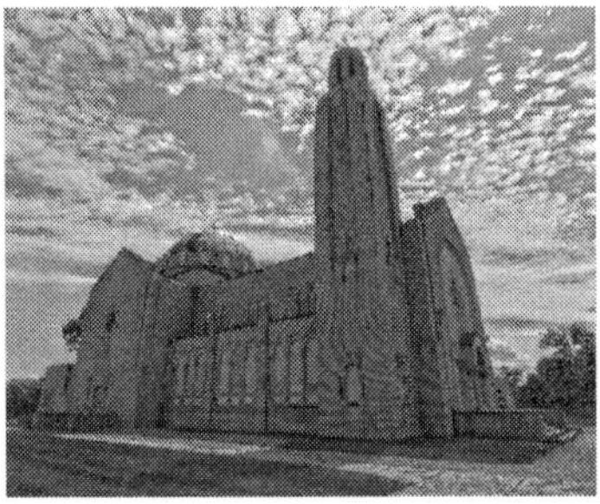

227. Assumption Greek Orthodox Church
(1948; Arthur Grieg, Jr.)
11000 Charlevoix St
Detroit, MI
[L]
Ledger details: Job #1008; 1960
"Assumption Ch Greek Orth."

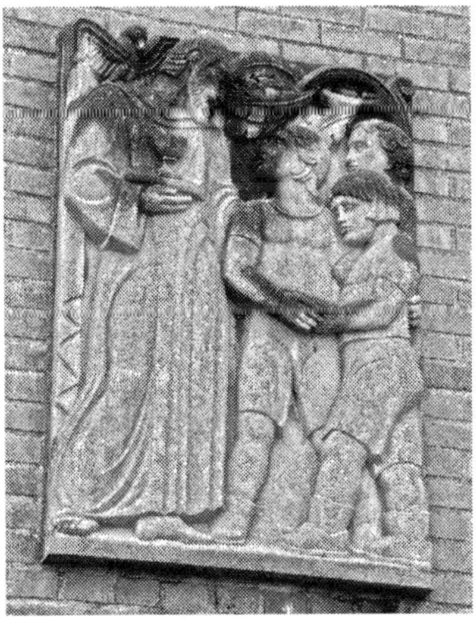

228. Old Redford Academy Auditorium
(1948; architect undetermined)
8001 W Outer Drive
Detroit, MI
[L]
Ledger details: Job #995; 1959
"St Benedict Statue"

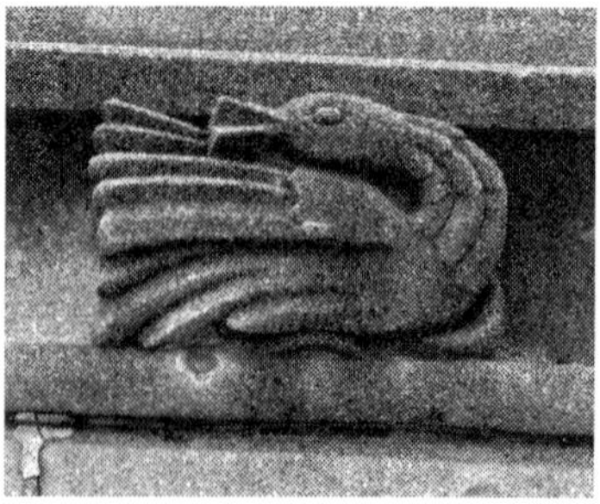

229. St. Suzanne School
(1950; McGrath & Dohmen)
19371 W Chicago
Detroit, MI
[L]
Ledger details: Jobs #922/#1037
1954/1962
"St Susanna (sic) Ch"

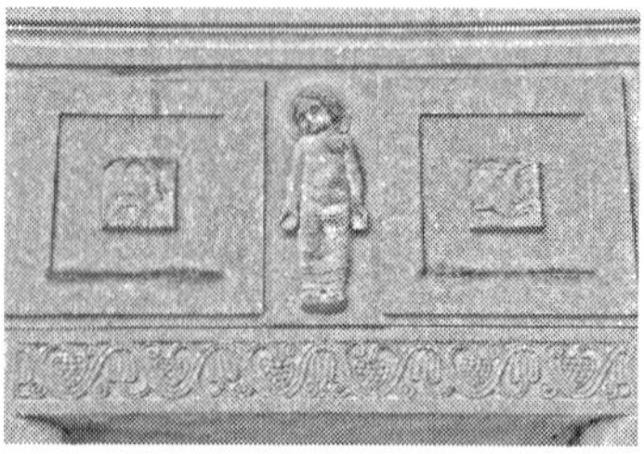

230. Nativity High School
(1949; architect undetermined)
5900 McClellan Ave
Detroit, MI
[L, SB]
Ledger details: Job #796; 1949
"Nativity Ch"

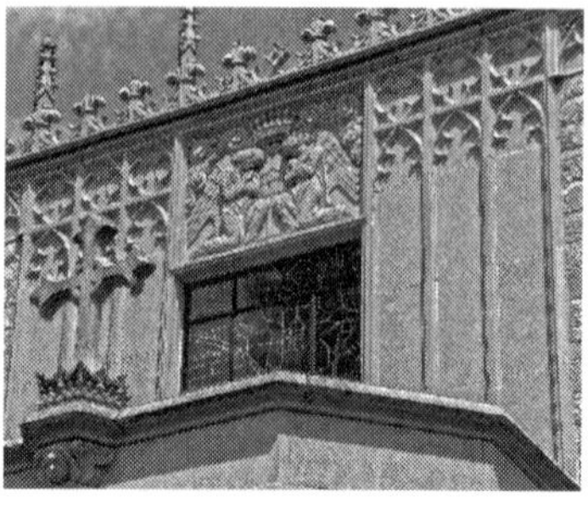

231. Queen of Heaven Cemetery Mausoleum ~ Exterior Elements
(c.1950; Harley, Ellington & Day)
1400 S Wolf Rd
Hillside, IL
[L, SB]
Ledger details: Jobs #801/
#934, #941/#968; 1949/1955/1957
"Our Lady Gate of Heaven (sic)"
"Queen of Heaven Maus Chicago"
"Our Lady Queen of Heaven (sic)"

One of the grandest commissions of Parducci's career, largely unknown to Michiganders. Individual sculptural works by Parducci at this site easily number in the hundreds.

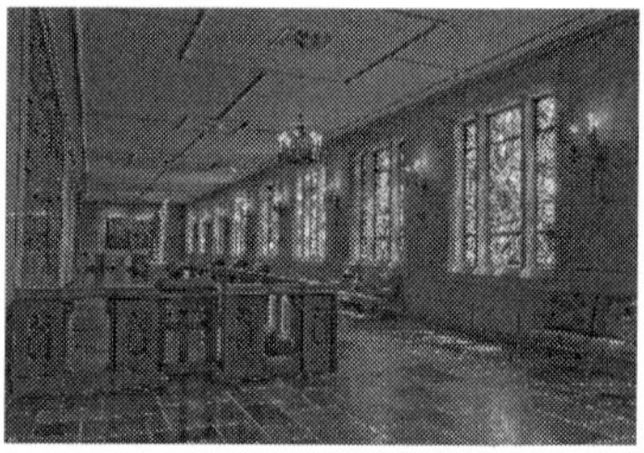

232. Queen of Heaven Cemetery Mausoleum ~ Interior Elements
(c.1950; Harley, Ellington & Day)
1400 S Wolf Rd
Hillside, IL
[L, SB]
Ledger details: Jobs #801/
#934, #941/#968; 1949/1955/1957
"Our Lady Gate of Heaven (sic)"
"Queen of Heaven Maus Chicago"
"Our Lady Queen of Heaven (sic)"

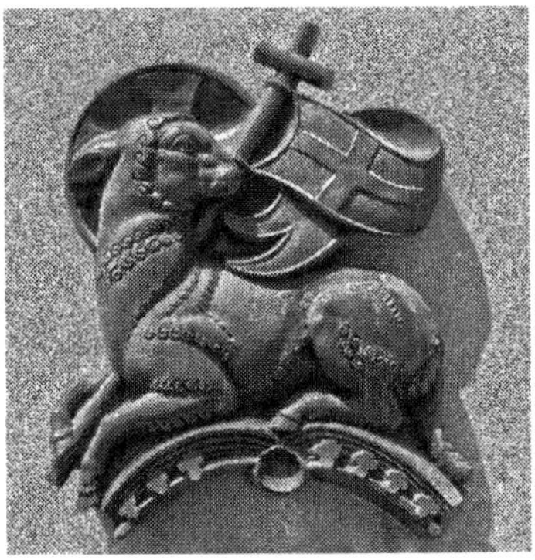

233. Queen of Heaven Cemetery Interment Chapel
(c.1950; Harley, Ellington & Day)
1400 S Wolf Rd
Hillside, IL
[L, SB]
Ledger details: Jobs #801/#934, #941/#968; 1949/1955/1957
"Our Lady Gate of Heaven (sic)"
"Queen of Heaven Maus Chicago"
"Our Lady Queen of Heaven (sic)"

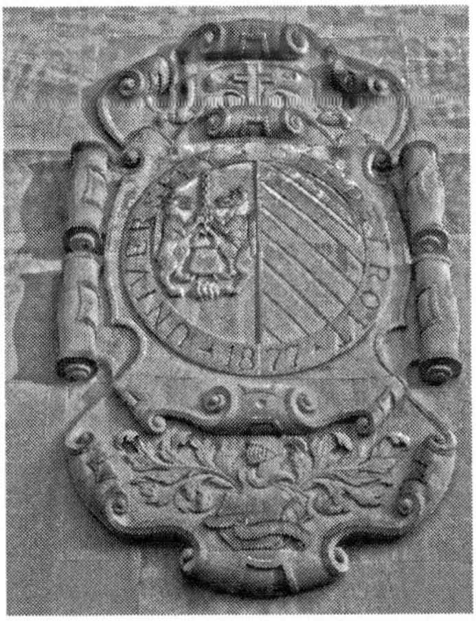

234. University of Detroit Library
(1949; Harley, Ellington & Day)
4001 W McNichols Rd
Detroit, MI
[L, SB]
Ledger details: Job #805; 1949
"University of Detroit Library"

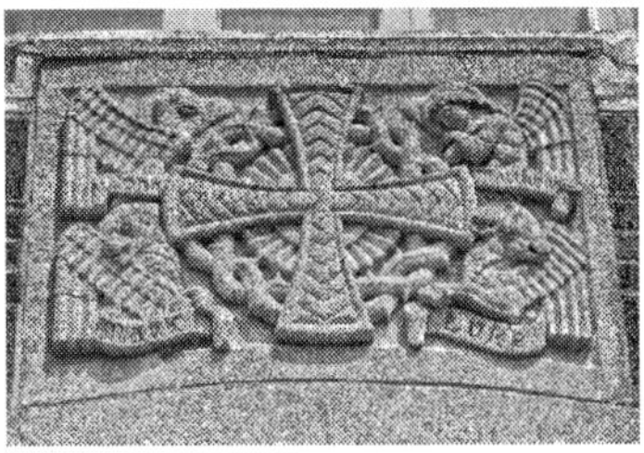

235. Grace Lutheran Church
(1949; Manson, Jackson & Kane)
591 N Martin Luther King Blvd
Lansing, MI
[L, FH]
Ledger details: Job #807; 1949
"Grace Lutheran Ch. Lansing Mich"

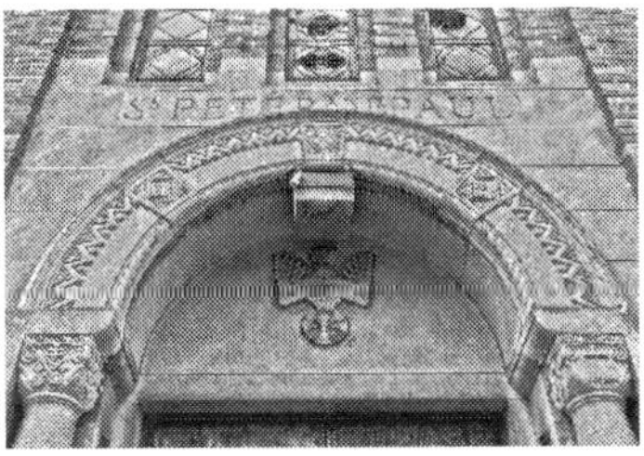

236. Saints Peter & Paul Russian Orthodox Church
(1948; Herman & Simons)
3810 Gilbert Ave
Detroit, MI
[L]
Ledger details: Jobs #811, #817/#954/#992; 1949/1955/1959
"Peter & Paul Ch."
"Russian Orth. Ch."

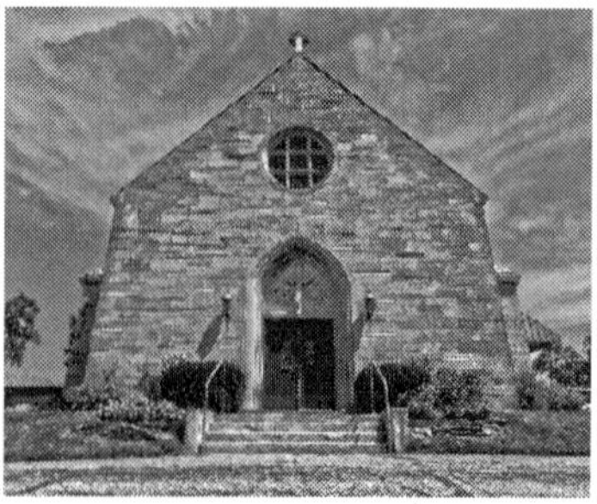

237. Church of the Holy Name
(1950; architect undetermined)
2448 Auburn Ave
Cincinnati, OH
[L, SB]
Ledger details: Job #813; 1949
"Holy Name Ch Cincinnati Ohio"

238. Assumption Catholic School
(c.1950; architect undetermined)
1500 McMakin Ave
Mt Healthy, OH
[L]
Ledger details: Job #814; 1949
"Assumption Sch. Mt Healthy Ohio"

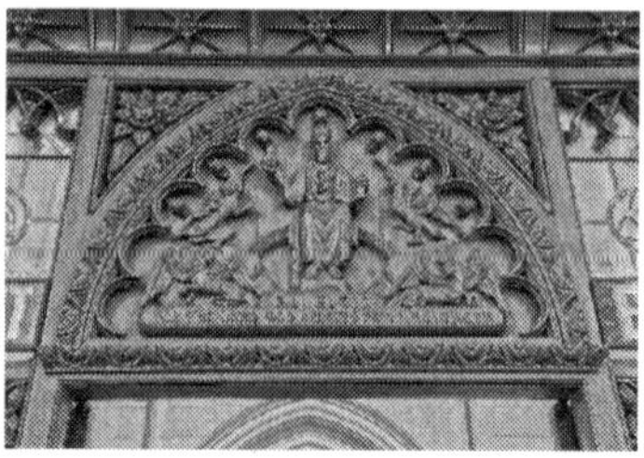

239. Kirk in the Hills Presbyterian Church ~ Interior Elements
(1948-1958; Wirt Rowland and George D. Mason, Inc.)
1340 W Long Lake Rd
Bloomfield Township, MI
[L, SB, DB]
Ledger details:
Jobs #815/#827/#876, #881/#933
1949/1950/1952/1955
"Kirk in the Hills"

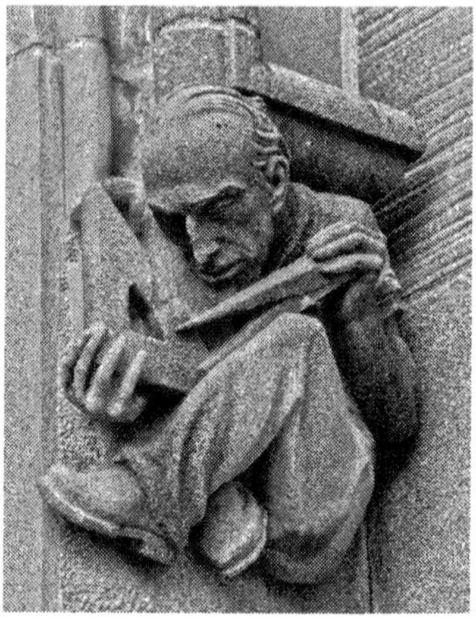

240. Kirk in the Hills Presbyterian Church ~ Exterior Elements
(1948-1958; Wirt Rowland and George D. Mason, Inc.)
1340 W Long Lake Rd
Bloomfield Township, MI
[L, SB, DB]
Ledger details:
Jobs #815/#827/#876, #881/#933
1949/1950/1952/1955
"Kirk in the Hills"

Architect Wirt Rowland spent over a decade developing the Kirk design in very close cooperation with project financier Colonel Edwin S. George, upon whose property it was constructed. It was built after Rowland's death and Mason's firm acted as the architects of record, but Rowland's indisputable contributions were recognized and immortalized by Parducci's sculpture, as evidenced by our photo.

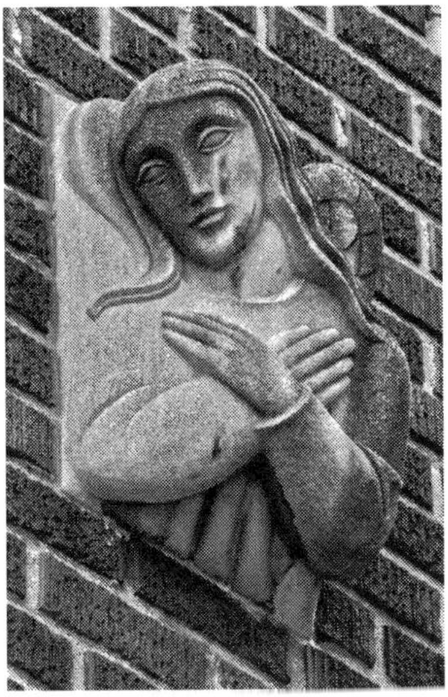

241. St. Ambrose Parish ~ Convent
(c.1950, Diehl & Diehl?)
1200 Alter Rd
Detroit, MI
[L]
Ledger details:
Jobs #816/#831, #838; 1949/1950
"St Ambrose Convent"

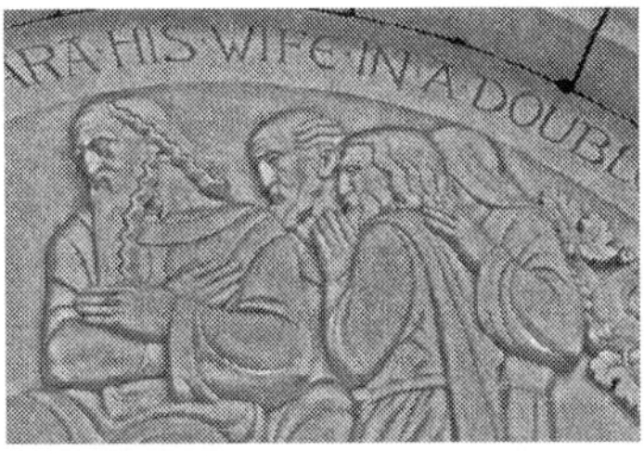

242. Fort Lincoln Cemetery Mausoleum
(1948; Harley, Ellington & Day)
3401 Bladensburg Rd
Brentwood, MD
[L, SB]
Ledger details: Jobs #818/#856
1949/1951
"Fort Lincoln Cemetery"

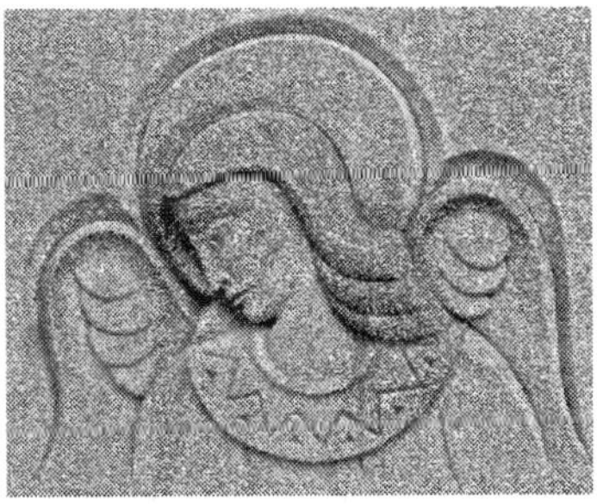

243. Garden of Meditation at Fort Lincoln Cemetery
(1948; N/A)
3401 Bladensburg Rd
Brentwood, MD
[L, SB]
Ledger details: Job #818/#856
1949/1951
"Fort Lincoln Cemetery"

244. Gesu Parish ~ Rectory
(c.1950; Diehl & Diehl)
17180 Oak Dr
Detroit, MI
[L]
Ledger details: Jobs #821, #839
1950
"Gesu Administration Bldg"

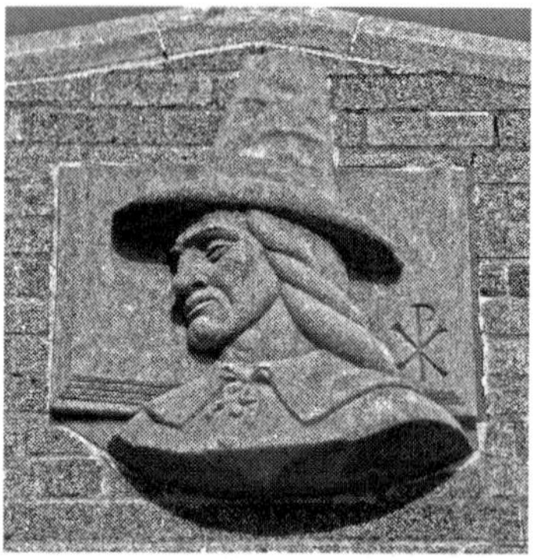

245. Pilgrim Congregational Church
(c.1950; Manson, Jackson & Kane)
125 S Pennsylvania Ave
Lansing, MI
[L, SB, FH]
Ledger details: Job #822; 1950
"Pilgrim Congr. Ch. Lansing"

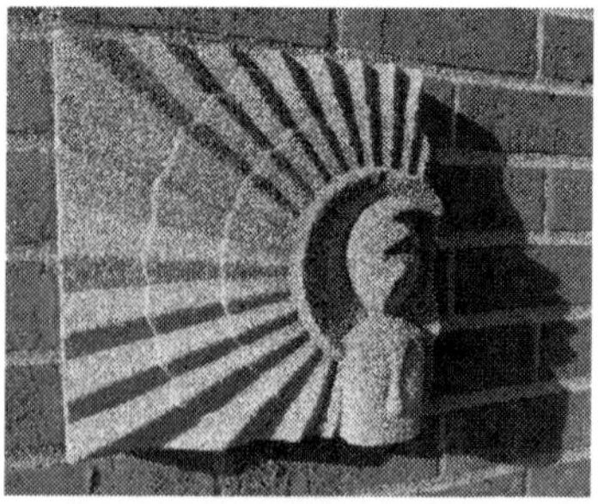

246. Mt. Hope United Methodist Church
(1949; architect undetermined)
15400 E Seven Mile Rd
Detroit, MI
[L, SB]
Ledger details: Job #824; 1950
"Mt. Hope Ch."

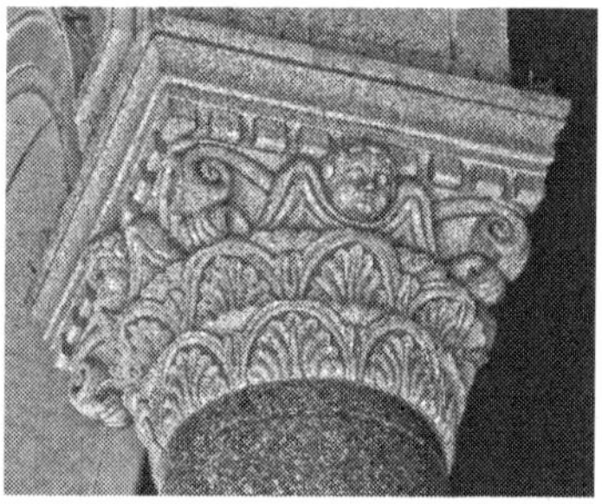

247. Precious Blood Catholic Church formerly known as St. Peter Claver Catholic Church now known as The Grove Street Cornerstone Community
(c.1950; Maguolo & Quick)
13305 Grove St
Detroit, MI
[L, SB]
Ledger details:
Jobs #825/#848/#1018/#1027/#1044
1950/1951/1960/1961/1963
"Precious Blood Ch."

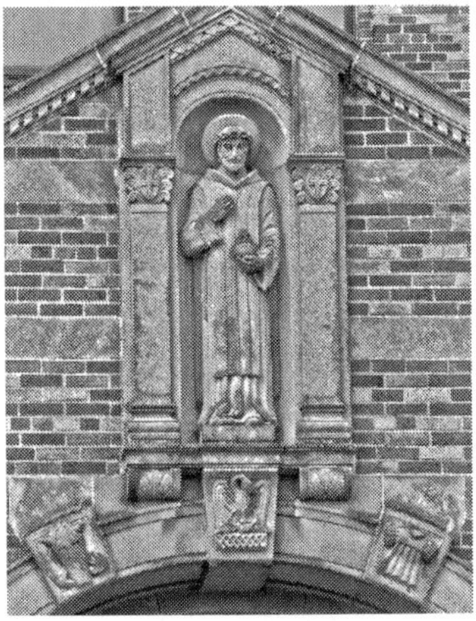

248. St. John Hospital now known as Ascension St. John Hospital
(1948-1951; Maguolo & Quick)
22101 Moross Rd
Detroit, MI
[L, SB]
Ledger details: Jobs #826/#868
1950/1951
"St. John's Hospital"

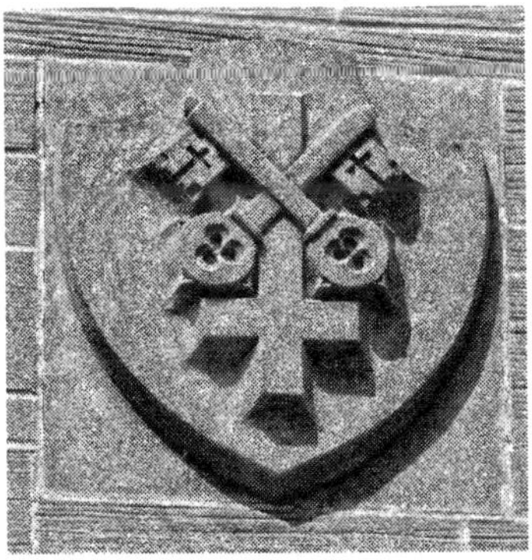

249. Grosse Pointe United Methodist Church
(1949-1950; David H. Williams of George D. Mason, Inc.)
211 Moross Rd
Grosse Pointe Farms, MI
[L]
Ledger details: Jobs #830/#975
1950/1957
"Grosse Pointe Methodist"

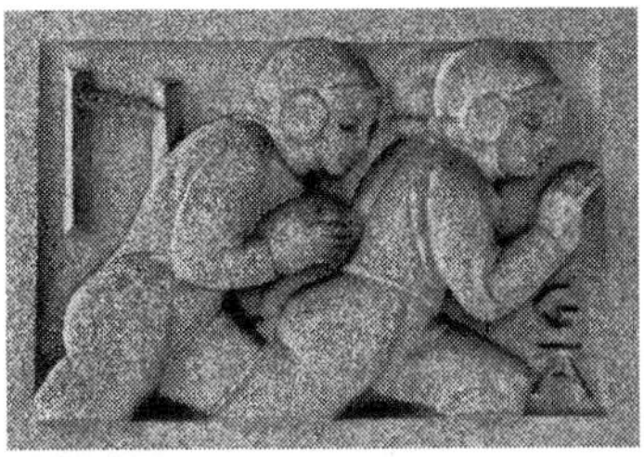

250. Guardian Angel School
(1948; Diehl & Diehl)
521 E Fourteen Mile Rd
Clawson, MI
[L, SB]
Ledger details: Job #833; 1950
"Guardian Angel Ch"

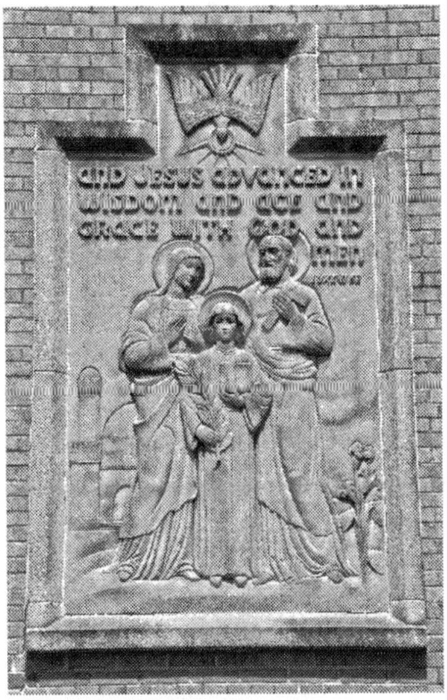

251. St. Ignatius School
(c.1950?; Maguolo & Quick?)
5222 N Bend Rd
Cincinnati, OH
[L, SB]
Ledger details: Job #837; 1950
"St. Ignatius Cincinnati"

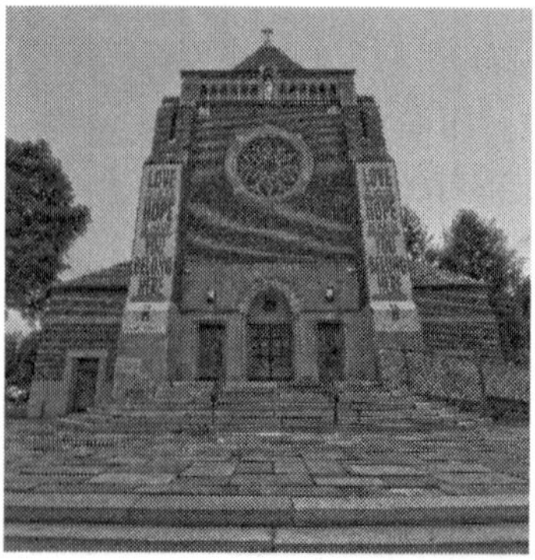

252. St. Gregory Catholic Church
(1950; Herman & Simons)
15031 Dexter Ave
Detroit, MI
[L, SB, WK]
Ledger details: Job #840#878
1950/1952
"St Gregory Church"

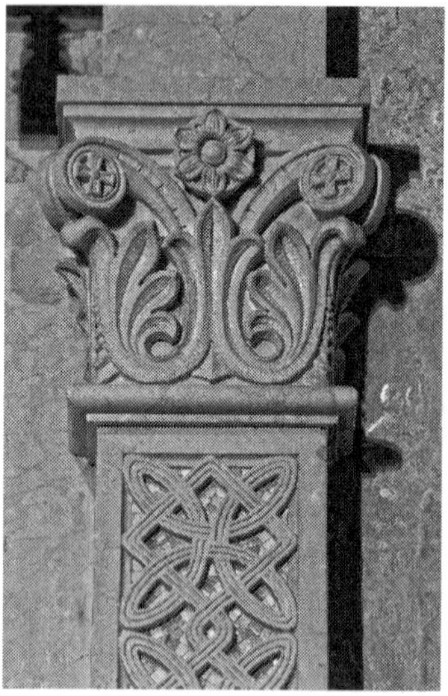

253. St. John's Chapel at Ascension Mercy Hospital formerly known as St. John's Hospital
(c.1950; Maguolo & Quick)
1235 E Cherokee St
Springfield, MO
[L]
Ledger details: Jobs #841/ #858, #868/#884; 1950/1951/1952
"St. John's Hosp. Springfield Mo"

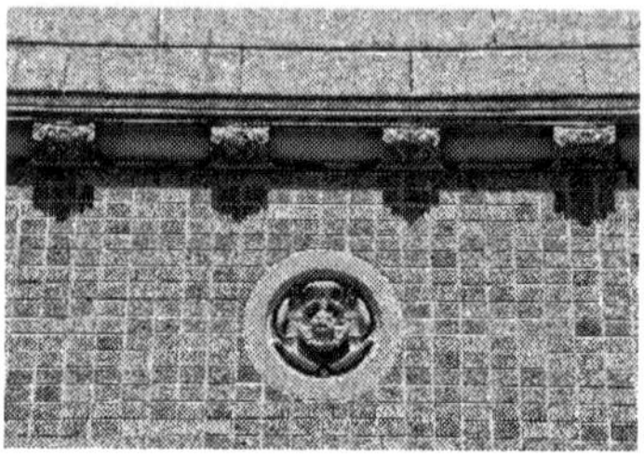

254. St. Martin of Tours Catholic Church
(1950; McGrath & Dohmen)
13100 Averhill Ct
Detroit, MI
[L, SB]
Ledger details: Jobs #844/#854, 860
1950/1951
"St. Martins Ch."

255. Detroit Historical Museum
(c.1950; William E. Kapp)
5401 Woodward Ave
Detroit, MI
[L, SB, DB]
Ledger details: Job #845; 1950
"Det. Historical Museum"

Regarding this commission Parducci states in the 1975 Smithsonian interview: *"You take the Historical Museum. I got a little work on that, building flagpole and the drawings over the entrance."*

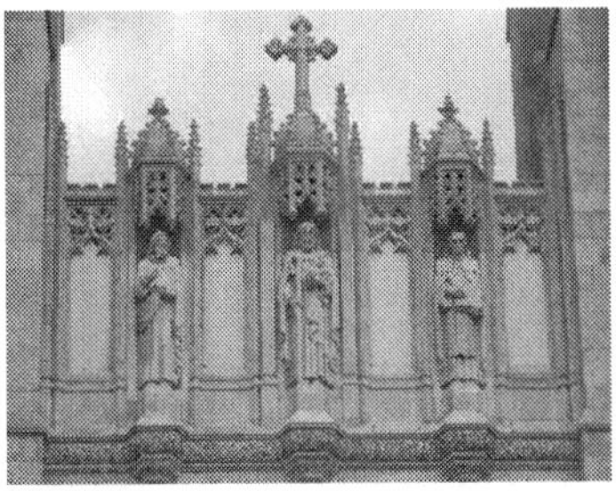

256. Cathedral of the Most Blessed Sacrament ~ Towers Addition
(c.1951; Diehl & Diehl)
9844 Woodward Ave
Detroit, MI
[L, SB, WK]
Ledger details: Jobs #720, #738/#847; 1945/1951
"Blessed Sacrament Cath."

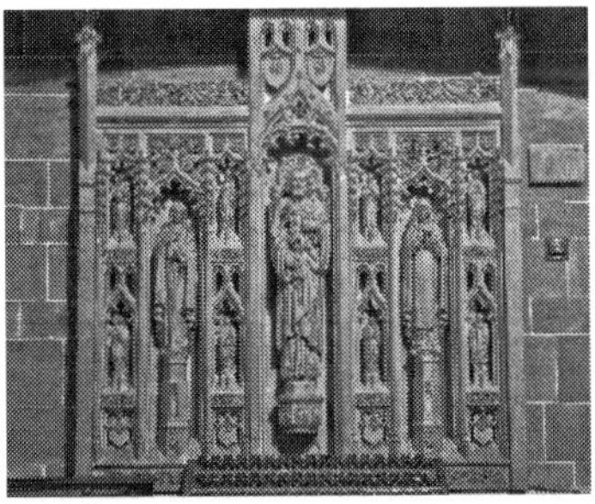

257. Cathedral of the Most Blessed Sacrament ~ Interior Additions
(c.1942-1951; Diehl & Diehl)
9844 Woodward Ave
Detroit, MI
[L, SB, WK]
Ledger details: Jobs #675/#712/ #738/#847; 1942/1944/1945/1951
"Blessed Sacrament Cath."

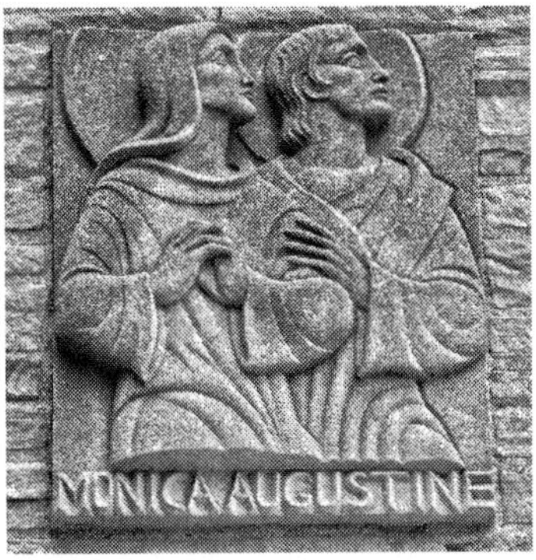

258. St. Clare of Montefalco Catholic Church
(1951-1953; Charles M. Valentine?)
16231 Charlevoix St
Grosse Pointe Park, MI
[L, SB]
Ledger details: Jobs #850, #864
1951
"St. Clare Ch."

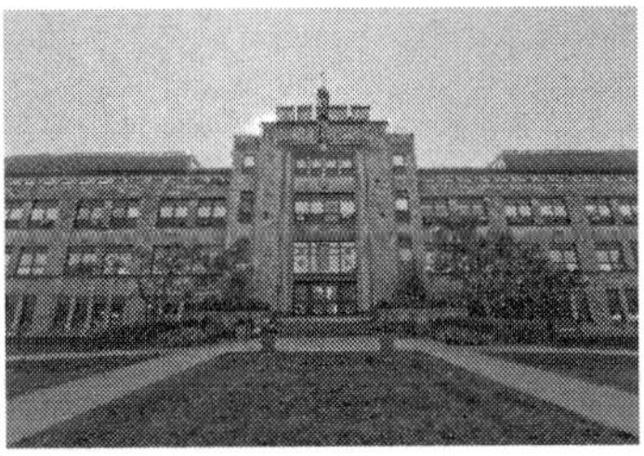

259. Alverno College ~ Founder's Hall
(1951-1954; Maguolo & Quick)
3400 S Forty-third St
Milwaukee, WI
[L]
Ledger details: Jobs #865/ #920, #929; 1951/1954
"Alverno Colledge (sic)"
"Alverno Training Sch"

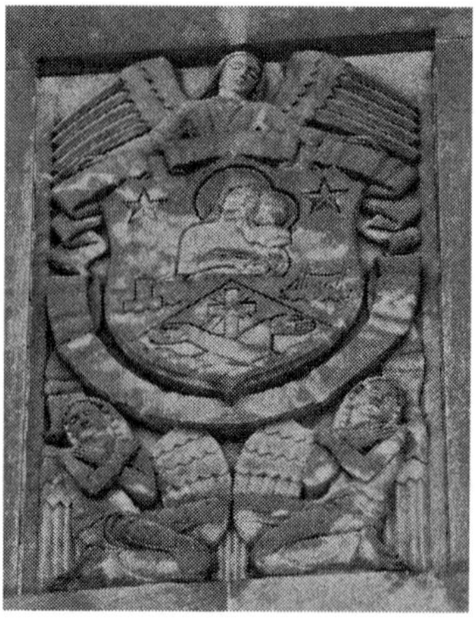

260. Alverno College ~ Pitman Theatre
(1951-1954; Maguolo & Quick)
3400 S Forty-third St
Milwaukee, WI
[L]
Ledger details: Jobs #865/ #920, #929; 1951/1954
"Alverno Colledge (sic)"
"Alverno Training Sch"

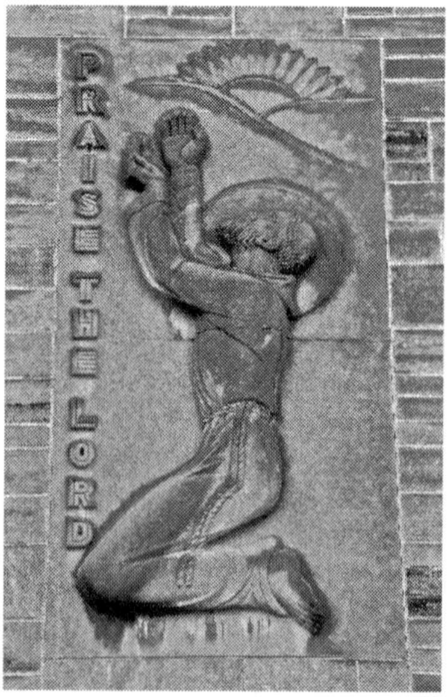

261. Alverno College Library
(1951-1954; Maguolo & Quick)
3400 S Forty-third St
Milwaukee, WI
[L]
Ledger details: Jobs #865/ #920, #929; 1951/1954
"Alverno Colledge (sic)"
"Alverno Training Sch"

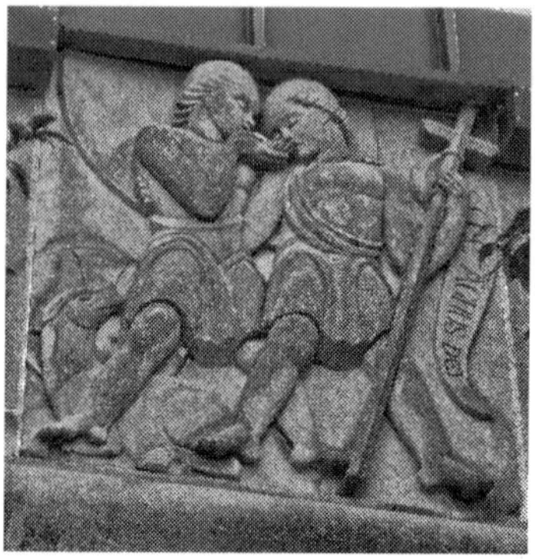

262. Alverno College ~ Elementary School
(1951-1954; Maguolo & Quick)
3400 S Forty-third St
Milwaukee, WI
[L]
Ledger details: Jobs #865/ #920, #929; 1951/1954
"Alverno Colledge (sic)"
"Alverno Training Sch"

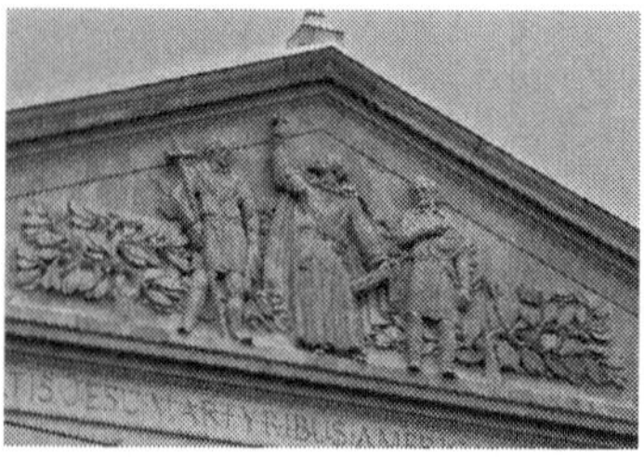

263. Jesuit High School Palmyra Street Addition ~ Exterior Elements
(1953; Wogan & Bernard)
4133 Banks St
New Orleans, LA
[L, SB]
Ledger details:
Jobs #866/#888, #901; 1952/1953
"Jesuit High Sch. New Orleans La"

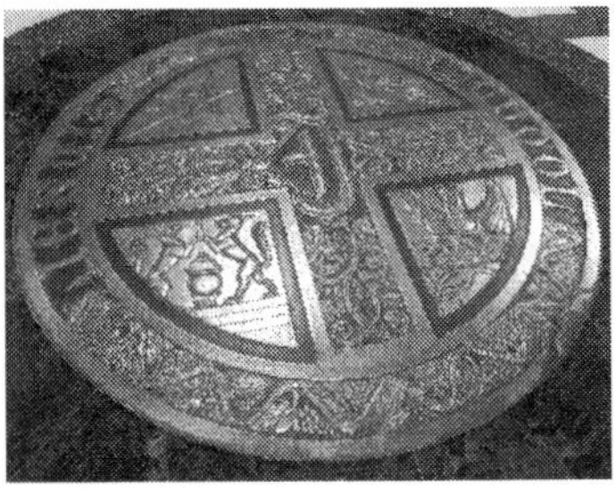

264. Jesuit High School Palmyra Street Addition ~ Interior Elements
(1953; Wogan & Bernard)
4133 Banks St
New Orleans, LA
[L, SB]
Ledger details:
Jobs #866/#888, #901; 1952/1953
"Jesuit High Sch. New Orleans La"

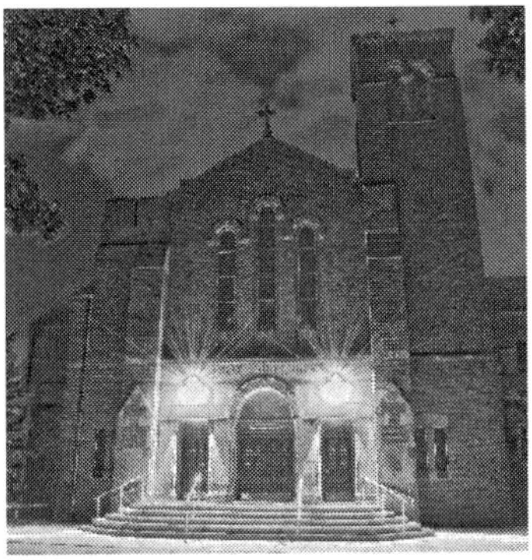

265. St. Cunegunda Catholic Church
(1951; architect undetermined)
5900 St Lawrence St
Detroit, MI
[L, SB]
Ledger details: Jobs #869/#887
1951/1952
"St Cunegunda"

266. St. Paul's Episcopal Church Addition
(1952; Manson, Jackson & Kane)
218 W Ottawa St
Lansing, MI
[L, SB, FH]
Ledger details: Job #875; 1952
"St. Paul's Episcopal Ch"

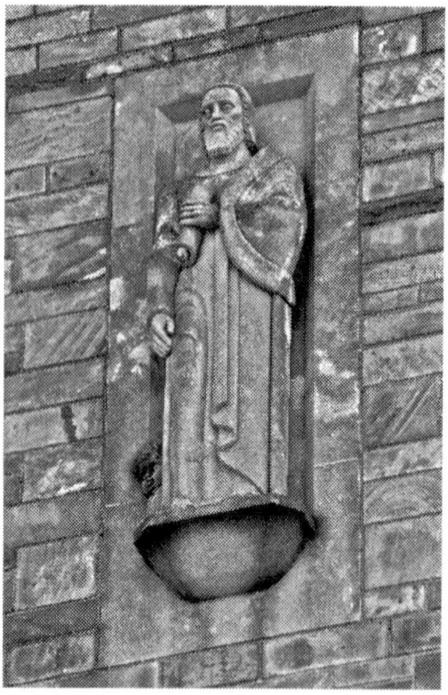

267. St. Matthew Catholic Church
(1954; Donaldson & Meier)
6021 Whittier Ave
Detroit, MI
[L, SB]
Ledger details: Job #879/#919
1952/1954
"St Matthew"

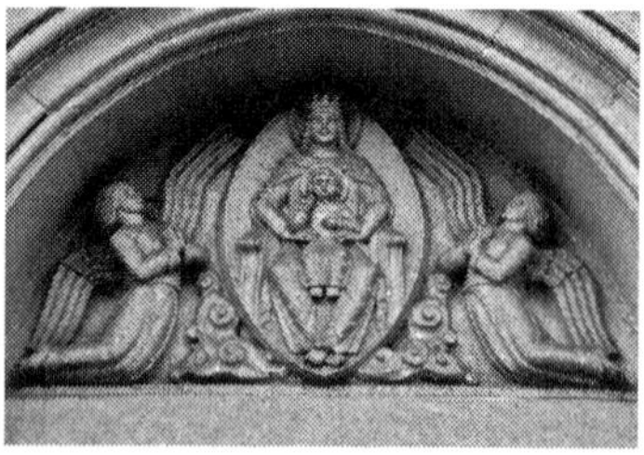

268. Our Lady Queen of Angels Catholic Church
(1951; Herman & Simons)
4200 Martin Rd
Detroit, MI
[L,SB, WK]
Ledger details: Job #882; 1952
"Our Lady Queen of Angels"

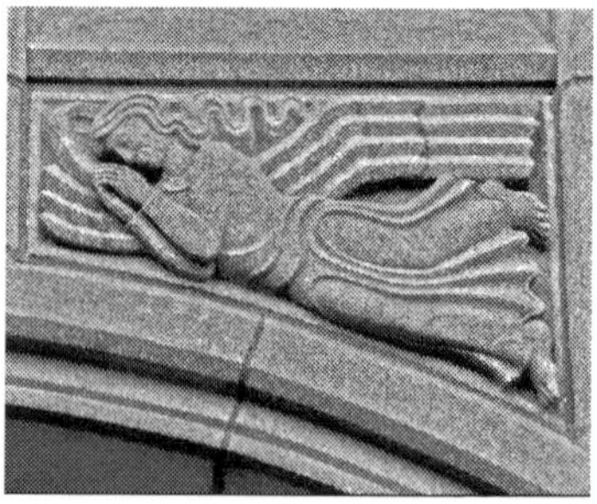

269. First United Methodist Church
(1951; architect undetermined)
204 W Cass St
Greenville, MI
[L, SB]
Ledger details: Job #883; 1952
"Greenville Methodist Ch. Lansing"

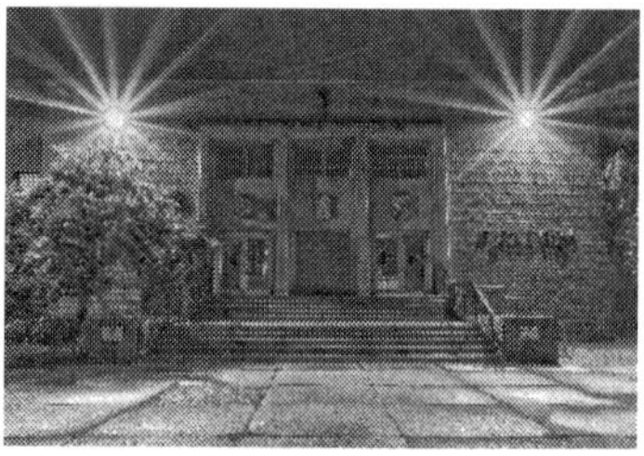

270. St. Joan of Arc School
(c.1952; architect undetermined)
22412 Overlake St
St Clair Shores, MI
[L, SB]
Ledger details: Job #885; 1952
"St. Joan of Arc Ch."

Entries #271 and #272 are confirmed only by images found in Parducci's personal scrapbook.

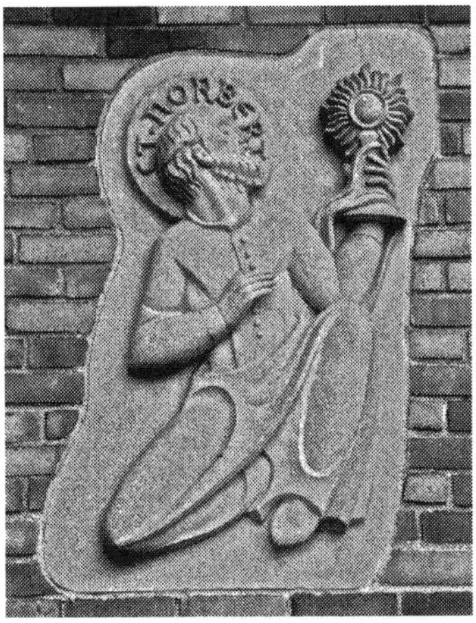

271. St. Norbert Catholic Church
(1952; Diehl & Diehl)
615 Inkster Rd
Inkster, MI
[SB]
Ledger details: N/A

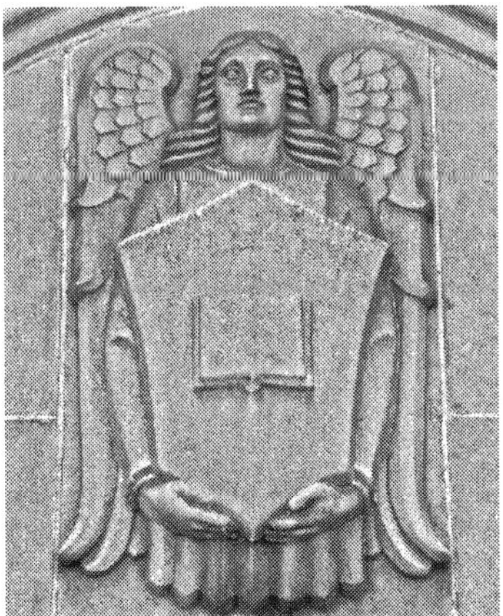

272. First Lutheran Church now known as Rhema Church of the Living God
(1952; architect undetermined)
4719 Cadieux Rd
Detroit, MI
[SB]
Ledger details: N/A

273. St. Cecilia Parish ~ Convent
(c.1953?; architect undetermined)
Burlingame St at Monica St
Detroit, MI
[L]
Ledger details: Job #892; 1953
"St Cecelia"

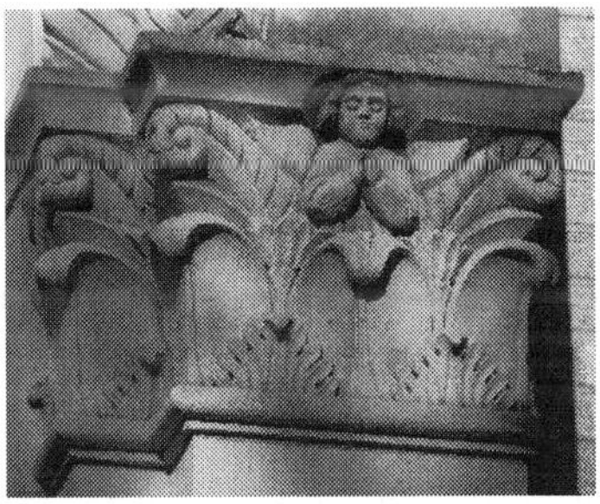

274. Holy Trinity Parish ~ Convent
(1953; architect undetermined)
3811 Oak Lawn Ave
Dallas, TX
[L]
Ledger details: Job #900; 1953
"Holy Trinity Parrish (sic) Dallas Tex"

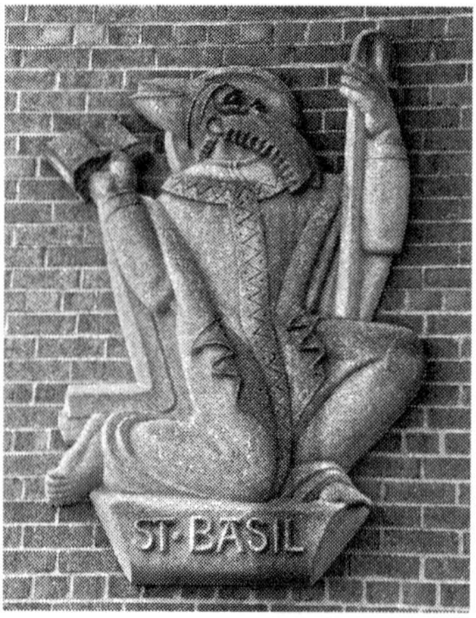

275. St. Basil the Great Catholic Church
(c.1953?; architect undetermined)
22851 Lexington Ave
Eastpointe, MI
[L, SB]
Ledger details: Job #903; 1953
"St Basil East Detroit Ch"

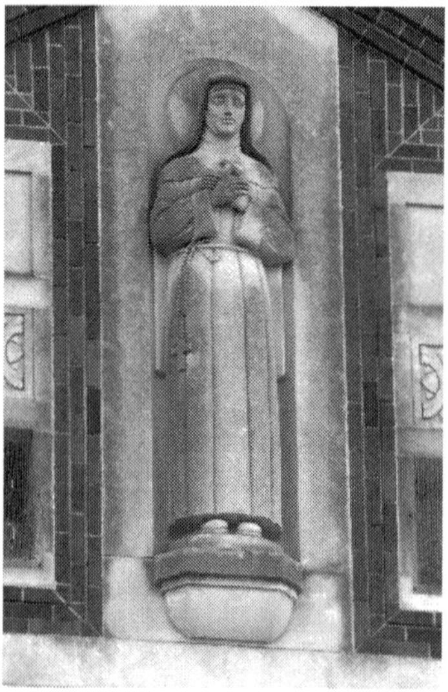

276. St. Rita Catholic Church
(1953; Donaldson & Meier)
1044 E State Fair Ave
Detroit, MI
[L, WK]
Ledger details: Job #904; 1953
"St. Rita Ch."

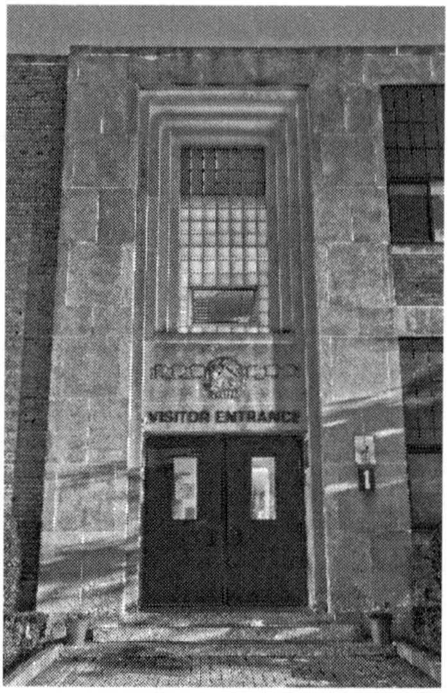

277. Divine Child Elementary School
(1953; Herman & Simons?)
25001 Herbert Weier
Dearborn, MI
[L, SB]
Ledger details: Job #905; 1953
"Divine Child Ch"

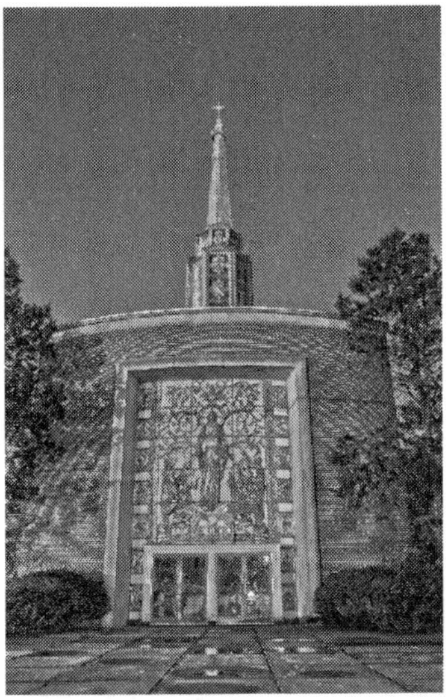

278. Westminster Presbyterian Church
(1953; Harold H. Fisher)
17567 Hubbell Ave
Detroit, MI
[HF]
Ledger details: N/A

279. Marathon County Courthouse
(1955; Childs & Smith)
500 Forest St
Wausau, WI
[L, SB]
Ledger details: Jobs #909/#931 1953/1954
"Marathon County Court House Wausau Wis"

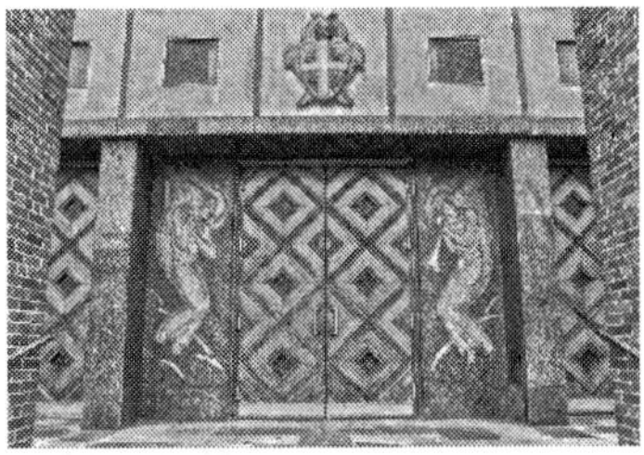

280. St. Gabriel Catholic Church
(1955; Diehl & Diehl)
8118 W Vernor Hwy
Detroit, MI
[L, SB]
Ledger details: Job #910; 1953
"St Gabriel Ch."

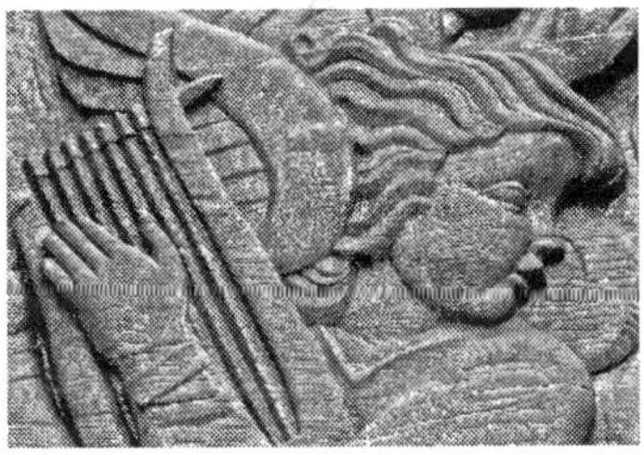

281. Hollywood Memorial Park Cemetery Mausoleum
(c.1954?; Harley, Ellington & Day?)
1500 Stuyvesant Ave
Union, NJ
[L, SB]
Ledger details: Job #916; 1954
"Hollywood Park Maus"

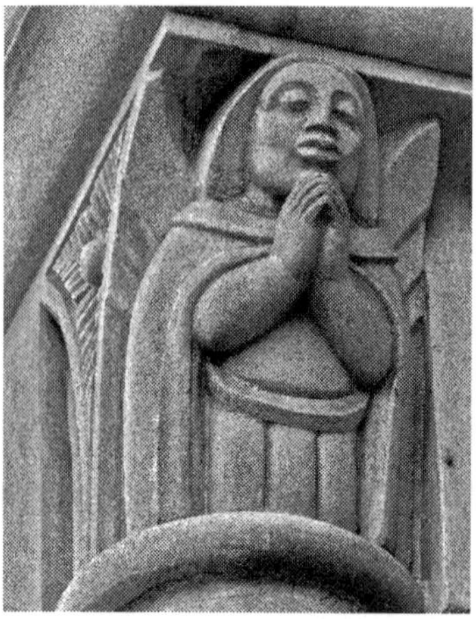

282. Epiphany Catholic Church
(1955; McGrath & Dohmen)
Mendota St at Crocuslawn Ave
Detroit, MI
[L]
Ledger details: Jobs #917, #927
1954
"Epiphany Parish Ch"

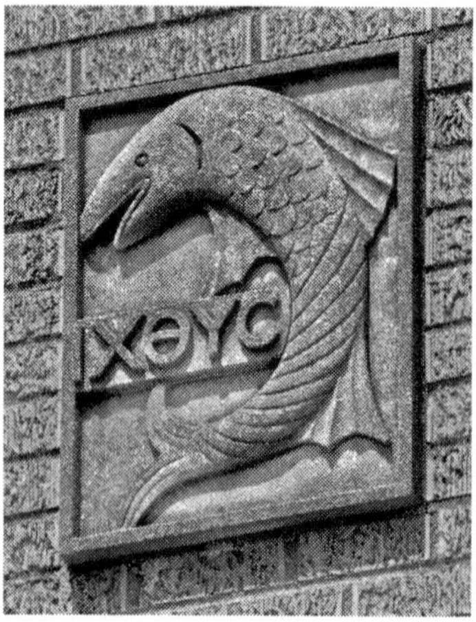

283. Redford Presbyterian Church Addition now known as Old Redford Academy Middle School
(1954; architect undetermined)
22122 W McNichols Rd
Detroit, MI
[L]
Ledger details: Job #918; 1954
"Redford Ave Presbyterian Ch."

284. Church of the Resurrection
(1954; Maguolo & Quick)
1740 First Ave
Cincinnati, OH
[L, SB]
Ledger details: Job #930; 1954
"Ressurection (sic) Ch Cin"

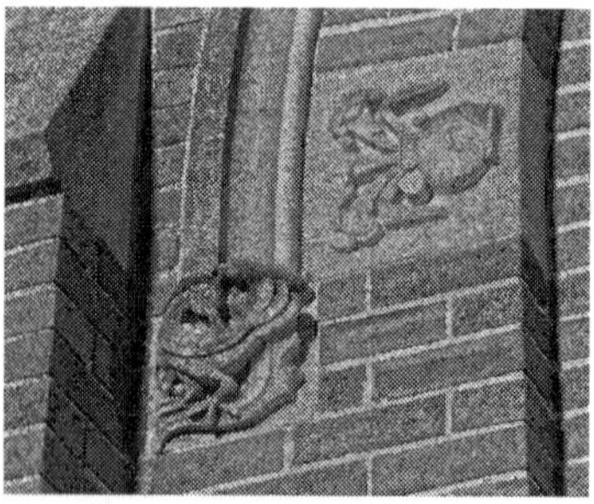

285. Our Lady Gate of Heaven Catholic Church now known as Fountain of Life Church and Kronk Boxing Community Center
(1954; McGrath & Dohmen)
9555 St Marys St at W Chicago
Detroit, MI
[L, SB]
Ledger details: Job #1043; 1964
"Our Lady Gate of Heaven"

As with entry #179, we classify the prior commission's inexplicable chronological misplacement in the ledgers as support for our theory that Parducci created his ledgers from less than flawless memories and incomplete records at some point late in his career.

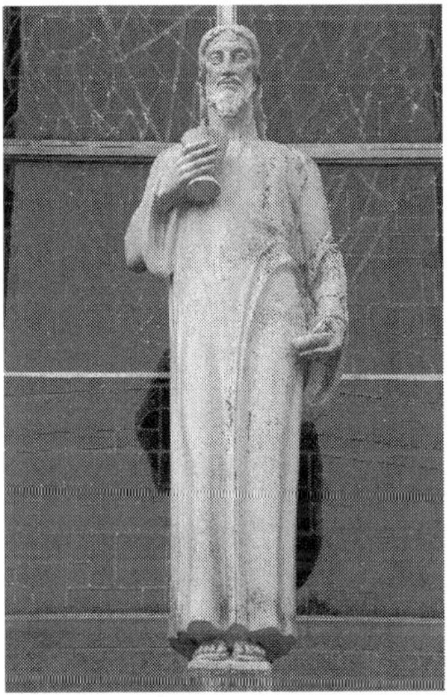

286. Holy Name Catholic Church ~ Exterior Elements
(1954; Diehl & Diehl)
630 Harmon St
Birmingham, MI
[L, SB, WK]
Ledger details: Jobs #932, #938
1955
"Holy Name Ch."

A rare rendering of a Parducci design in fiberglass.

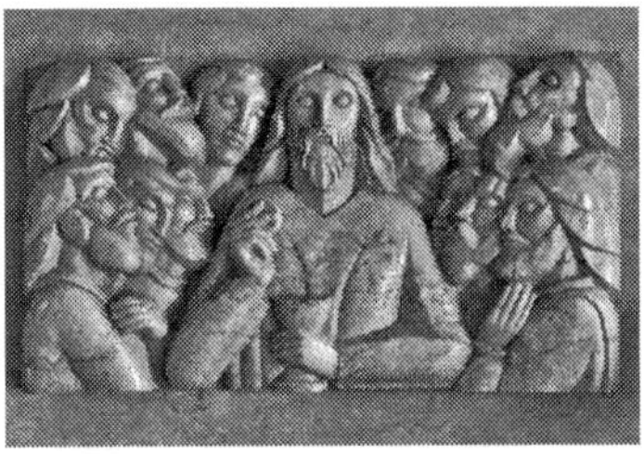

287. Holy Name Catholic Church ~ Interior Elements
(1954; Diehl & Diehl)
630 Harmon St
Birmingham, MI
[L, SB, WK]
Ledger details: Jobs #932, #938
1955
"Holy Name Ch."

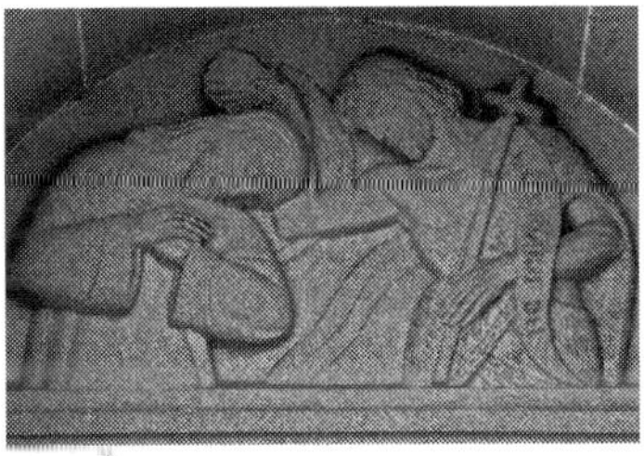

288. St. John the Baptist Romanian Byzantine Catholic Church
(1955; Diehl & Diehl)
2371 Woodstock Dr
Detroit, MI
[L, SB]
Ledger details: Jobs #936, #940
1955
"St John the Baptist"

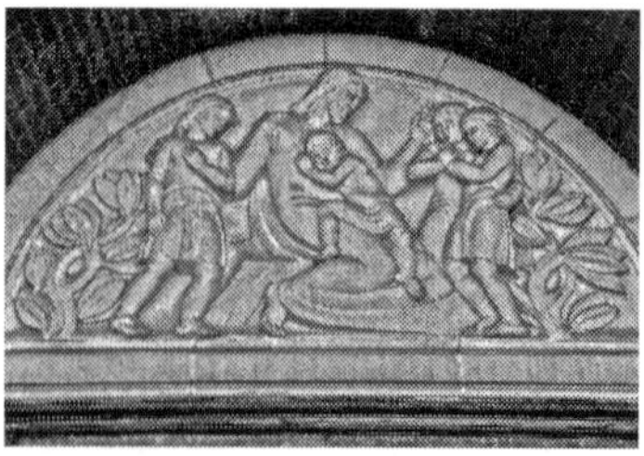

289. First Baptist Church now known as Christ Community Church ~ Children's Center Addition
(1955; Manson, Jackson & Kane)
227 N Capitol Ave
Lansing, MI
[SB, FH]
Ledger details: N/A

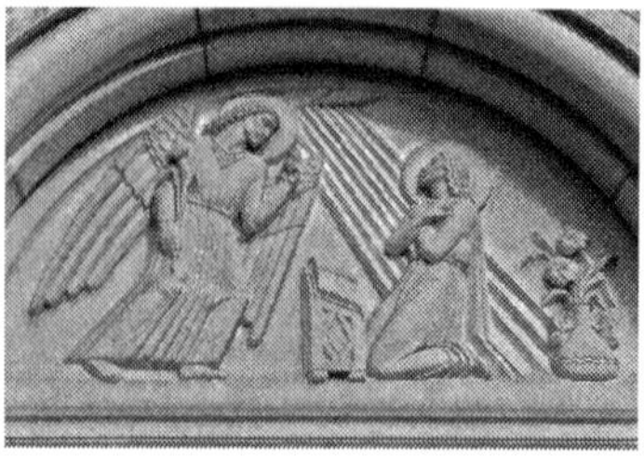

290. Cathedral of Our Lady of the Rosary
(1957; Maguolo & Quick)
2801 E Fourth St
Duluth, MN
[L, SB]
Ledger details: Job #937; 1955
"Our Lady of the Rosary DeLuth (sic) Minn"

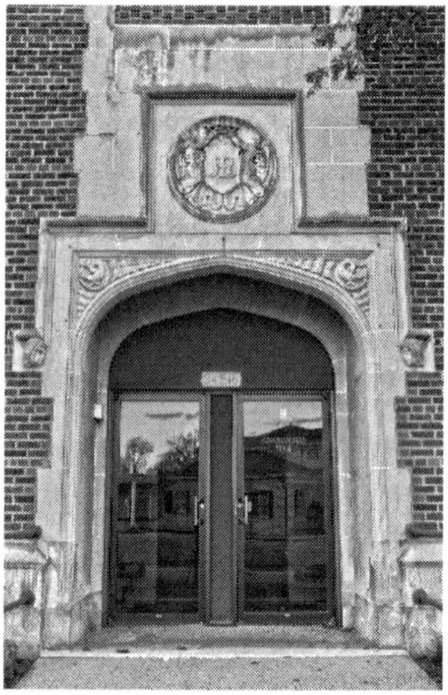

291. St. Mary School
(c.1953; Diehl & Diehl)
34516 W Michigan Ave
Wayne, MI
[L]
Ledger details: Job #939, #949 1955
"St Mary's Ch. Wayne"

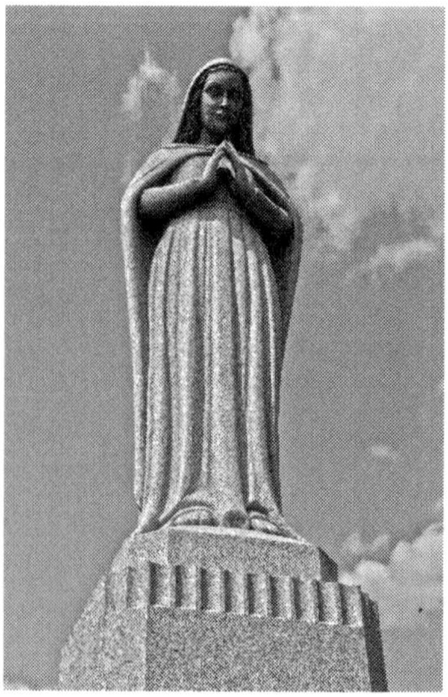

292. Garden of the Rosary at Mt. Olivet Cemetery
(c.1955; N/A)
17100 Van Dyke Ave
Detroit, MI
[L, SB]
Ledger details: Jobs #943/#1014
1955/1960
"Mount Olivet Cem."

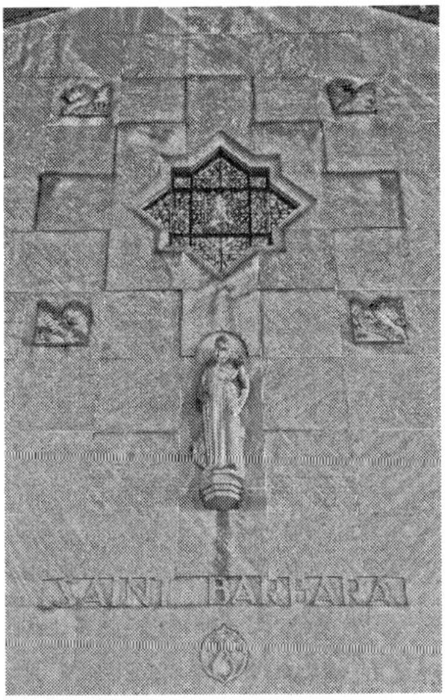

293. St. Barbara Catholic Church
(1955; Herman & Simons)
13534 Colson St
Dearborn, MI
[L, SB]
Ledger details: Jobs #944/#966
1955/1956
"St Barbara Ch"

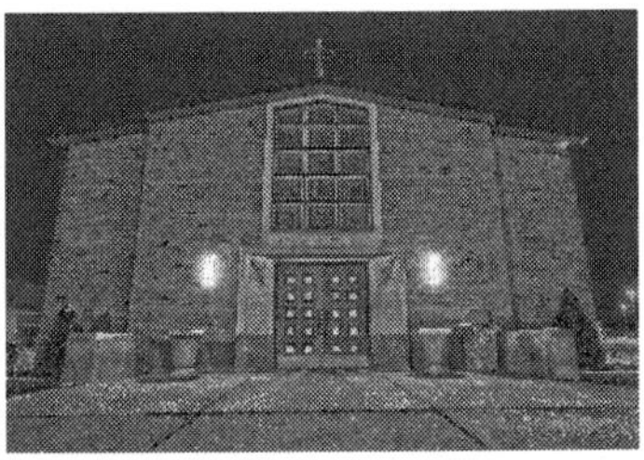

294. Holy Family Catholic Church
(1953; Diehl & Diehl)
11804 S Saginaw St
Grand Blanc, MI
[L]
Ledger details: Jobs #945, #947;
1955
"Holy Name (sic) Ch"

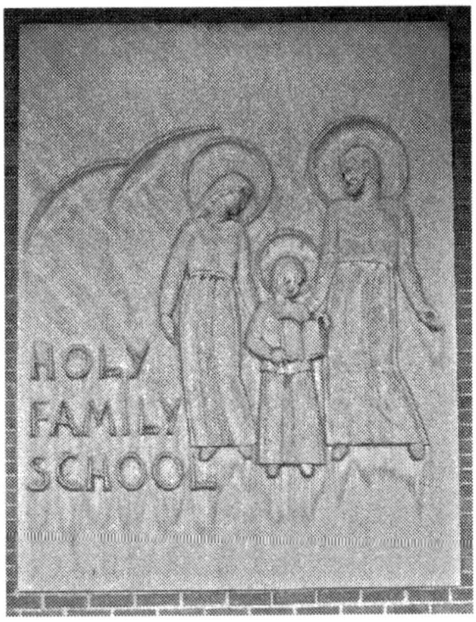

295. Holy Family Elementary School
(1956; Diehl & Diehl)
11804 S Saginaw St
Grand Blanc, MI
[L, SB]
Ledger details: Jobs #945, #947;
1955
"Holy Name (sic) Ch"

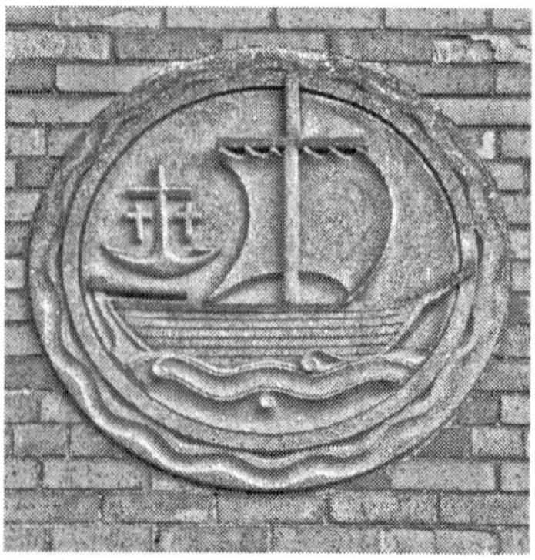

296. Mariners Inn
(1955; architect undetermined)
445 Ledyard St
Detroit, MI
[L, SB]
Ledger details: Job #953; 1955
"Mariner Emblem"

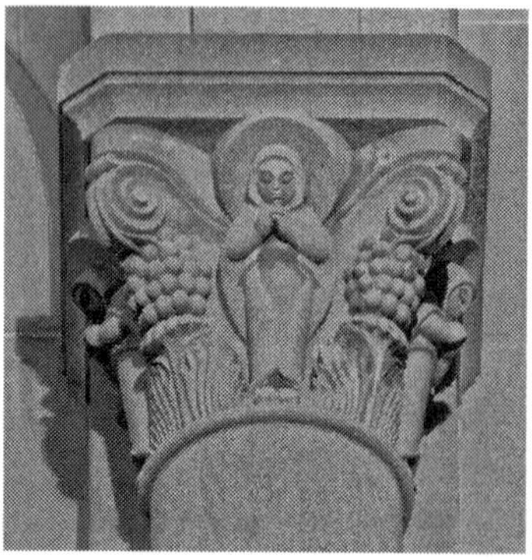

297. St. Veronica Catholic Church
(1956; McGrath & Dohmen)
21440 Universal Ave
Eastpointe, MI
[L, SB]
Ledger details: Jobs #955, #961; 1956
"St Veronica Ch"

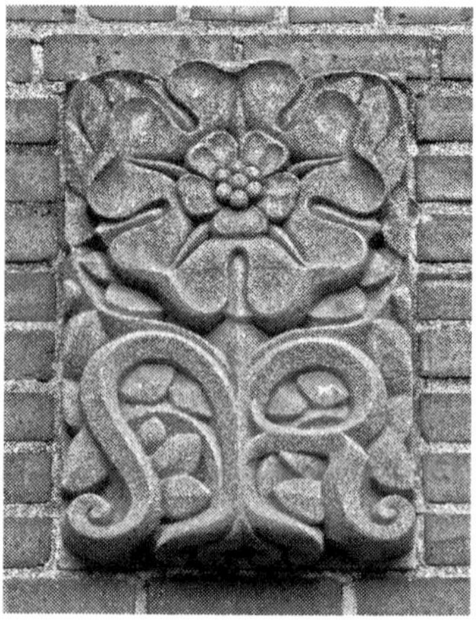

298. Our Lady of Good Counsel School Additions
(c.1955; Diehl & Diehl)
17260 Rowe St
Detroit, MI
[L, SB]
Ledger details: Jobs #963/#967 1956/1957
"Our Lady of Good Counsel"

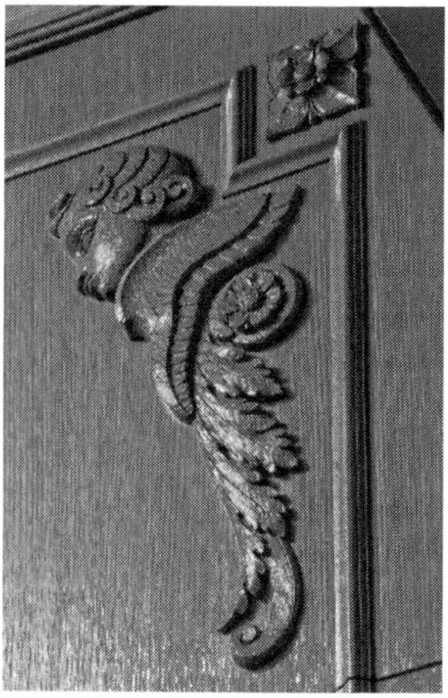

299. Peter Whyte Memorial inside Holy Sepulchre Catholic Cemetery Mausoleum
(Memorial: 1956)
(Mausoleum: 1948;
Harley, Ellington & Day)
25800 W Ten Mile Rd
Southfield, MI
[L]
Ledger details: Job #965; 195
"Whyte Mem"

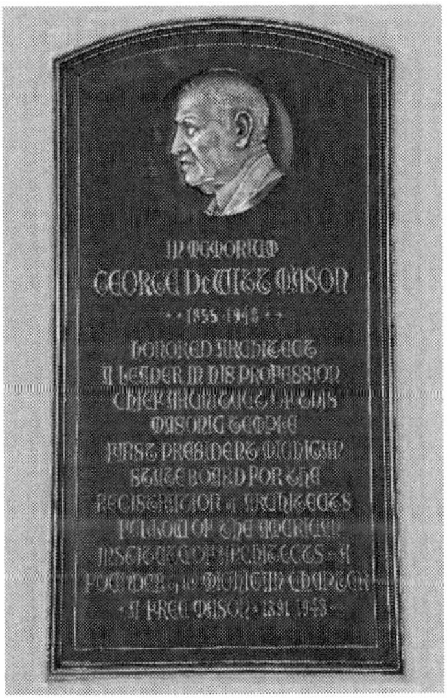

300. George D. Mason Memorial at Detroit Masonic Temple
(Memorial: c.1957; N/A)
(Masonic Temple: 1920-1926;
George D. Mason)
500 Temple St
Detroit, MI
[SB, WK]
Ledger details: N/A

Located in the Temple's 'George Mason Room'. Though Mason passed away in 1948, a typewritten note in William Kapp's presentation notes for Parducci's 1958 American Institute of Architects honorary membership ceremony reveals to us the approximate date of this memorial's creation. It also tells us that the ceremony in question took place at the Detroit Masonic Temple, unsurprisingly.

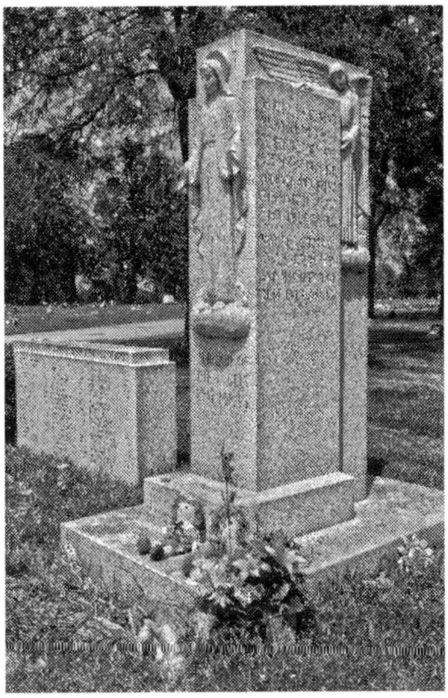

301. Our Lady of the Angels School Fire Memorial at Queen of Heaven Cemetery
(c.1959; N/A)
1400 S Wolf Rd
Hillside, IL
[Speculative]
Ledger details: N/A

The basis of our case for this attribution is formed by Parducci's long-standing professional relationship with Queen of Heaven Cemetery architects and administrators, plus this memorial's undeniable similarity to other Parducci works of the era.

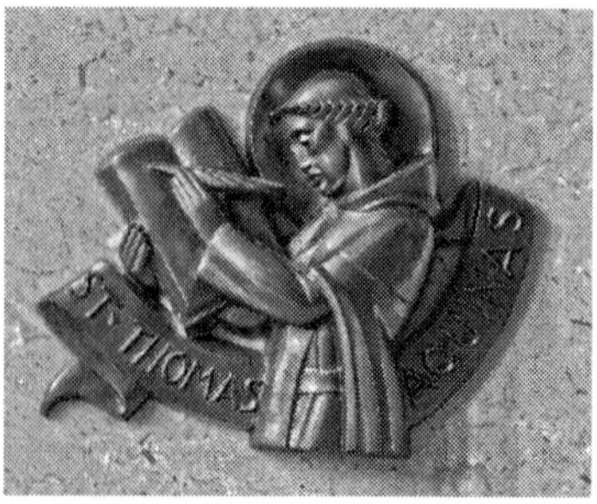

302. St. Columba Cathedral
(1958; Diehl & Diehl)
159 W Rayen Ave
Youngstown, OH
[L, SB]
Ledger details: Jobs #970/#988 1957/1959
"St. Columba Cath Youngstown Ohio"

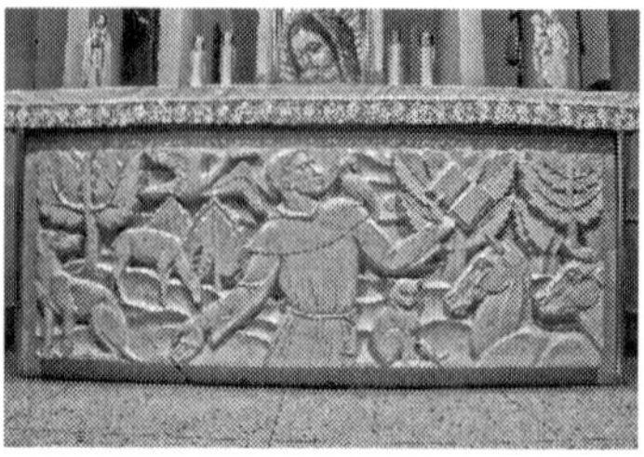

303. Franciscan Friars Shrine of Our Lady Comforter of the Afflicted
(Unknown year; architect undetermined)
517 S Belle Vista Ave
Youngstown, OH
[L, SB]
Ledger details: Jobs #970/#988 1957/1959
"St. Columba Cath Youngstown Ohio"

This altar was created in 1958 for the sanctuary of St. Columba Cathedral in Youngstown. Sometime over the last couple of decades it was moved to the Franciscan Friars Shrine after developing a hairline fracture in its marble stretching from top to bottom.

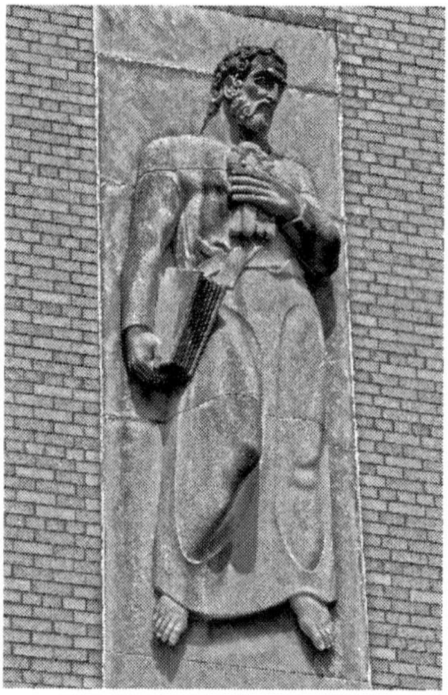

304. Saints Peter & Paul Catholic Church
(1957; Donaldson & Meier)
7685 Grandville Ave
Detroit, MI
[L, SB, WK]
Ledger details: Job #972; 1957
"Peter & Paul Ch"

305. Zion Evangelical Lutheran Church
(1957; George D. Mason, Inc.)
1501 W Liberty St
Ann Arbor, MI
[L]
Ledger details: Job #973; 1957
"Zion Evangelical Lutheran Ch"

Dedication literature for Zion Evangelical Lutheran authored by "George D. Mason & Co." tells us that a second Detroit based architectural sculptor identified as "D. Varga Studios" also contributed to this structure's embellishments.

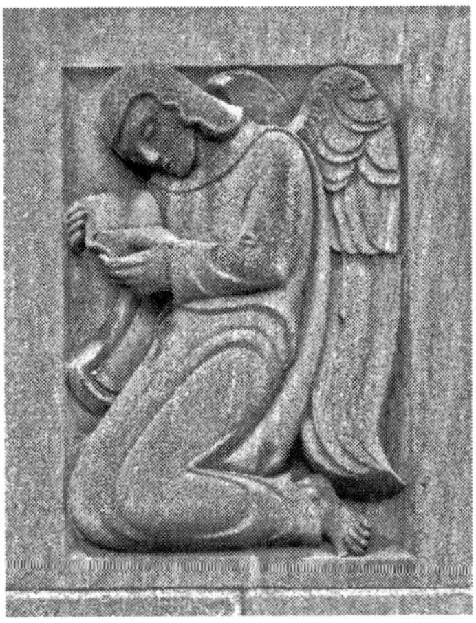

306. Drayton Avenue Presbyterian Church
(1957; Herman & Simons)
2441 Pinecrest Dr
Ferndale, MI
[L]
Ledger details: Job #974; 1957
"Drayton Ave. Pres. Ch"

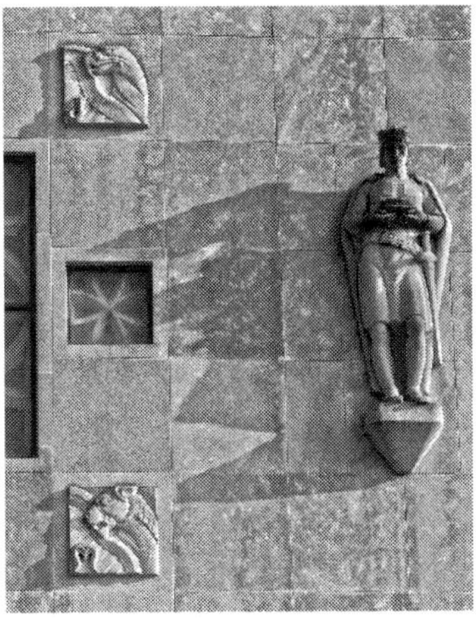

307. St. Louis the King Catholic Church now known as New Greater Zion Hill Church
(1959; Charles M. Valentine)
18891 St Louis St
Detroit, MI
[L]
Ledger details: Job #976; 1957
"St. Louis Roman Cath. Ch."

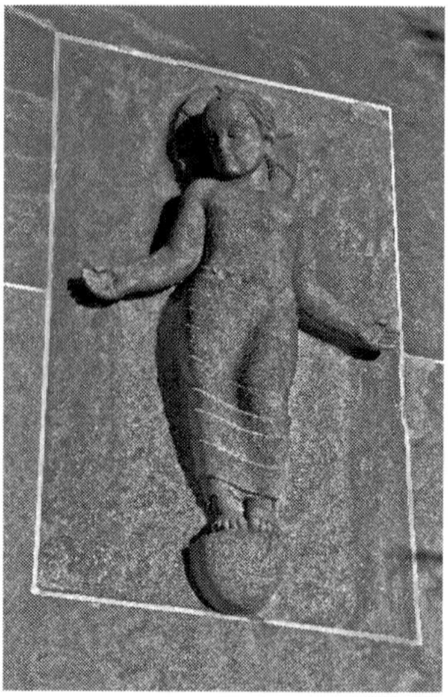

308. Divine Child High School
(1958; Herman & Simons)
1001 N Silvery Ln
Dearborn, MI
[L]
Ledger details: Job #978; 1958
"Divine Child High Sch"

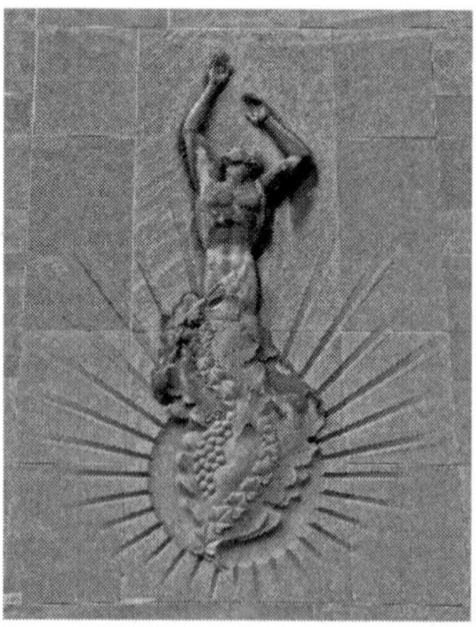

309. Oak Woods Cemetery Mausoleum
(c.1958; Harley, Ellington & Day)
1035 E Sixty-seventh St
Chicago, IL
[L, SB]
Ledger details: Job #983; 1958
"Oak Woods Maus. Chic."

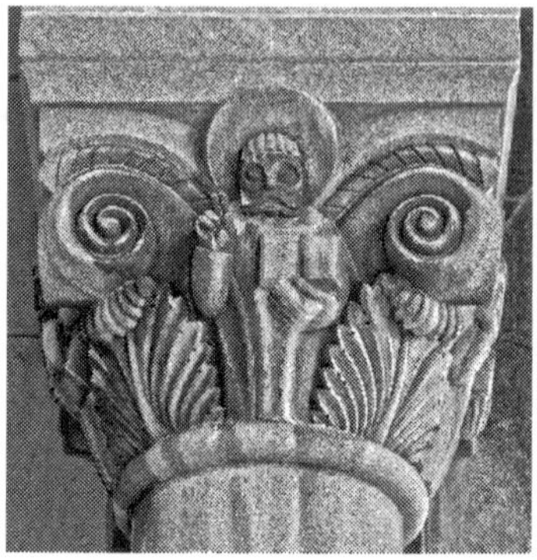

310. St. Luke Catholic Church
(1958; architect undetermined)
8017 Ohio St
Detroit, MI
[L, SB]
Ledger details: Jobs #985, #986; 1958
"St. Lukes Ch"

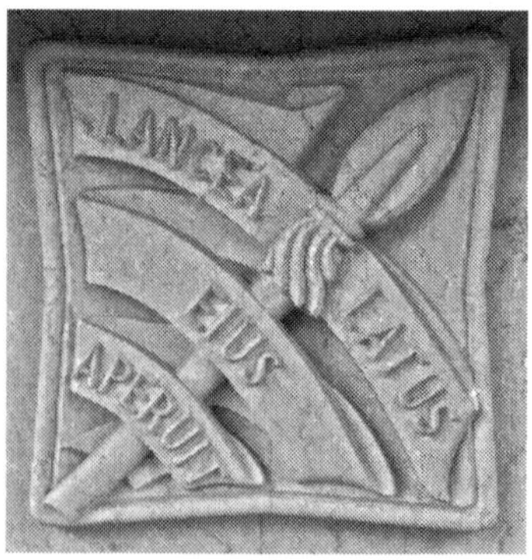

311. Colombiere Seminary now known as Colombiere College/Retreat and Conference Center ~ Chapel
(c.1959; Diehl & Diehl)
9075 Big Lake Rd
Clarkston, MI
[L, SB]
Ledger details: Job #990; 1959
"St. Columbiere (sic)"

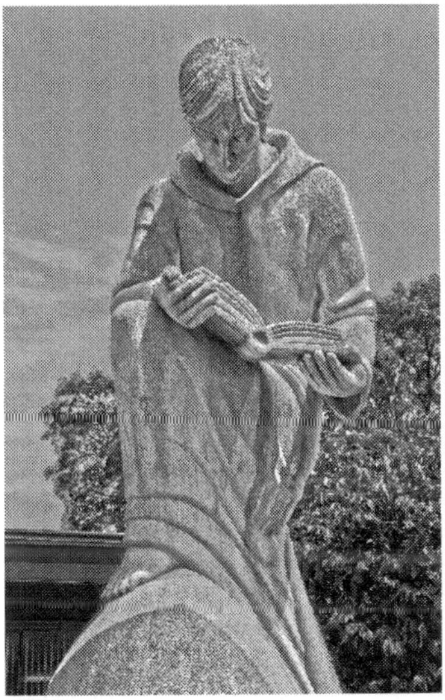

312. Old Redford Academy High School ~ St. Benedict Statue
(c.1959; N/A)
8001 W Outer Drive
Detroit, MI
[L, SB]
Ledger details: Job #995; 1959
"St. Benedict Statue"

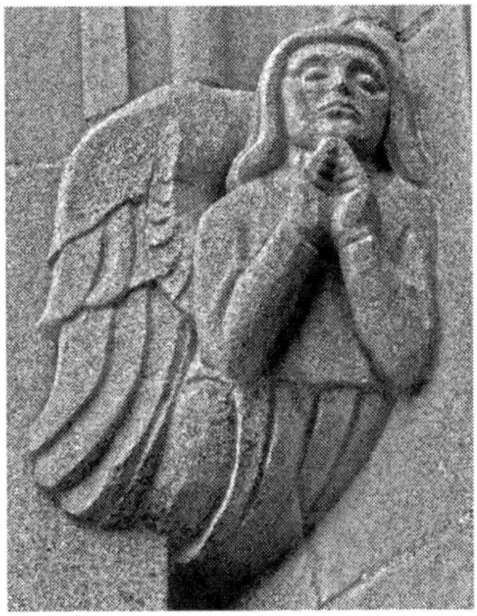

313. St. Peter Catholic Church
(1960; McGrath & Dohmen)
95 Market St
Mt. Clemens, MI
[L, SB]
Ledger details: Jobs #996, #997; 1959
"St Peters Ch Mt Clemmens (sic)"

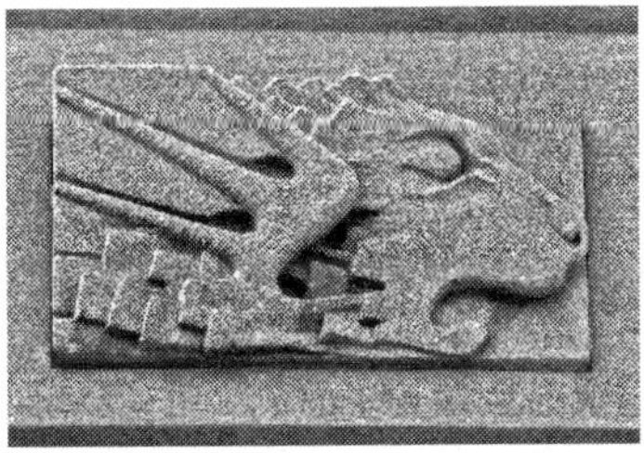

314. Brother Rice High School
(1959; Charles M. Valentine)
7101 Lahser Rd
Bloomfield Township, MI
[L, SB]
Ledger details: Jobs #998, #1004; 1959
"Brother Rice High Sch"

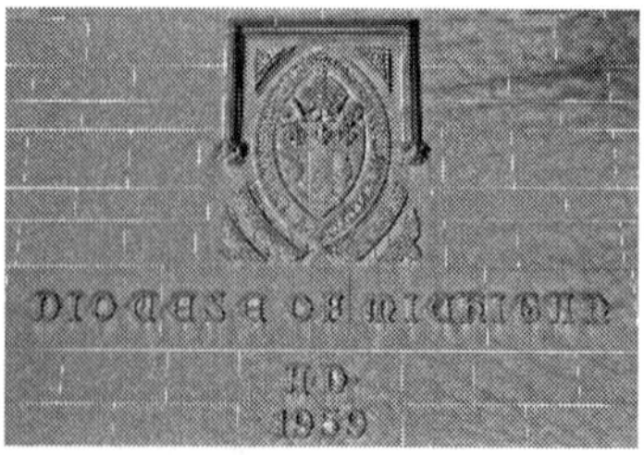

315. Cathedral Church of St. Paul School Addition
(1959; Harley, Ellington & Day)
4800 Woodward Ave
Detroit, MI
[L, SB]
Ledger details: Job #1000; 1959
"St Pauls Cath. Detroit"

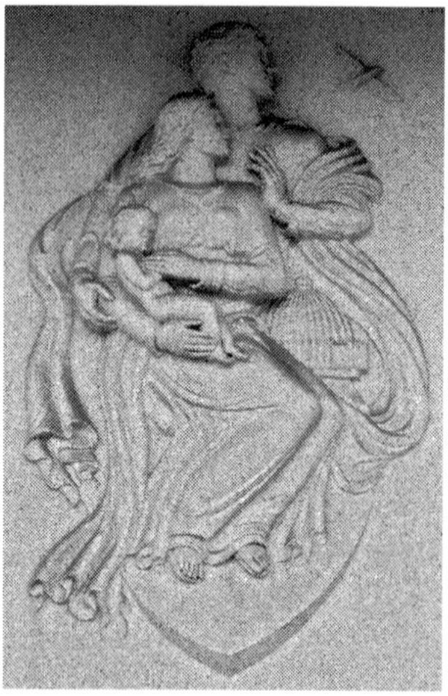

316. Allegheny Cemetery Mausoleum ~ Exterior Elements
(1960; Harley & Ellington)
4734 Butler St
Pittsburgh, PA
[L, SB]
Ledger details: Jobs #1006/#1050/ #1075; 1960/1964/1971
"Allegheny Maus. Pitts Pa"

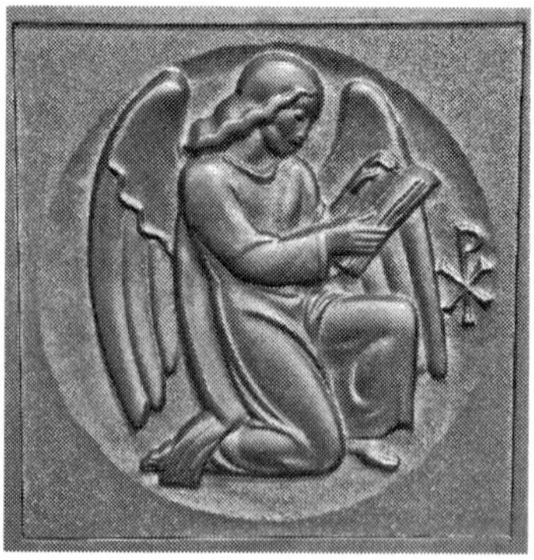

317. Allegheny Cemetery Mausoleum ~ Interior Elements
(1960; Harley & Ellington)
4734 Butler St
Pittsburgh, PA
[L, SB]
Ledger details: Jobs #1006/#1050/ #1075; 1960/1964/1971
"Allegheny Maus. Pitts Pa"

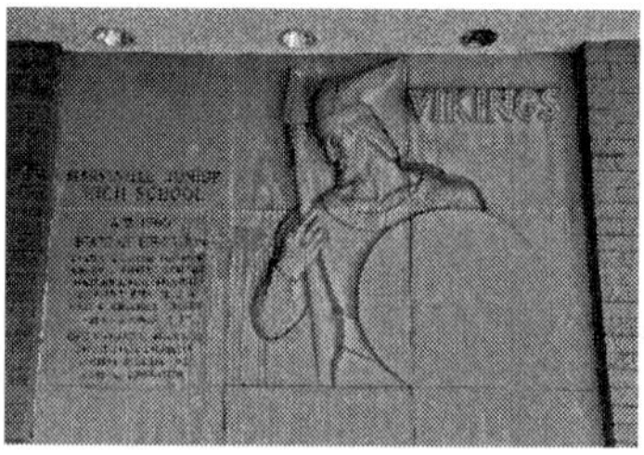

318. Marysville Junior High School
(1960; Charles M. Valentine)
400 Collard Dr
Marysville, MI
[L, SB]
Ledger details: Job #1011; 1960
"Mary'sville (sic) Junior High Sch"

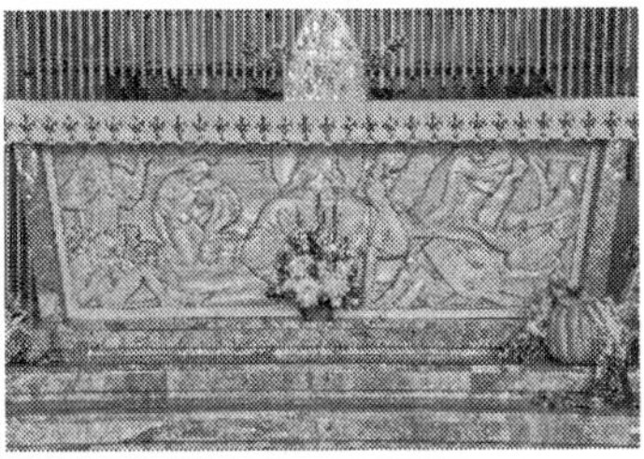

319. St. Clement Catholic Church Now known as St. Mary, Our Lady Queen of Families Catholic Church
(1960-1961: Diehl & Diehl)
25320 Van Dyke Ave
Center Line, MI
[L, SB]
Ledger details: Job #1012; 1960
"St Clement's Ch"

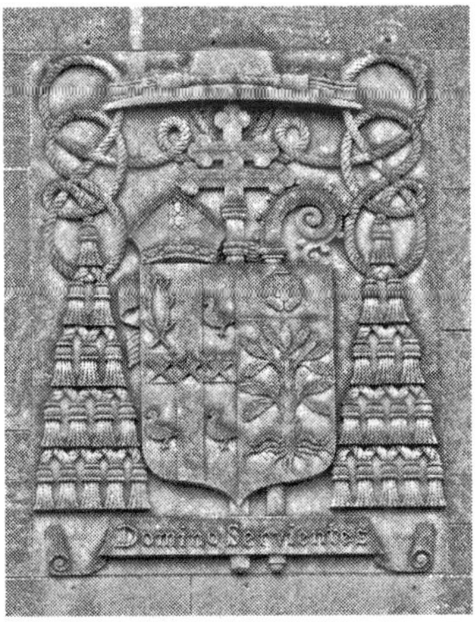

320. Cardinal Mooney Latin School at Sacred Heart Major Seminary
(1961; Charles M. Valentine)
Approximately 9401 Linwood St
Detroit, MI
[L, SB]
Ledger details: Job #1017; 1960
"Cardinal Mooney Latin Sch"

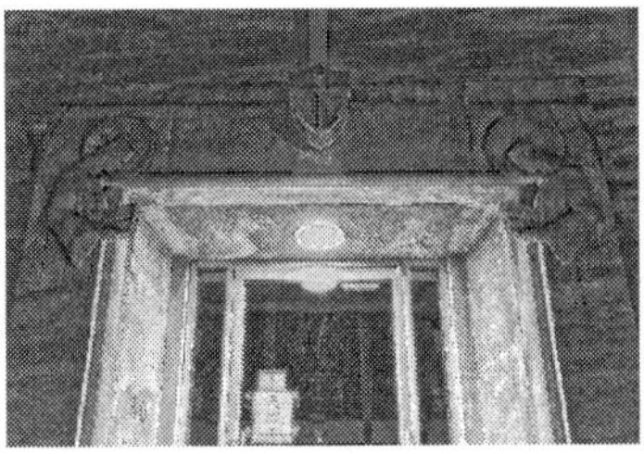

321. Hope Lutheran Church
(1960; Harold H. Fisher)
3640 Madison St
Dearborn, MI
[HF]
Ledger details: N/A

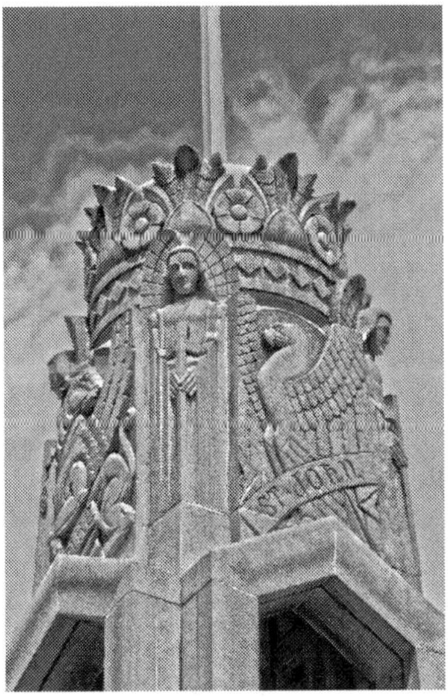

322. Christ Presbyterian Church
(1963; Harold H. Fisher)
944 E Gorham St
Madison, WI
[L, SB]
Ledger details: Jobs #1019/#1035
1960/1962
"Christ Presbyterian Ch. Madison Wisc"

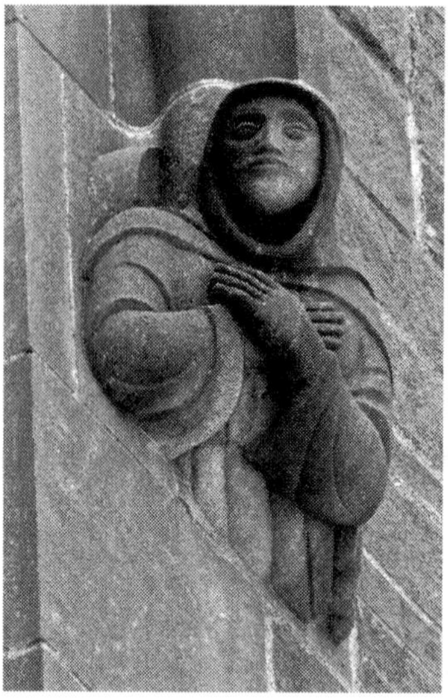

323. St. Mary Catholic Church
(1960; McGrath & Dohmen)
201 N Westphalia St
Westphalia, MI
[L]
Ledger details: Jobs #1020, #1022; 1961
"St. Mary's Westphalia"

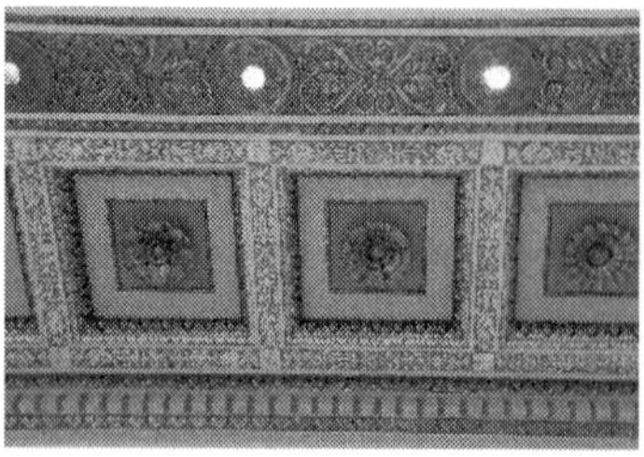

324. Viola Bray Gallery Addition at Flint Institute of Arts
(1961; Smith, Hinchman & Grylls)
1120 E Kearsley St
Flint, MI
[L]
Ledger details: Job #1021; 1961
"DeWaters Art Center"

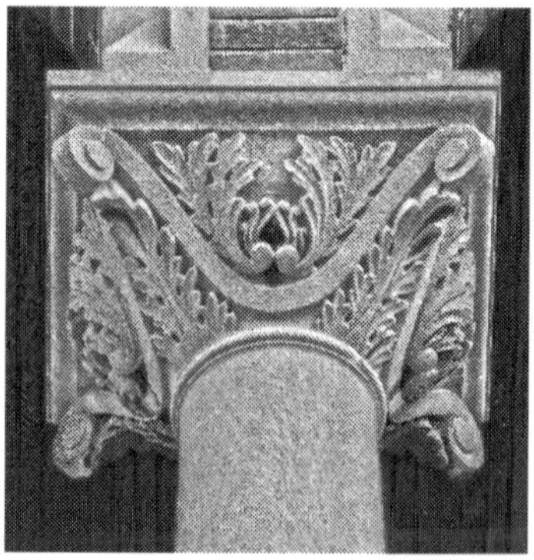

325. Evangelical Lutheran Church of Our Savior ~ Bell Tower Addition
(c.1961; Charles M. Valentine)
12844 Elmdale St
Detroit, MI
[L]
Ledger details: Job #1029; 1961
"Our Savior Luth. Ch"

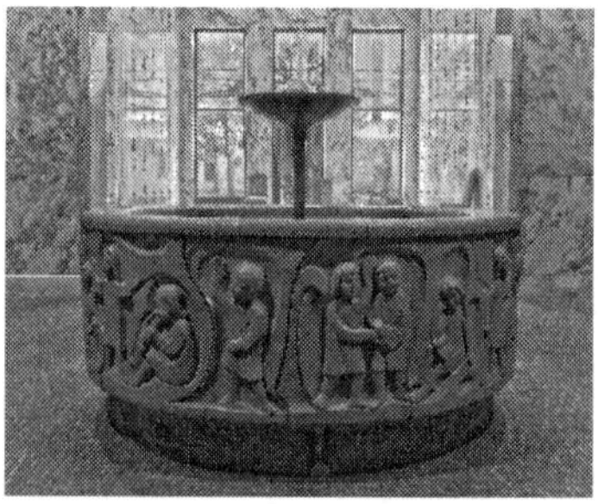

326. All Saints Cemetery Mausoleum and Interment Chapel
(c. 1961; Harley, Ellington, Cowin & Stirton)
700 N River Rd
Des Plaines, IL
[L]
Ledger details: Job #1031; 1961
"Queen of All Saints Maus. Chic."

No scrapbook images illuminate our thinking regarding Parducci's contributions to this mausoleum full of sculptural embellishment. Two fountains featuring reliefs of children appear to our eyes the pieces most likely to have been created by Parducci.

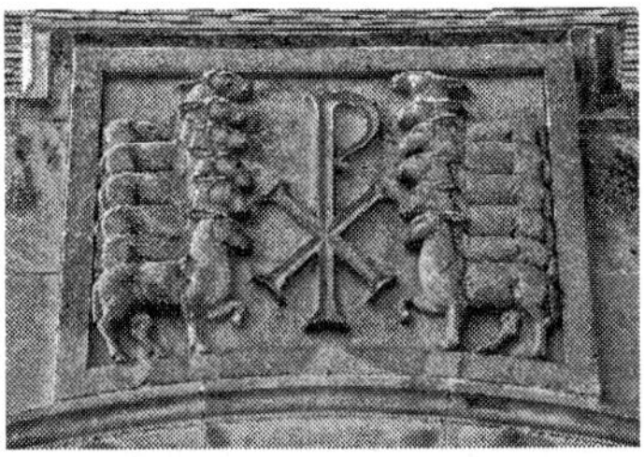

327. Christ United Methodist
(1962; Manson, Jackson & Kane)
517 W Jolly Rd
Lansing, MI
[L, SB]
Ledger details: Job #1036; 1962
"Christ Methodist Ch Lansing"

328. Lansing Public Library ~ Clarence H. Rosa Branch
(1964; Kenneth C. Black)
401 S Capitol Ave
Lansing, MI
[L, SB, FH]
Ledger details: Job #1039; 1962
"Lansing Library"

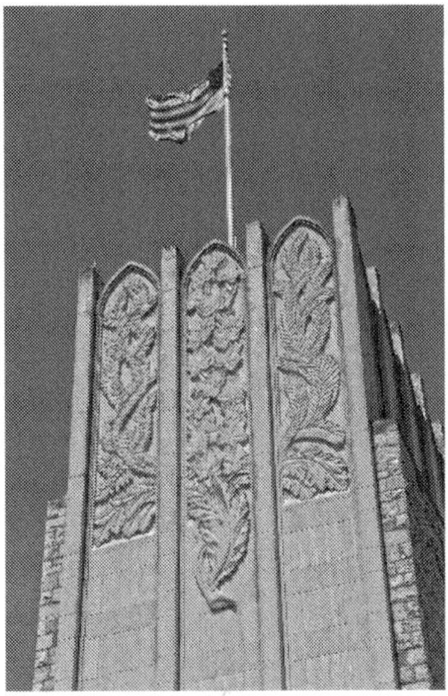

329. Cedars of Lebanon Mausoleum at Spring Grove Cemetery
(c.1963; Harley, Ellington, Cowin & Stirton)
4521 Spring Grove Ave
Cincinnati, OH
[L, SB]
Ledger details: Job #1040; 1962
"Spring Grove Maus Columbus (sic) Ohio"

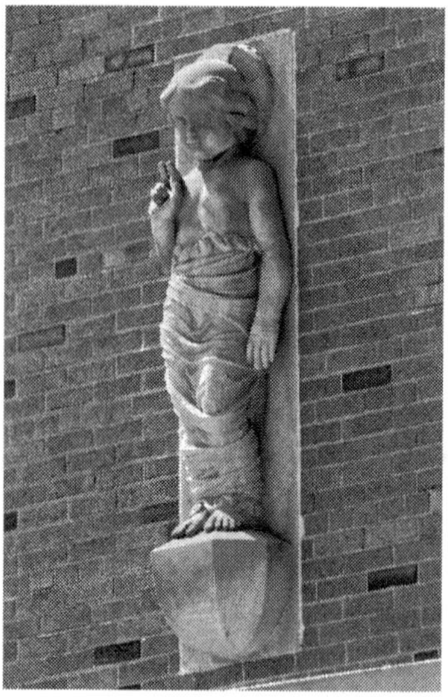

330. Church of the Divine Child
(1962-1963; Herman & Simons?)
1055 N Silvery Ln
Dearborn, MI
[L]
Ledger details: Job #1041; 1963
"Devine (sic) Child"

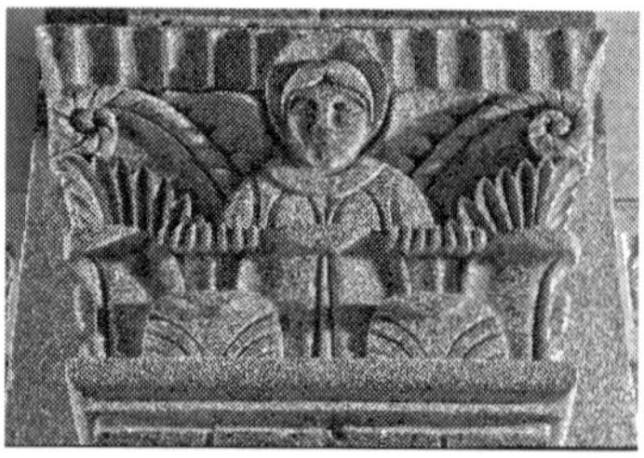

331. Christ the King Catholic Church
(c.1962; McGrath & Dohmen)
20800 Grand River Ave
Detroit, MI
[L, SB]
Ledger details: Jobs #914/#1042/#1052; 1953/1963/1965
"Christ the King"

How this church, built around 1962, made it onto Parducci's 1953 ledger page is beyond us. The last of a handful of inconsistencies that convince us Parducci created the ledgers from flawed memories and incomplete records years after executing the commissions.

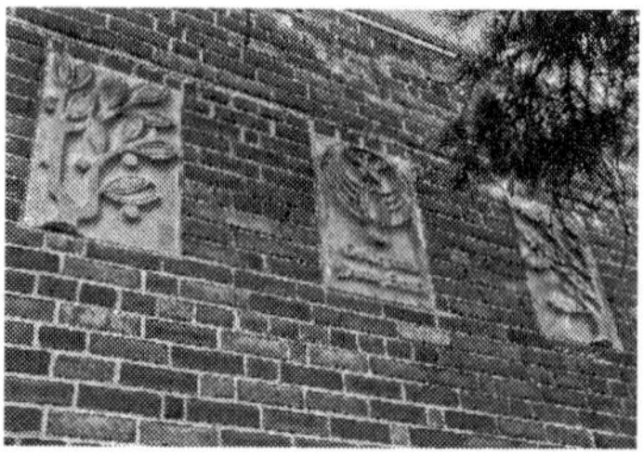

332. Duns Scotus College now known as Word of Life Church ~ Additions
(c.1964?; Charles M. Valentine?)
20000 W Nine Mile Rd
Southfield, MI
[L]
Ledger details: Job #1046; 1964
"Duns Scotus College"

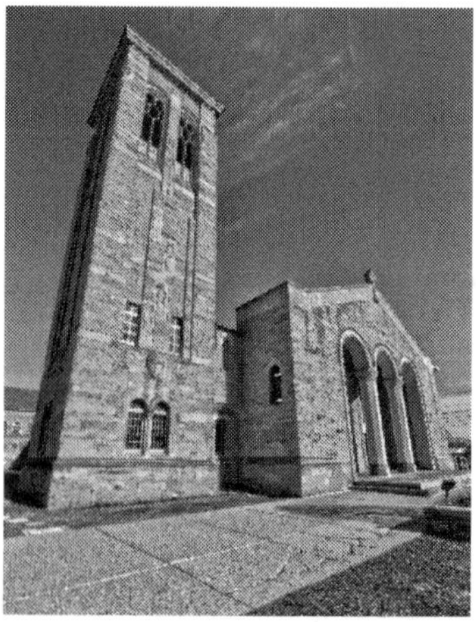

333. St. Anne Catholic Church
(1964; Charles M. Valentine)
32000 Mound Rd
Warren, MI
[L, SB]
Ledger details: Job #1048; 1964
"St Annes Ch."

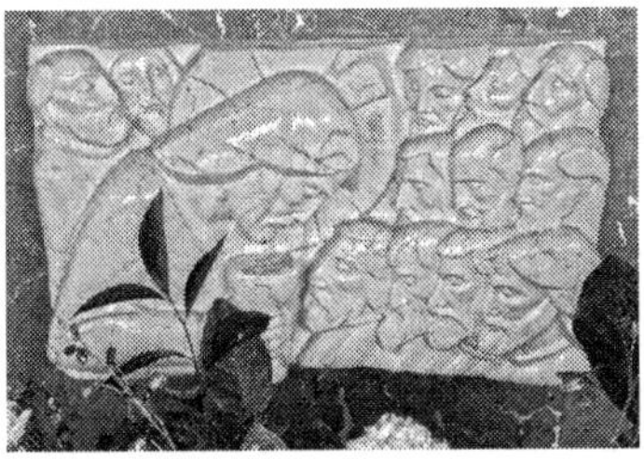

334. St Scholastica Catholic Church
(1965; Diehl & Diehl)
8201 W Outer Drive
Detroit, MI
[L;SB]
Ledger details: Job #1053; 1965
"St Scholastica Ch"

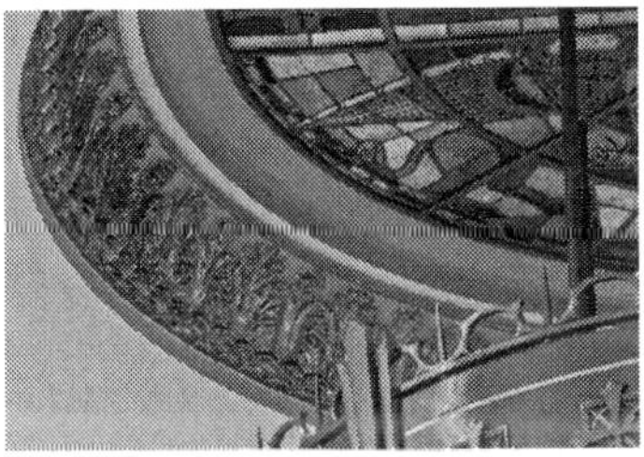

335. St. Edward Chapel at St. John Hospital now know as Ascension St. John Hospital
(1965; Maguolo & Quick)
22101 Moross Rd
Detroit, MI
[L]
Ledger details: Job #1055; 1965
"St. John's Hospt. Chapel ceiling"

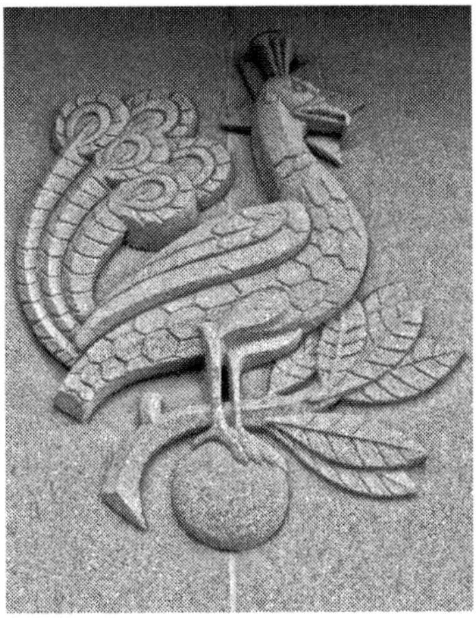

336. St. Casimir Cemetery Offices and Chapel
(c.1965; Harley, Ellington, Cowin & Stirton)
4401 W 111th St
Chicago, IL
[L, SB]
Ledger details: Job #1057; 1965
"St. Casimer (sic) Cem."

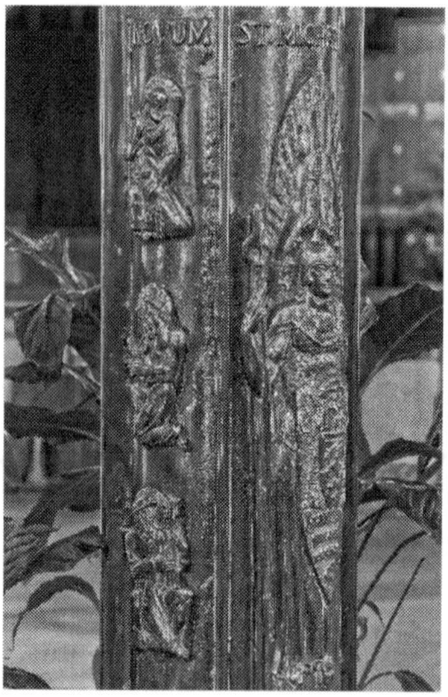

337. National Shrine of the Little Flower ~ Lectern
(Lectern: 1965; N/A)
1621 Linwood Ave
Royal Oak, MI
[L, SB, DB]
Ledger details: Job #1058; 1965
"Shrine of the Little Flower Lectern"

A late addition to the Shrine's interior that Parducci specifically references in the 1975 Smithsonian interview.

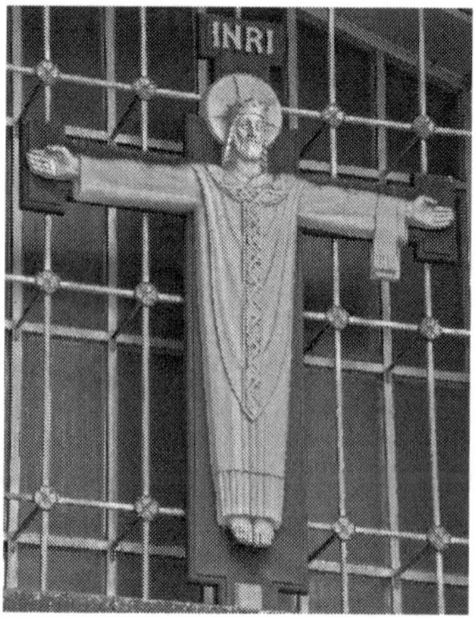

338. Monastery of the Blessed Sacrament
(1964; Diehl & Diehl)
29575 Middlebelt Rd
Farmington Hills, MI
[L, SB]
Ledger details: Job #1059; 1965
"Blessed Sac. Monastery"

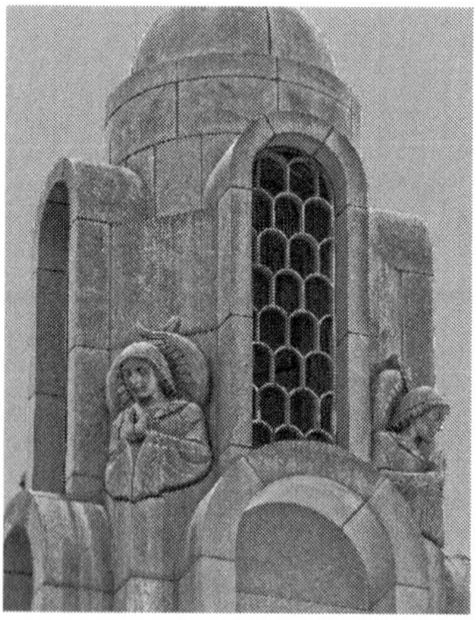

339. St. Lazarus Serbian Orthodox Church
(1965; Harold H. Fisher)
4575 E Outer Drive
Detroit, MI
[L, SB]
Ledger details: Jobs #1060/#1064
1965/1967
"St. Lazarus Ch."

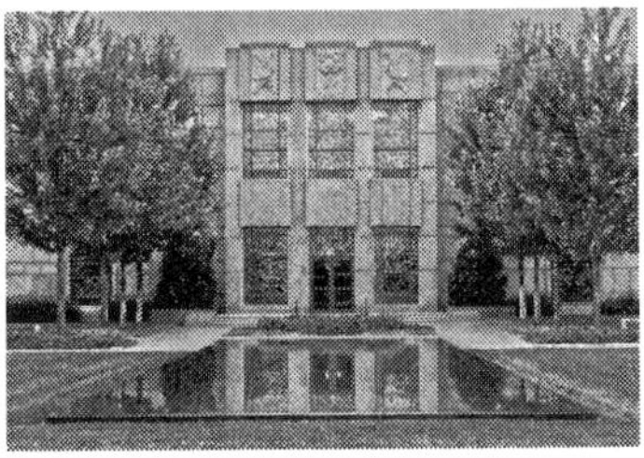

340. Lakewood Cemetery Mausoleum
(1967; Harley, Ellington, Cowin & Stirton)
3600 Hennepin Ave
Minneapolis, MN
[L, SB]
Ledger details: Job #1061; 1966
"Lakewood Maus. Minn. Min"

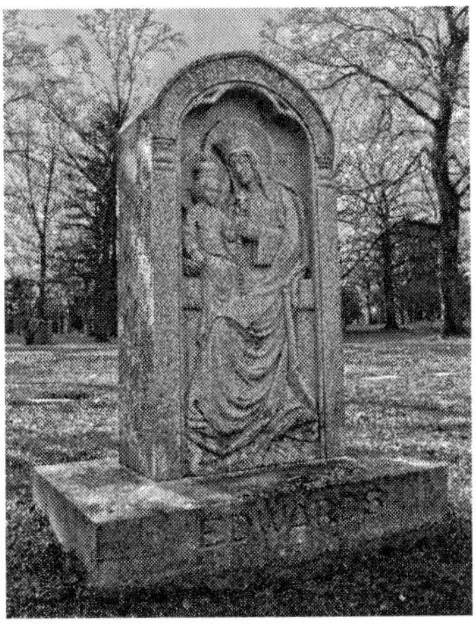

341. L.A. Edwards Memorial at Holy Sepulchre Catholic Cemetery
(c.1967; N/A)
25800 W Ten Mile Rd
Southfield, MI
[L, SB]
Ledger details: Job #1066; 1967
"Tombstone Mr. L.A. Edwards"

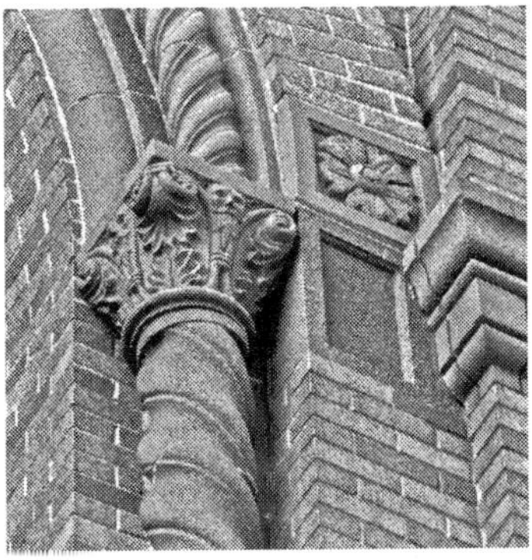

342. Michigan National Bank Tower now known as Boji Tower ~ 1965-1967 Addition
(1965-1967; Kenneth C. Black)
124 W Allegan S
Lansing, MI
[L, FH]
Ledger details: Job #1068; 1967
"Mich. Nat. Bk Lansing"

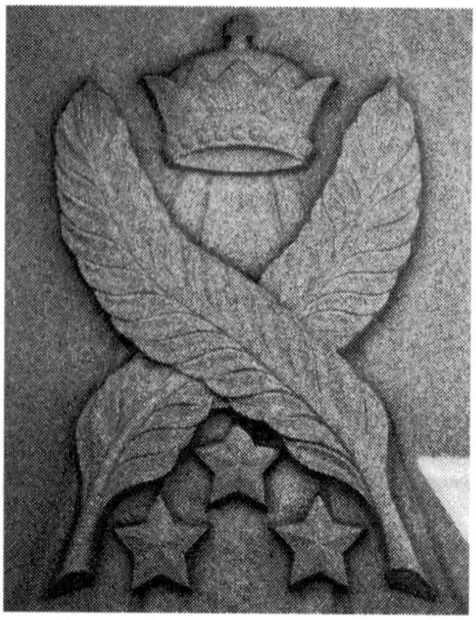

343. Resurrection Cemetery Offices
(1968; Malcolm Stirton? Harley, Ellington, Cowin & Stirton? Harley Ellington Associates?)
9400 W Donges Bay Rd
Mequon, WI
[L]
Ledger details: Job #1070; 1967 "Resurrection Cem Mau. Milwaukee Wisc"

We personally examined blueprints for this building signed by Malcolm Stirton. It is unclear to us if Stirton, at this point in his career, was still partnered with Harley, Ellington & Cowin, or if he was engaged in a solo venture. This consideration also applies to entry #346.

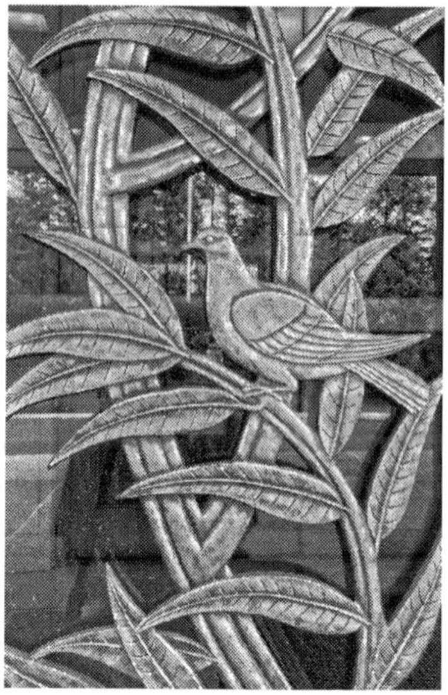

344. Woodland Cemetery Mausoleum
(c.1969; Harley Ellington Associates)
118 Woodland Ave
Dayton, OH
[L, SB]
Ledger details: Job #1073; 1969 "Woodland Cem Maus"

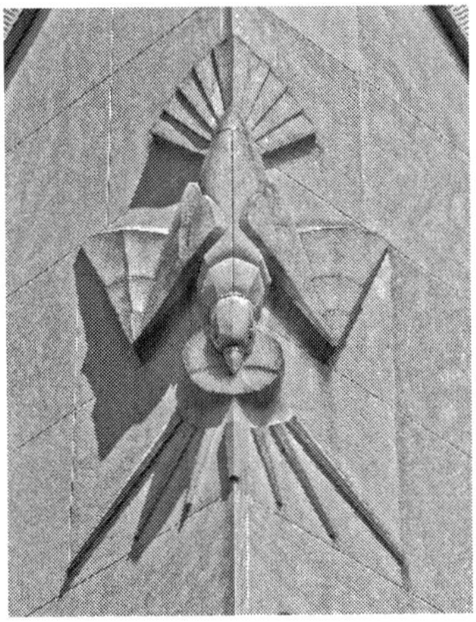

345. Redeemer Baptist Church now known as Woodside Bible Church ~ Warren Campus
(c.1970; Harold H. Fisher)
27300 Hoover Rd
Warren, MI
[L]
Ledger details: Job #1074; 1970 "Redeemer Baptist Ch."

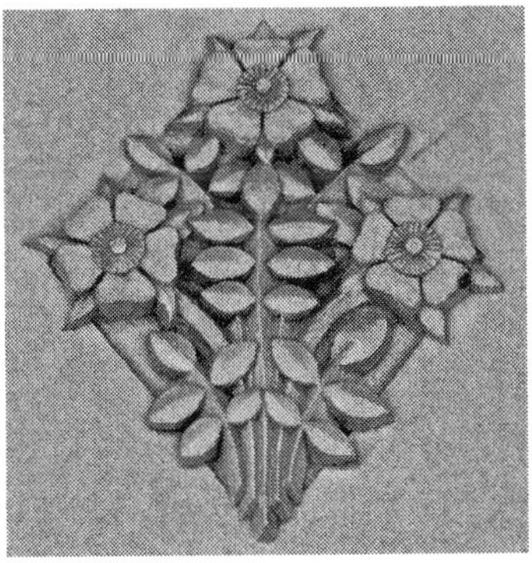

346. Loudon Park Cemetery Offices and Chapels
(c.1972; Malcolm Stirton? Harley, Ellington, Cowin & Stirton? Harley Ellington Associates?)
3620 Wilkens Ave
Baltimore, MD
[L]
Ledger details: Job #1076; 1972 "Louden (sic) Park Cem. Maus"

347. George J. Maguolo Family Memorial at Calvary Cemetery
(c.1975; N/A)
5239 W Florissant Ave
St. Louis, MO
[SB]
Ledger details: N/A

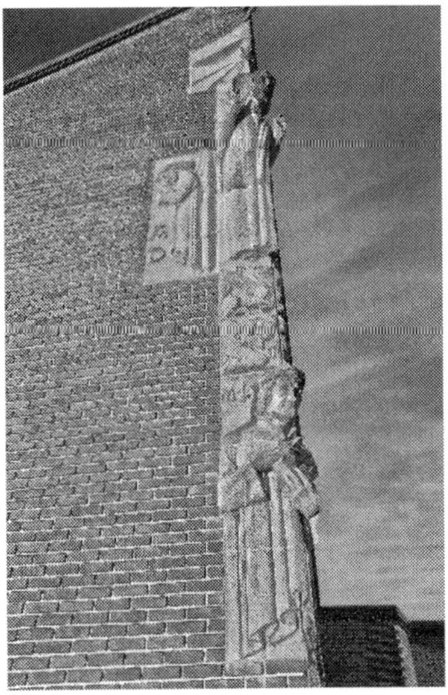

348. St. Thomas Lutheran Church
(1976; Harold H. Fisher)
23801 Kelly Rd
Eastpointe, MI
[SHG, MSA]
Ledger details: N/A

349. New York State Capitol Senate Chamber
(1881; Henry Hobson Richardson with Stanford White)
165 State St
Albany, NY
[C, SB, FH]
Ledger details: N/A

(*See Figure H, page 136*)

Regarding the New York State Capitol Senate Chamber commission, Parducci states in the 1979 Fay Hendry interview that Stanford White left the mantle uncarved. White, a legendary figure in American architectural history is said to have designed, in part, the New York State Capitol Senate Chamber while working as a draftsman in the employ of the even more legendary Henry Hobson Richardson. In addition to the uncarved mantle, Parducci also created designs for five lintels, referred to in correspondence with the commissioning architects as "overdoor panels." Difficulties in contracting an adequately skilled stone carver plus an unwieldy State Senate schedule prevented these designs from being carved until 1981. This date, as well as stone carver Vincent Leggiadro's surname, is chiseled into one of Parducci's foliage designs surrounding his bust of Richardson in shallow relief.

Incidentally, in the 1975 Smithsonian interview, Parducci references White's very direct influence upon Ulysses Ricci under whom Parducci apprenticed:

"CORRADO PARDUCCI: *You know, Stanford White started something you know when he . . . You know, before there was Richardson Romanesque. You know those?*
DENNIS BARRIE: *Right.*
CORRADO PARDUCCI: *And Stanford White came up with the Greek and the Roman and, you know, he built the Madison Square Garden. You remember the old, with the terra cotta? All that terra cotta work was all done by the Riccis at Perth Amboy.*
DENNIS BARRIE: *Hmm.*
CORRADO PARDUCCI: *And they were actually the pupils of Stanford White!"*

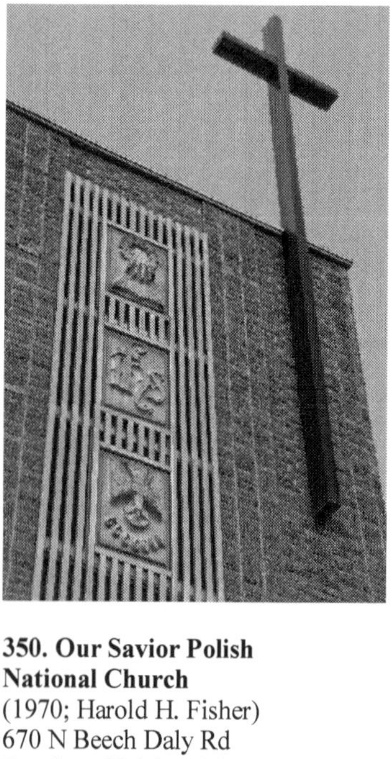

350. Our Savior Polish National Church
(1970; Harold H. Fisher)
670 N Beech Daly Rd
Dearborn Heights, MI
[C]
Ledger details: N/A

Parducci's last known commission, executed in 1980, is confirmed by photocopies of correspondence with church officials. We speculate that the fully detached tower to which Parducci's sculpture is affixed is actually a 1980 addition to the original 1970 construction.

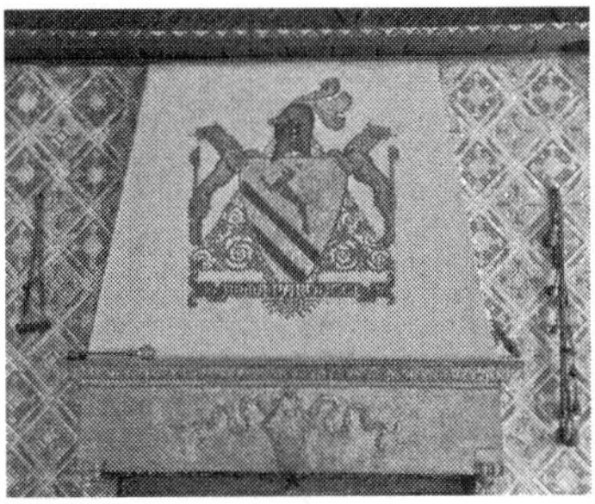

351. Corrado Parducci Residence
(1928; J. Robert F. Swanson)
Colonial Rd
Grosse Pointe Shores, MI
[SB, DB, AP]
Ledger details: N/A

Allen Parducci tells us that his father worked closely with Swanson on the design of his Grosse Pointe Shores home of over fifty years. Allen also tells us that shortly after his death in 1981 he personally deposited his father's ashes in the massive urn at the center of the home's circle drive. Over the course of many years, Parducci embellished his home with custom decorations throughout, in paint, plaster, metals and stone.

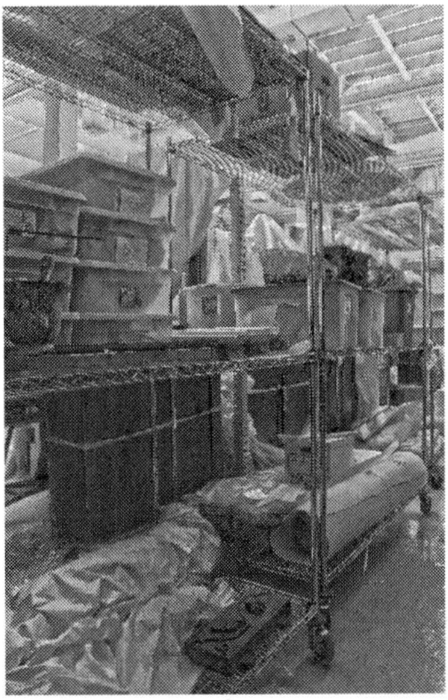

352. Corrado Parducci Collection at Detroit Historical Museum Storage Facility
(1924-1981; N/A)
Detroit, MI
[DHM]
Ledger details: N/A

Image courtesy Detroit Historical Society

Dale A. Carlson, Photographer

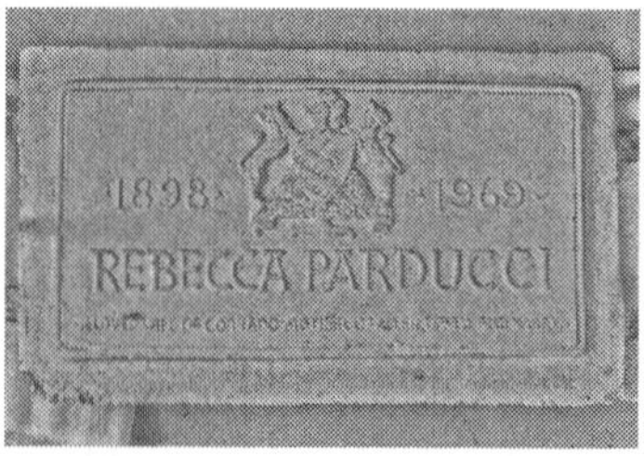

353. Corrado Parducci Collection at Detroit Historical Museum Storage Facility ~ Rebecca Parducci Headstone Model
(c.1969; N/A)
Detroit, MI
[DHM]
Ledger details: N/A

Image courtesy Detroit Historical Society

Dale A. Carlson, Photographer

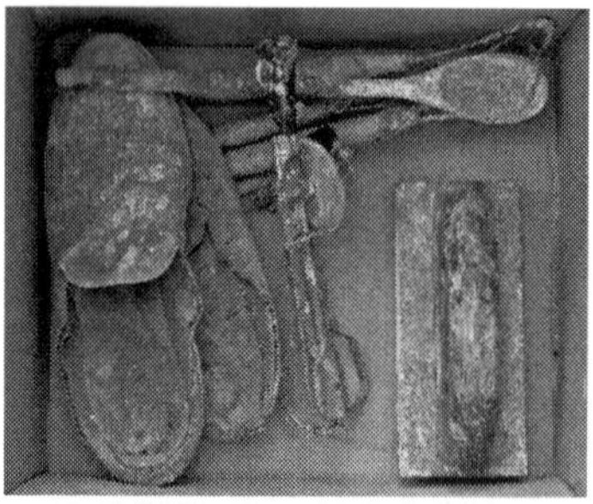

354. Corrado Parducci Collection at Detroit Historical Museum Storage Facility ~ Parducci Studio Shoes and Plaster Tools
(1924-1981; N/A)
Detroit, MI
[DHM]
Ledger details: N/A

Image courtesy Detroit Historical Society

Dale A. Carlson, Photographer

The following seven entries, #354 through #359, are all personal possessions of Parducci's son, Allen.

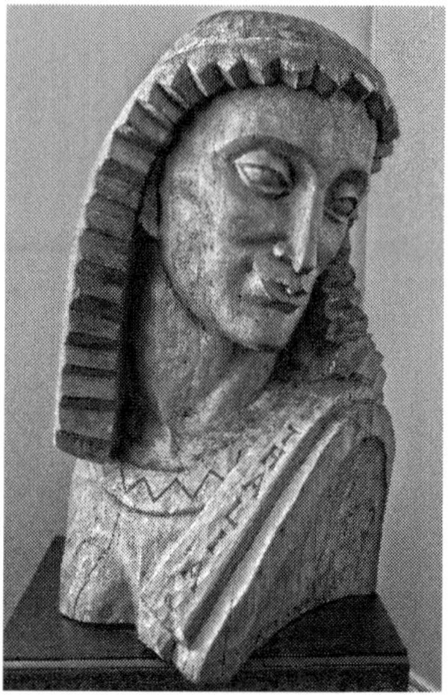

355. Corrado Parducci Personal Sculpture
(Unknown year; N/A)
Pacific Palisades
Los Angeles, CA
[AP]
Ledger details: N/A

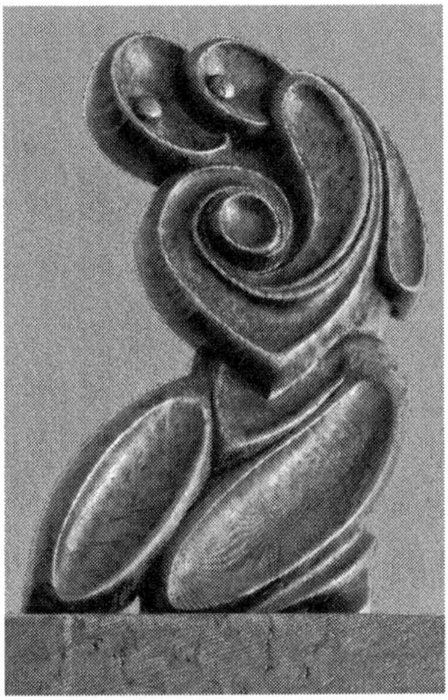

356. Corrado Parducci
Personal Sculpture
(Unknown year; N/A)
Pacific Palisades
Los Angeles, CA
[AP]
Ledger details: N/A

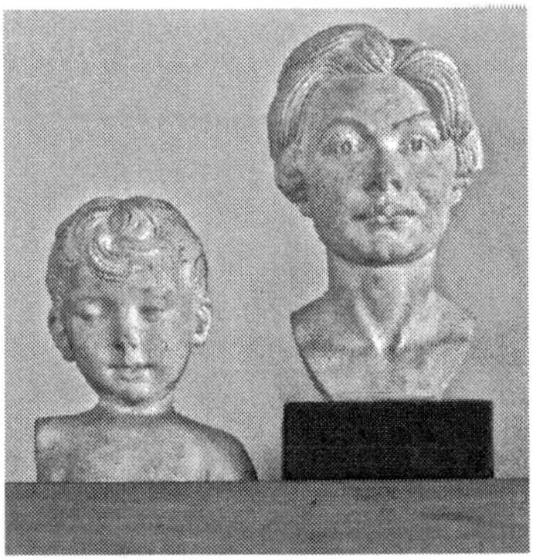

357. Corrado Parducci
Personal Sculpture
(c.1932; N/A)
Pacific Palisades
Los Angeles, CA
[AP]
Ledger details: N/A

Busts of son, Allen, and wife, Rebecca, rendered in plaster. Our date of 1932 is based on Allen's appearance which we estimate to be around seven years.

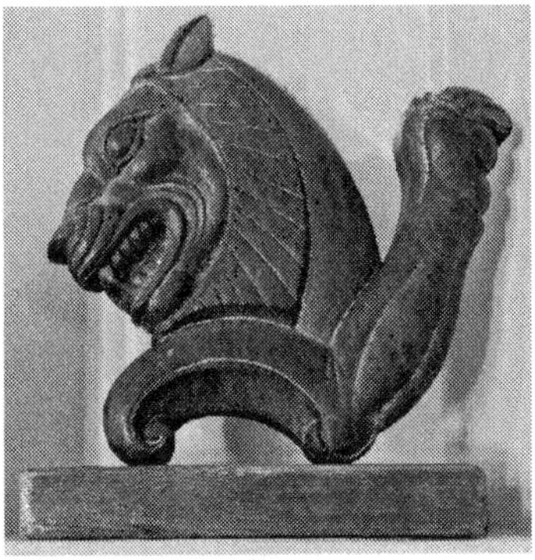

358. Corrado Parducci
Personal Sculpture
(Unknown year; N/A)
Pacific Palisades
Los Angeles, CA
[AP]
Ledger details: N/A

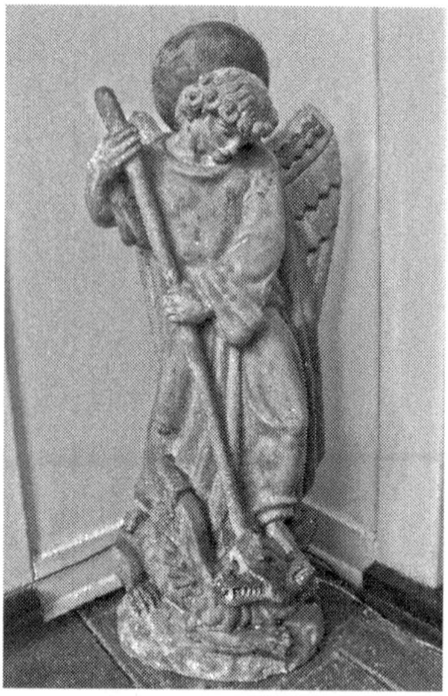

359. Corrado Parducci Studio Model
(Unknown year; N/A)
Pacific Palisades
Los Angeles, CA
[AP]
Ledger details: N/A

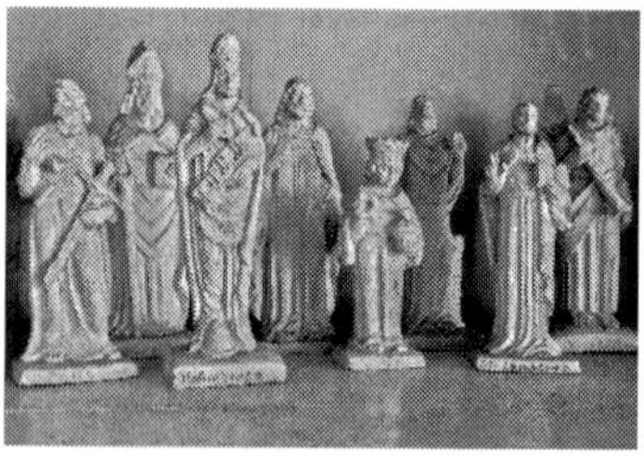

360. Corrado Parducci Maquettes
(1924-1981; N/A)
Pacific Palisades
Los Angeles, CA
[AP]
Ledger details: N/A

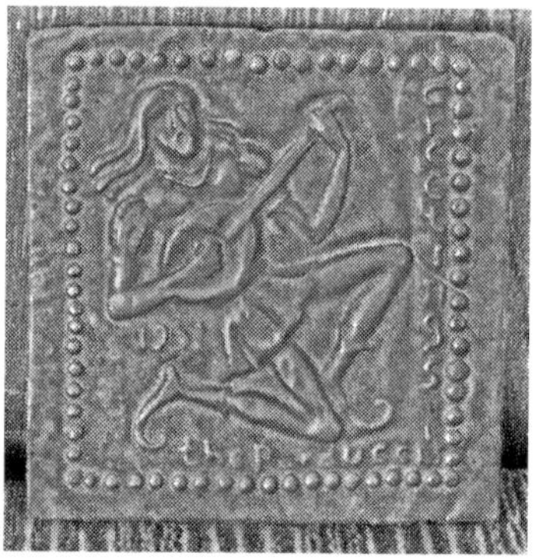

361. Corrado Parducci 1952 Christmas Card
(1952; N/A)
Pacific Palisades
Los Angeles, CA
[AP]
Ledger details: N/A

Creating a metal Christmas card was an annual tradition of Parducci's. They were generally ready right around the February following the holiday, Allen tells us.

APPENDIX

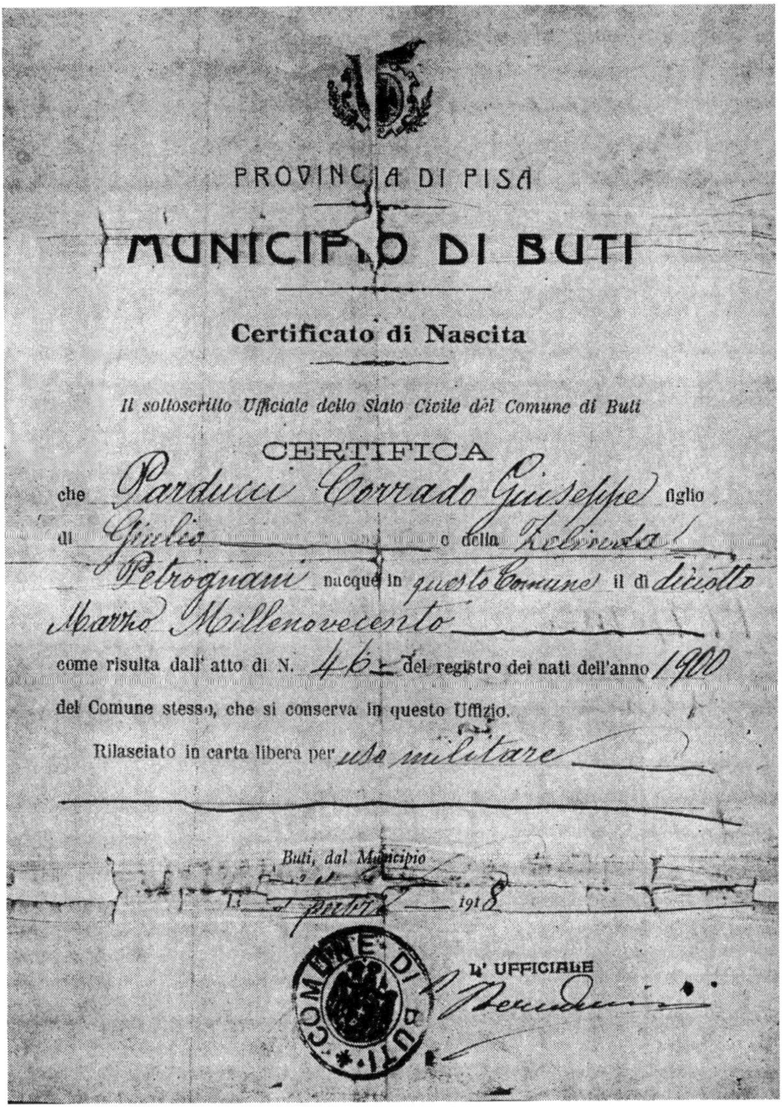

PROVINCIA DI PISA

MUNICIPIO DI BUTI

Certificato di Nascita

Il sottoscritto Ufficiale dello Stato Civile del Comune di Buti

CERTIFICA

che Parducci Corrado Giuseppe figlio
di Giulio e della Zelinda
Petrognani nacque in questo Comune il dì diciotto
Marzo Millenovecento
come risulta dall' atto di N. 46 del registro dei nati dell'anno 1900
del Comune stesso, che si conserva in questo Uffizio.

Rilasciato in carta libera per uso militare

Buti, dal Municipio
13 Aprile 1918

COMUNE DI BUTI

L' UFFICIALE

Figure A ~ Corrado Parducci birth certificate, issued by the municipality of Buti, Italy in 1918.

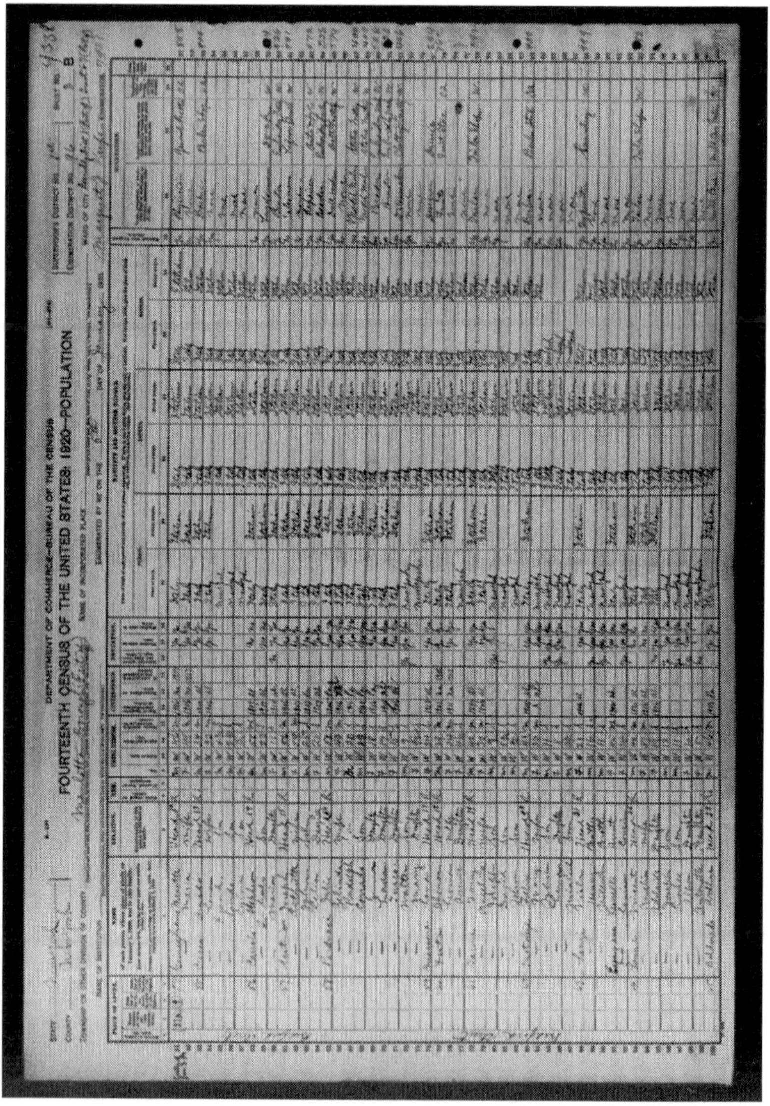
DEPARTMENT OF COMMERCE—BUREAU OF THE CENSUS

FOURTEENTH CENSUS OF THE UNITED STATES: 1920—POPULATION

Figure B ~ 1920 United State Census record with Parducci family, lines 65-73

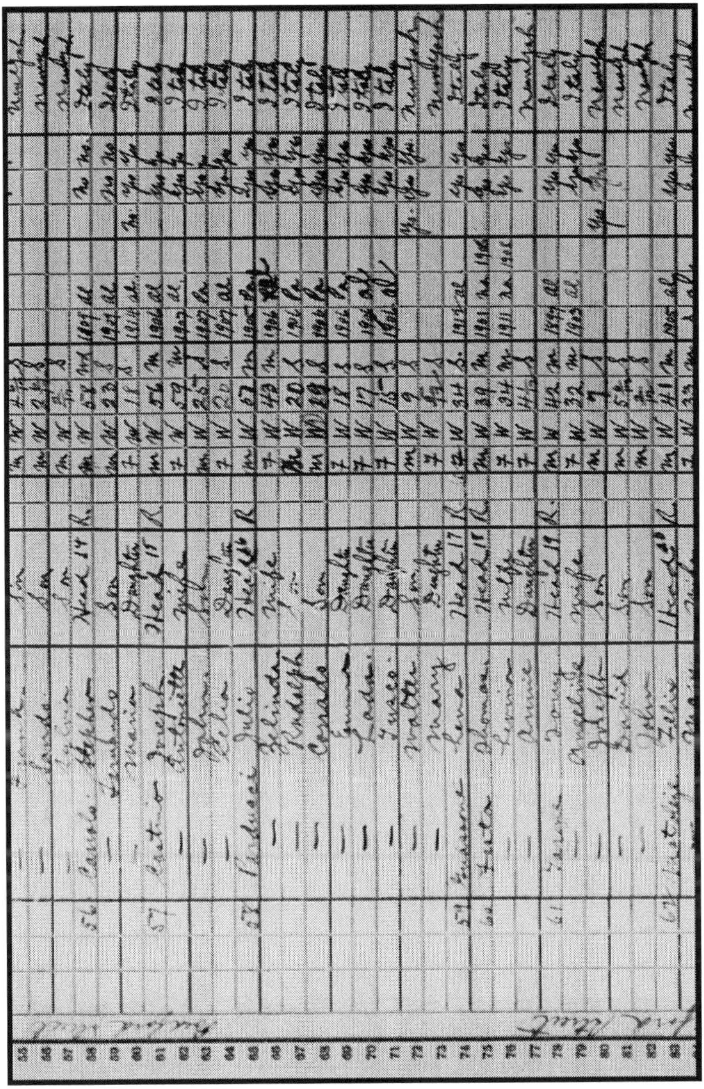

Figure C ~ Detail of 1920 United State Census Record with Parducci family, lines 65-73

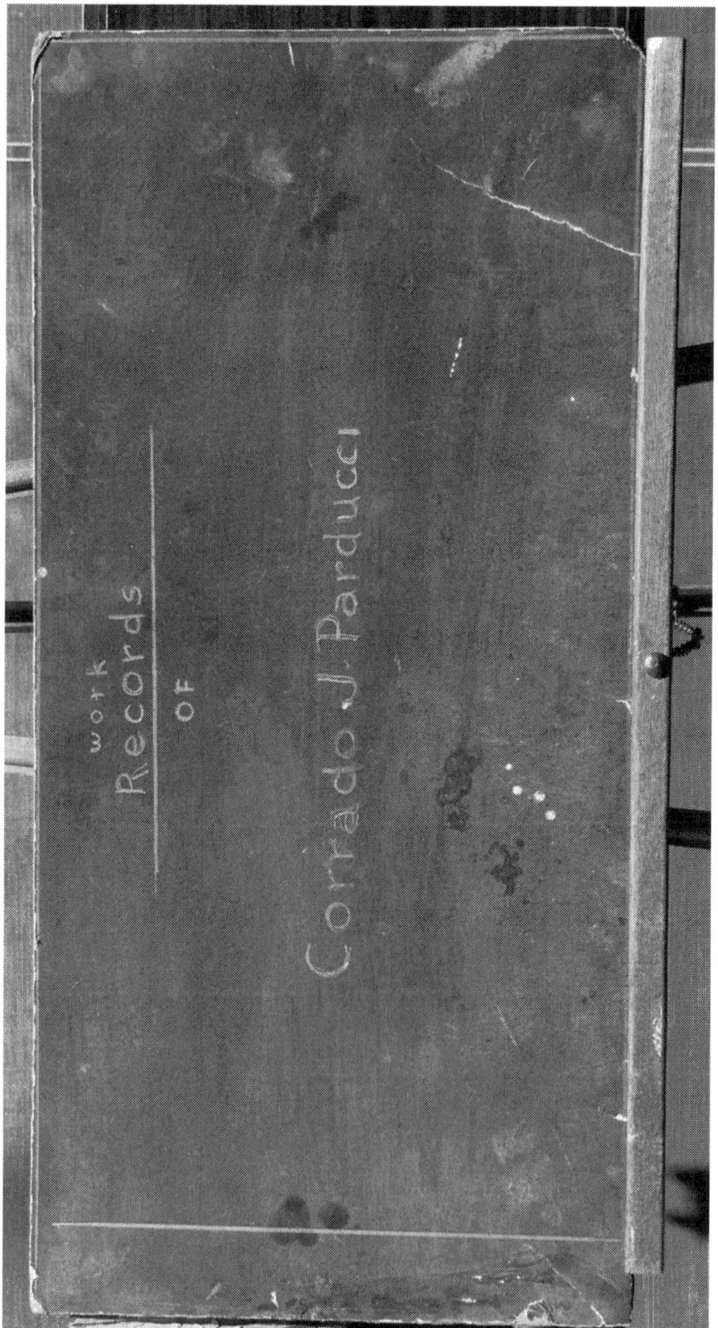

Figure D ~ Corrado Parducci ledger, cover

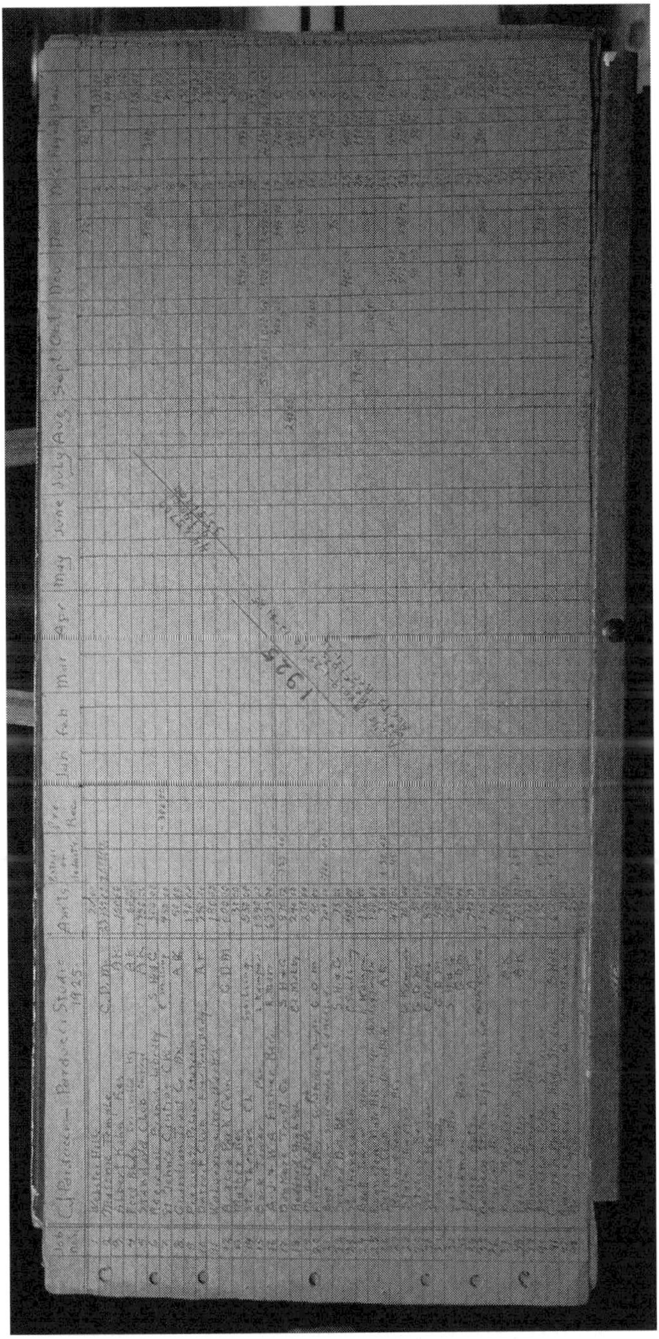

Figure E ~ Corrado Parducci ledger page, 1925

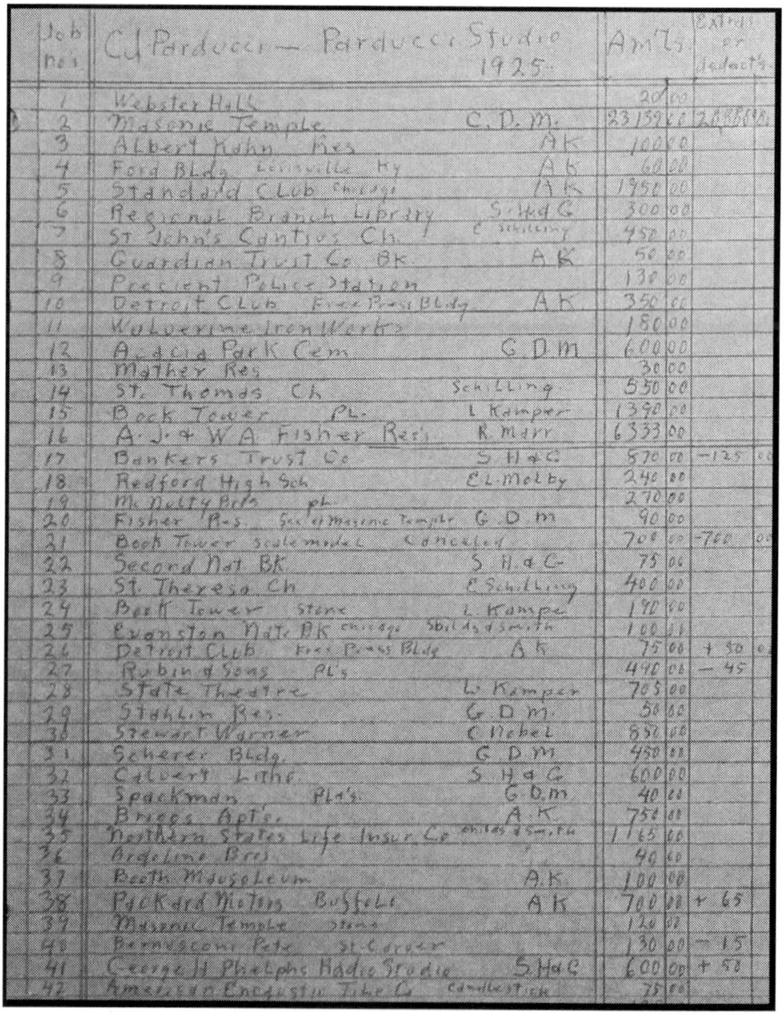

Job nos	CJ Parducci — Parducci Studio 1925		Am'ts	Extras or deducts
1	Webster Hall		20 00	
2	Masonic Temple	C. D. M.	23139 00	2488[illegible]
3	Albert Kahn Res	AK	100 00	
4	Ford Bldg Louisville Ky	AK	60 00	
5	Standard Club Chicago	AK	1950 00	
6	Regional Branch Library	S H & G	300 00	
7	St John's Cantius Ch	C Schilling	450 00	
8	Guardian Trust Co BK	AK	50 00	
9	Precinct Police Station		130 00	
10	Detroit Club Free Press Bldg	AK	350 00	
11	Wolverine Iron Works		180 00	
12	Acacia Park Cem	G D M	600 00	
13	Mather Res		30 00	
14	St. Thomas Ch	Schilling	550 00	
15	Book Tower PL	L Kamper	1390 00	
16	A. J. & W. A. Fisher Res	R. Marr	6333 00	
17	Bankers Trust Co	S H & G	570 00	-125 00
18	Redford High Sch	E L Malby	240 00	
19	McNulty Bros pl		270 00	
20	Fisher Res Sec of Masonic Temple	G D M	90 00	
21	Book Tower Scale model Canceled		700 00	-700 00
22	Second Nat BK	S H & G	75 00	
23	St. Theresa Ch	C Schilling	400 00	
24	Book Tower Stone	L Kamper	190 00	
25	Evanston Nat BK Chicago	[illegible]	100 00	
26	Detroit Club Free Press Bldg	AK	75 00	+ 30 00
27	Rubin & Sons PL's		490 00	— 45
28	State Theatre	L Kamper	705 00	
29	Stahlin Res	G D M	50 00	
30	Stewart Warner	C Nobel	850 00	
31	Scherer Bldg	G D M	450 00	
32	Calvert Litho	S H & G	600 00	
33	Spackman PL's	G D M	40 00	
34	Briggs Apt's	A K	750 00	
35	Northern States Life Insur Co	Childs & Smith	1165 00	
36	Ardeline Bros		40 00	
37	Booth Mausoleum	A K	100 00	
38	Packard Motors Buffalo	A K	700 00	+ 65
39	Masonic Temple stone		120 00	
40	Bernasconi Pete St Carver		130 00	— 15
41	George H Phelphs Radio Studio	S H & G	600 00	+ 50
42	American Encaustic Tile Co candlestick		75 00	

Figure F ~ Detail of Corrado Parducci ledger page, 1925

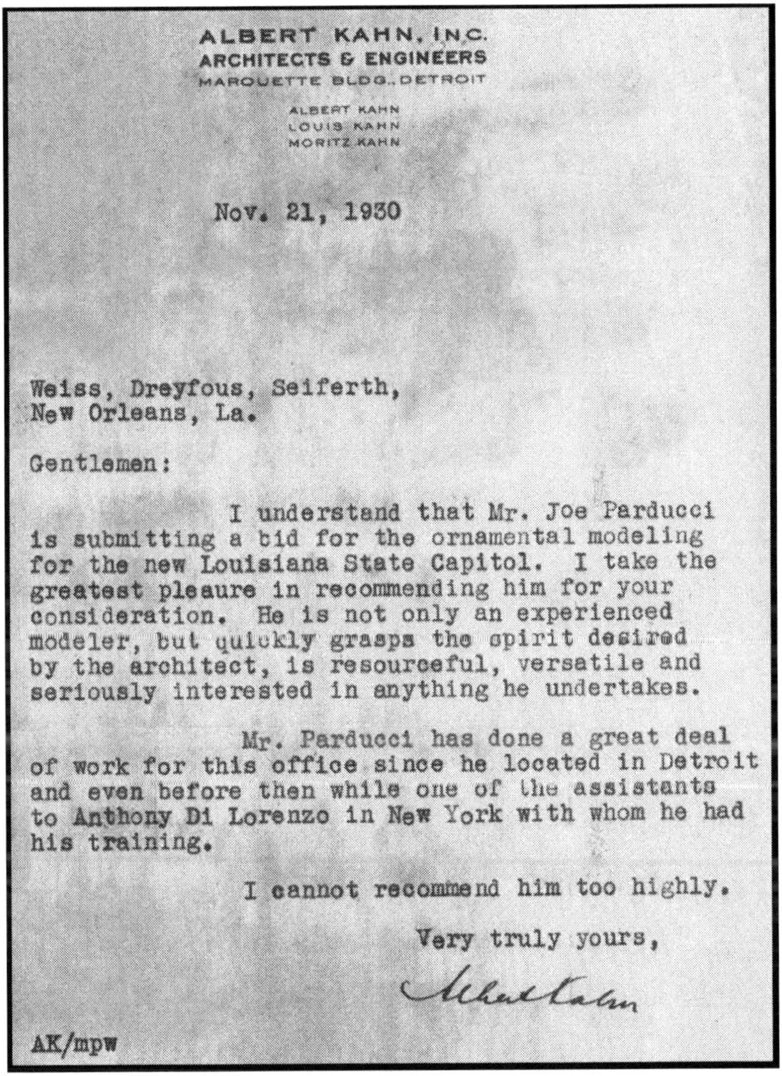

ALBERT KAHN, INC.
ARCHITECTS & ENGINEERS
MARQUETTE BLDG., DETROIT

ALBERT KAHN
LOUIS KAHN
MORITZ KAHN

Nov. 21, 1930

Weiss, Dreyfous, Seiferth,
New Orleans, La.

Gentlemen:

I understand that Mr. Joe Parducci is submitting a bid for the ornamental modeling for the new Louisiana State Capitol. I take the greatest pleaure in recommending him for your consideration. He is not only an experienced modeler, but quickly grasps the spirit desired by the architect, is resourceful, versatile and seriously interested in anything he undertakes.

Mr. Parducci has done a great deal of work for this office since he located in Detroit and even before then while one of the assistants to Anthony Di Lorenzo in New York with whom he had his training.

I cannot recommend him too highly.

Very truly yours,

Albert Kahn

AK/mpw

Figure G ~ Albert Kahn's letter of recommendation to Weiss, Dreyfous & Seiferth, 1930

MENDEL • MESICK • COHEN • ARCHITECTS

388 BROADWAY ALBANY, NEW YORK 12207 518 463-2278

June 26, 1978

Corrado J. Parducci
141 Sibley
Detroit, Michigan 48201

Dear Mr. Parducci:

In confirmation of our recent telephone conversation, we would like you to submit a proposal for the following items of architectural sculpture which are to be undertaken this year in the Senate Chamber of the Capitol Building in Albany:

1. Overdoor panels. There are five panels, one of which is larger than the others. Our feeling is that the subject matter for the portrait medallions should be the several architects of the Capitol. We can provide photographs of these individuals.

2. Corbels at doorways. Each door opening has a pair of these to be carved with foliate ornament of Romanesque Revival character. In keeping with the ornamental treatment elsewhere in the room it may not be desirable to have all of these carved to the same pattern.

3. Dentils above doorways. These now exist as finished blocks but according to all early sketches they were to be ornamentally carved.

It is our assumption that you will want to visit the Chamber to get a feeling for the existing stonework prior to making your designs. Your proposal should provide for travel as well as for time spent in supervising the stonecutters, if this is a service which you feel it desirable to provide.

Sincerely yours,

Craig Morrison
Project Architect

Figure H ~ Correspondence with acting architects of the New York State Capitol, 1978

INDEX of PEOPLE

(Numbers within brackets [*] indicate entries in the commissions list. Those without indicate page numbers.)

INDEX of BUILDINGS and SITES

BIBLIOGRAPHY

"AIA Guide to Detroit Architecture" Eric J. Hill & John Gallagher; Wayne State University Press, Detroit, 2003

"Alverno College Campus: Architectural Art and Building Exteriors" [Pamphlet]; Author unknown, 2012

The American Magazine of Art, January 1923, Vol. XIV, No. 1, pg. 52-56

“Architectural and Decorative Plaster Ornaments” Detroit Decorative Supply Co. Office & Studios [Merchandise Catalog]; Detroit, 1929

“Artists in California, 1786-1940” Edan Milton Hughes; Hughes Publishing Co., San Francisco, 1986

"Artist's Work is Widespread" Herman Wise; Detroit Free Press, May 10, 1931, pg. 18

“Bishop Dedicates East Side Church” Author unknown; Detroit Free Press, Oct. 4, 1920, pg. 5

"Buildings of Michigan" Kathryn Bishop Eckert; Oxford University Press, New York, 1993

"Carved into Detroit's heart, Parducci's art is unsigned and you'll have to look up to see it" Elaine Latzman Moon; Detroit Free Press, March 14, 1976, ‘Detroit’ section, pg. 18

“Catalog of Works of art by Carleton Watson Angell: Artist, University Museums, University of Michigan, 1926-1955” Author Unknown; Ann Arbor: University Museums, 1955

“Central Building - Lansing [School District] Libraries - Lansing, Michigan” [Dedication pamphlet for Clarence H. Rosa Branch of the Lansing Public Library] Author unknown; 1964

“Corrado Joseph Parducci, 81, architectural sculptor” [Obituary] Ric Bohy; Detroit News, Nov. 26, 1981, pg. 12-B

Corrado Parducci's Personal Scrapbook; Unpublished, 1910-1981

“Designing Detroit: Wirt Rowland and the Rise of Modern American Architecture” Michael G. Smith; Wayne State University Press, Detroit, 2017

"Detroit Bishop to Dedicate Church" Author unknown; Detroit Free Press, Oct. 4, 1930, pg. 8

"Detroit's Historic Places of Worship" Marla O. Collum, Barbara E. Krueger and Dorothy Kostuch; Wayne State University Press, Detroit, 2012

"Edsel B. Ford Office Papers, 1903-1945 (bulk 1920-1940) - Accession 6" Box 312; Benson Ford Research Center, Dearborn, MI

"Fay L. Hendry Outdoor Sculpture Project Records 00149"; Michigan State University Archives and Historical Collections, East Lansing, MI

"Géza Maróti and the Decoration of the Fisher Building Lobby" Joan Boddie; Unpublished Master's Thesis, 1978 [Held at the University of Michigan Fine Arts Library inside Tappan Hall, Ann Arbor, MI]

"Guardians of Detroit: Architectural Sculpture in the Motor City" Jeff Morrison; Wayne State University Press, Detroit, 2019

"A Half Century in Stone" Michigan Society of Architects with George F. Diehl and Malcolm R. Stirton; Michigan Society of Architects Monthly Bulletin, October 1975

"Heavenly Doors" Michael H. Margolin; Detroit Free Press, Nov. 26, 1978, 'Detroit' section, pg. 14

"The 'Henry Ford' of Detroit architecture" Beverly Eckman; Detroit News, Mar. 22, 1973, pg. unknown

"H.H. Richardson ~ Complete Architectural Works" Jeffrey Karl Ochsner; Massachusetts Institute of Technology, 1982

"A Historical Tour of the University of Michigan" Bentley Historical Library; An online presentation located at: http://bentley.umich.edu/legacy-support/campus_tour/

"History of Lansing: A Visitor's Guide" Unknown author, unknown year; an online publication located at: https://www.lansingmi.gov/DocumentCenter/View/377/Walking-Tour-Booklet-PDF

"Images of America: Detroit's Masonic Temple" Alex Lundberg and Greg Kowalski; Arcadia Publishing, 2006

"Kalamazoo County Building - Dedication - October 16th, 1937" [Dedication pamphlet] Author unknown; 1937

“Kirk Sculpture by Sculptor” Unknown author; Unpublished, unknown year [Inventory of sculptural works at Kirk in the Hills Presbyterian Church in Bloomfield Township, Michigan]

"Listening in on Detroit" H.C.L. Jackson; Detroit News, Unknown month and day, 1932, pg. unknown

“Masonic Temple: Rock of Ages” Gregg Sutter; Monthly Detroit, December 1980

"Meadow Brook Artisans Recall Hall's Origins and Days of Opulence" Jody Headlee; The Oakland Press, August 7, 1973, pg. A-6

“Meadow Brook Hall - Monument to a flamboyant era” [Pamphlet] Unknown author; Meadow Brook Hall, 1979

"Metal Crafts in Architecture" Gerald K. Geerlings; Bonanza Books, 1957

"The Michigan Law Quadrangle: Architecture and Origins" Kathryn Horste; The University of Michigan Press, 1997

Midland Theatre History Mural Installation @ Herbert D. Doan Midland County History Center, Midland, Michigan; Midland County Historical Society, 2003

“A Monumental Example of Structural Beauty” Louis D. Ray; Michigan Manufacturer and Financial Record, Vol. 42, No. 17, Oct. 27, 1928

"Oral History Interview with Corrado Parducci, 1975 Mar. 17. Archives of American Art, Smithsonian Institution"; Published online @ https://www.aaa.si.edu/collections/interviews/oral-history-interview-corrado-parducci-12608#transcript

"Outdoor Sculpture in Grand Rapids" Fay L. Hendry; *i*ota Press, 1980

"Outdoor Sculpture in Kalamazoo" Fay L. Hendry; *i*ota Press, 1980

"Outdoor Sculpture in Lansing" Fay L. Hendry; *i*ota Press, 1980

“The Pelican Guide to the Louisiana Capitol” Ellen Roy Jolly and James Calhoun; Firebird Press, a division of Pelican Publishing Company, 1980

"A Place in the Country - Matilda Wilson's Personal Guidebook to Meadow Brook Hall" Matilda Rausch Dodge Wilson; Oakland University Press, 1998

“Polk’s Detroit City Directory”; R.L. Polk & Co., Publishers; 1925-1926, 1926-1927, 1927-1928, 1928-1929, 1929-1930, 1930-31, 1931-1932, 1932-1933, 1934, 1935, 1936, 1937, 1938, 1939, 1940, 1941

"The Proposed Historic Detroit Financial District Final Report" City of Detroit City Council Historic Designation Advisory Board, 2010

"Rock Holds Spirit of Auditorium - Skillful Brothers Model for Beauty" Unknown author; Grand Rapids Press, June 21, 1932, pg. 17

"Sculptor, 79, has left his mark on Detroit" Andrea Ford; Detroit Free Press, Nov. 12, 1979, sec. A, pg. 3

"Sculpture and the Federal Triangle" George Gurney; Smithsonian Institution Press, 1985

"Souvenir Bulletin of the Dedication of St. Thomas the Apostle School, Ann Arbor, Mich. May Eleventh Nineteen Hundred and Thirty" Rev. Allen J. Babcock; Archdiocese of Detroit, 1930

"University of Michigan Public Art by Campus" Unknown author, unknown year; an online PDF located at: https://president.umich.edu/wp-content/uploads/sites/3/2019/03/PAConPA-Acquisition-List_Updated_3_1_2019-1.pdf

[Untitled Parducci Biography]; Unpublished, Smith, Hinchman & Grylls, c.1975

"White Footprints Say: 'Sculptor Lives Here'" Unknown author; Detroit Free Press, Feb. 1, 1953, pg. 92

[Notes for Corrado Parducci's American Institute of Architects honorary membership award ceremony] William E. Kapp; Unpublished, 1958

"Work Records of Corrado J. Parducci" [Ledgers]; Unpublished, 1924-1972

[Write the authors at 1971dac@gmail.com to obtain access to their complete research archive.]